HAIL REDSKINS

A Celebration of the Greatest Players, Teams, and Coaches

RICHARD WHITTINGHAM

TRIUMPH
BOOKS

CHICAGO

The publisher would like to thank Joe Gibbs for the Foreword and gratefully acknowledge the assistance of Ray Didinger and Craig Ellenport of the NFL.

Library of Congress Cataloging-in-Publication Data

Whittingham, Richard, date.
   Hail Redskins : a celebration of the greatest players, teams, and coaches
 / Richard Whittingham
     p. cm.
   Includes index.
   ISBN 1-57243-419-8 (hardcover)
    1. Washington Redskins (Football team) I. Title

   GV956.W3 W46 2001
   769.332'64'09753—dc21

                                  2001027989

This book is available in quantity at special discounts for your group or organization. For further information, contact:

Triumph Books
601 South LaSalle Street
Suite 500
Chicago, Illinois 60605
(312) 939-3330
Fax (312) 663-3557

Printed in the United States of America

ISBN 1-57243-688-3

Interior and jacket design by Eileen Wagner

Top front cover photo courtesy of Scott Cunningham
Bottom front cover photo courtesy of AP/Wide World Photos
Back cover photo courtesy of Vernon Biever

Except where otherwise credited, all photos in this book are from the personal collection of the author, Richard Whittingham.

Contents

Foreword

My decision to return to coaching after 12 years away was the result of a long process of reflection, prayer, and discussion with my family. This was a huge step, and I was well aware of the challenge. It was daunting, to say the least. But when I returned to Redskin Park on January 8, 2004, any doubts I might have had about the wisdom of my decision were put to rest. That was the day I was officially introduced—for the second time—as head coach of the Washington Redskins. Hundreds of fans gathered outside in the cold, cheering and playing "Hail to the Redskins." Inside, a number of my former players, including Art Monk, Darrell Green, and Gary Clark, were waiting to welcome me home.

The emotions I felt that day were overwhelming and, while I fully understood the magnitude of the task at hand and the fact that there was no guarantee of success, I knew I had done the right thing. There are a lot of football teams and coaching jobs, but there is no team and no job quite like this one. The Washington Redskins are one of the greatest franchises in all of professional sports. They have a passionate fan base with thousands of season tickets passed down from generation to generation. Many of the people who attend Redskins games today are the grandchildren of fans who watched Sammy Baugh play in old Griffith Stadium. The team has a rich tradition that I came to appreciate and embrace.

I felt fortunate to coach the Redskins from 1981 through 1992. Given the opportunity to return by owner Daniel Snyder, I feel fortunate again. I just hope we can achieve the same level of success. We certainly will strive to do so.

Even in my years away from football, when I was operating my racing team in Charlotte, North Carolina, and winning NASCAR championships, I still had an emotional bond with the Redskins and the Washington fans. When you share the experience of winning three Super Bowls and you see that pride reflected in the community, that feeling never leaves you. Over the past decade, I was approached by a number of NFL teams, asking if I would consider a return to coaching. Each time I said no. In my heart, I think the only job I could have taken was this one. I'm a Washington Redskin. It just so happened that this year, when I finally reached a point in my life when I could seriously consider such a move, the Redskins job became available and Daniel Snyder called. And here I am.

I left the Redskins after the 1992 season because I was whipped, physically and emotionally. The stories about our coaching staff working until 4:00 in the morning, living on candy bars and pizza, were no exaggeration. It drained me to the point where, finally, it was necessary for me to walk away. But I never lost my love for the game, even though I've enjoyed my involvement in the racing industry. There are moments you experience as a coach that you cannot experience anywhere else. By moments, most people would assume I'm referring to our three Super Bowl wins—the moment when the game ended and the celebration began. I remember those moments, but it is the relationships I cherish most of all. I remember going back on the field after one of our Super Bowls. The stadium was empty, the field was deserted, and Charles Mann, our great defensive end, was there looking around. He said, "You know, Coach, getting here was the fun." It was so true. Getting there, building the team, climbing that mountain, was something we all shared. That was the fun—meeting that challenge.

We had a unique group in Washington. We turned the roster over a dozen times and players came and went, but they all contributed. Some of my favorite guys were the special teams players, like Pete Cronan, Greg Manusky, and Larry Kubin. You need stars like John Riggins and Darrell Green to win championships, but you need those blue-collar guys too, because they are an important part of your team chemistry. I still remember one practice where everyone was taking it easy on Riggins. No one wanted to hit him because we all knew he was our leader on offense. But as practice was winding down, we were running a goal-line series and Larry Kubin gave John a shot. Nothing dirty—just a good hard lick. It woke everyone up. John kind of glared and pushed up his sleeves.

I said, "OK, last play, full go. Offense, call any play you like." Of course, we all knew they'd give the ball to Riggins. He took the handoff and Kubin smacked him head on. John's helmet went flying and down he went. The players put Kubin on their shoulders and carried him to the locker room, chanting, "Ku-bin, Ku-bin."

It was one of those moments that no one saw, other than the coaches and players, and it never made it into the newspapers. It was just another day on the practice field, but it is those moments I missed in my years away from football—and, in the end, it was the memory of those moments that brought me back.

—JOE GIBBS

Introduction

In 1961 I was in the military, stationed at Fort Meade, Maryland, and playing for the Browns on weekends. I was a halfback then, in the backfield with Jim Brown, and we had a very good team. But Paul Brown wanted Ernie Davis, who was just coming out of Syracuse, where Jim had played. Ernie was a very good running back. He was a Heisman Trophy winner and was sure to be the No. 1 pick in the draft. The Redskins had that pick.

Paul Brown wanted to trade for Ernie and, as it turned out, it seems I was one of the only guys [George Preston] Marshall said he would take. They didn't have any blacks on the team then, never had, and Marshall had been told that if he didn't put some blacks on the team, they weren't going to play in the D.C. stadium any more. So I was the guy.

I was also the last guy to learn about the trade. Everybody thought I knew about the trade but I didn't. After the last game of the season, against the Giants in Yankee Stadium in 1961, Paul Brown came over and said, "Sometimes we do things we don't want to do," and shook his head. I didn't know what he was talking about. And Jim Brown, whose locker was next to

Bobby Mitchell became one of the greatest receivers in Redskins history. During his career in Washington (1962–1968), the fleet Mitchell (he ran the 100-yard dash in 9.7 seconds) caught 393 passes for 6,491 yards, 58 for touchdowns. His most productive year was 1963, when his reception yardage was 1,436, a Redskins record that has never been bettered. Mitchell was inducted into the Pro Football Hall of Fame in 1983.

mine, said something like, "I didn't have anything to do with this. I want you to know that." I said to myself, "What the hell's he talking about?" Apparently, the papers in Cleveland had carried some articles saying that Jim Brown had been talking to Ernie Davis about coming to the Cleveland Browns. Jim thought I had read about it, although I hadn't.

But I was on my way to Washington to begin what turned out to be a career with the Redskins that's now 40 years long. I was concerned. I was leaving a team that had been a real contender, always winning seasons, and joining one that had won only one game the year before, the worst record in the NFL. And a team that had never fielded a black player before.

Bill McPeak, the Redskins head coach, called and asked me to come in and talk. He had hoped that while I was there I could meet Mr. Marshall. I did meet him, and later we got an opportunity to talk regarding my contract. I'd met an attorney in Washington, Turk Thompson, who later became a respected judge in that city, and he offered to accompany me, help me out in the negotiation. What I didn't know then was that they didn't allow representation, not in the early sixties. Mr. Marshall asked him what he was doing there.

"I'm with Bobby . . . to help him out," he replied.

"No you're not," Marshall said. "Get out of here." Ran him right out of the office. Anyway, we talked and finally came to an agreement. I got a raise. He didn't want to give it to me, thought that what I did the year before was for the Browns and therefore he shouldn't have to reward me. But he did. Then he gave me three pieces of advice before I left: "This is Washington; don't get involved with politics." "Be a good man" (I think he actually said "boy"). And "Don't ask for too much money."

I reported to training camp in California, and I could tell they didn't have a lot of good ballplayers. I watched the [offensive] line, and as a running back I felt there was cause for some real concern. Coach McPeak said to me, "You can tell we don't have much of a line, but I've got a pretty good quarterback, Norm Snead. What would you think about playing outside?" I took another look at that line and said, "Yup."

I'd never played as a receiver before but I was sure I could do it. Throughout the training camp that summer I worked with Norm. There was no receivers coach in those days, so we just worked it out among ourselves, and by the time the season was ready to start we had connected pretty good.

It was a really different time then. To give an example, after we broke camp, we went back to Washington. They always had a "Welcome Home" luncheon. It was at the Shoreham Hotel and there were six or seven hundred people there. It was to present the team and introduce the new players. At the end, Marshall got everybody up to sing. The band played. The song was "Dixie." I wasn't singing. Marshall shouted over at me, "You sing, Bobby Mitchell . . . sing!" I mouthed like I was singing, but I didn't.

We opened against the Browns in Cleveland and I really wanted to do well against them. They were a big favorite that day. I didn't get the ball as much as I would've liked, but I did get it at the end and scored the game-winning touchdown. It was one of the most memorable moments of my career. Later that season the Browns came to Washington, and we beat them again. Then the next year I caught a pass for a 99-yard touchdown against the Browns, another moment I really cherish, which was a Redskins record [and still is, but shared].

Bill McPeak was a good coach, in my opinion, and he did a good job with the little he had to work with. We never had a winning season, however. Then Vince Lombardi came. He scared us into a winning season. We were the same team that had won only 5 of 14 games in 1968. In 1969 we were 7–5–2, a big turnaround.

Lombardi was determined to make us into the Green Bay Packers. But we had different personnel; we were a much faster team. We had Charley Taylor by then, and Larry Brown; and Sonny Jurgensen had the quickest release. He spent most of the training camp getting us to run the "Lombardi Sweep," but we were too fast for it; our timing was always off and we couldn't slow down to make the cuts. Green Bay was a precision team; it was perfect for them with Paul Hornung and Jim Taylor, but not right for us. By the end of training camp Coach Lombardi realized that. I remember he said to me, "I made a mistake. We've got to do it differently." We did, and it worked.

After that season I retired. It was Coach Lombardi who talked me into staying with the organization. I had some other offers, but he was forceful and he convinced me it would be best to stay. I started out in scouting, traveling all over the country, looking at the college talent.

We lost Coach Lombardi that year. Coach George Allen came along shortly thereafter and he really got things going for the Redskins. He moved me to another position, one he created: director of pro scouting. I believe we were the first team to ever have that position. George, of course, was much more interested in veteran players than the college kids. He got his "Over-the-Hill Gang" and he

was happy. George took us to the Super Bowl. He was a great motivator, and I learned as much if not more from him about football than I had from anyone in all my years.

After George Allen was released, Bobby Beathard was brought in as general manager. He was an exceptional personnel man, a great scout, and excellent at assessing talent. Where Bobby was most impressive was in his drafting between the third and seventh rounds. Anybody can get the first two rounds down; you just have to go to the magazines and newspapers for that. But from three to seven, that's really important; that is, in fact, where he built much of the team that was to go to the Super Bowls for Washington under Joe Gibbs.

Beathard went out and got Gibbs for the Redskins [1981]. It was one of the most important and successful moves in Redskins history. After Joe took over the team, we took off like a bat out of hell. We had a great run with Joe, four Super Bowls, three world championships.

I was on Redskins teams with some great players: Norm Snead, Sonny Jurgensen, Charley Taylor, Jerry Smith, Pat Richter. . . . But one I especially note is John Nisby. John was a guard and he arrived the same year I did, 1962; he came over from the Steelers. John was small, but a great lead guard and one of the best blockers in the game. He was smart and he was a leader of the offensive line, and that line surely needed one.

I've been very fortunate to have been involved with the game I love so much for so long. I've been especially fortunate to be with the Redskins through all the ups and downs, the thrills and the disappointments. I've played for them, scouted for them, handled so many different kinds of front office assignments. I'm glad I listened to Coach Lombardi when my playing days ended. It's been a great time, and Washington is a great place to be.

—BOBBY MITCHELL

HAIL REDSKINS

TRIUMPH
BOOKS
CHICAGO

1
The Redskins' Heritage

The year was 1932. The United States was well into the Great Depression, Franklin Delano Roosevelt was out campaigning for the first time for the presidency of the United States, while in Germany, rabble-rousing Adolf Hitler was coming into power. Amelia Earhart had just become the first woman to fly across the Atlantic solo, famine was sweeping the Soviet Union, and a tall, arrogant, flamboyant laundry tycoon decided to diversify his business interests and launch a professional football team in Boston.

George Preston Marshall, who owned a string of laundries in the Washington, D.C., area, as well as a team in the old National Basketball League, was persuaded by two acquaintances from the basketball circuit—National Football League president Joe Carr and Chicago Bears owner George Halas—to take on the newly available Boston NFL franchise. Marshall lined up three partners: Larry Doyle, a New York stockbroker; Jay O'Brien, a New York investment banker; and Vincent Bendix, an automotive supplier in South Bend, Indiana. The franchise's self-appointed chief executive officer, Marshall, then signed a contract to play the team's games at Braves Field, home of the Boston Braves of baseball's National League. The laundryman promptly dubbed his team the Braves as well.

The Boston Braves were not the first professional football team to appear in Beantown. Back in 1926, in the first American Football League, which had been founded by C. C. "Cash and Carry" Pyle to compete with the NFL, there had been a Boston franchise known as the Bulldogs. However, that league had lasted only a year. The Boston Bulldogs were revived in 1929 as an NFL franchise, but after a lackluster season (4–4–0), and a profound failure to attract fans, the team went out of business.

Marshall was told that Boston was a wonderful baseball town; it supported two teams in the major leagues, the Braves and the Red Sox. College football also had a dedicated following at institutions like Harvard, Boston University, Boston College, and nearby schools such as Amherst, Holy Cross, Dartmouth, and Tufts. Marshall was warned, though, that Boston was not a city that waxed warmly to professional football, a game that, in those days, still drew the disdain of college football coaches and the apathy of many otherwise devoted sports fans. After all, it was less than a decade since the legendary coach of the University of Chicago, Amos Alonzo Stagg, had condemned pro football as an insidious force, referring to it as a menace on a par with gambling. And Red Grange's coach at the University of Illinois, Bob Zuppke, had refused to talk to his great running back for several years after the Galloping Ghost signed with the NFL's Chicago Bears in

1925. Many of those same sentiments still lingered in ever-proper Boston, Marshall was informed. But with consummate faith in his entrepreneurial talents and his flair for promotion, the laundry magnate ignored the warning and set about organizing his team.

In 1932, the National Football League was a world away from the NFL of today. There were only eight teams, no divisions or conferences, no playoffs or formal championship game. Of the eight teams, only five franchises besides Mr. Marshall's would survive into the modern NFL: the Chicago Bears, the Green Bay Packers, the New York Giants, the Chicago (later St. Louis and still later Phoenix) Cardinals, and the Portsmouth (Ohio) Spartans, who would eventually relocate to Detroit and change their name to the Lions. There was no uniformity of schedule in those early years of the league either. The Bears, for example, played 14 games in 1932, the Spartans 12, and Marshall's Braves just 10.

The NFL was still very young. Only 12 years had elapsed since Ralph Hay of the Canton Bulldogs, George Halas of the Decatur Staleys (soon to become the Chicago Bears), and several other pro football owners met at the now famous Hay's Hupmobile showroom in Canton, Ohio, on September 17, 1920, to organize what would become the National Football League. And it was only seven years since pro football had been put on the proverbial sports map by the game's most dazzling and most publicized running back, Red Grange. After joining the Chicago Bears in 1925, Grange was sent with them on a whirlwind barnstorming tour that took pro football from the Midwest to the East Coast, down to Florida, across the country to California, and up to the state of Washington. (During the first part of the junket the Bears played an incredible eight games in 11 days in eight different cities.) When it was over, professional football had stepped out of its infancy with a following that had not been there before. No longer would teams perform on Sunday afternoons to crowds as small as two or three thousand, nor would game results and league standings be relegated to some inconspicuous slot inside the various newspapers' sports pages. It was, however, still a long way from filled stadiums and front-page headlines, which would not come until after World War II.

By 1932 the league had had to withstand a variety of perils. Besides fan indifference during its first five years, there had also been the competition from a new league, the first AFL, to which Grange and a number of other important NFL players defected in 1926. There was also, of course, the onslaught of the worst economic depression in the nation's history.

None of this fazed George Preston Marshall. A supreme optimist—with an ego to match—he looked with relish on the challenge of endearing professional football to the citizens of Boston, Massachusetts.

After securing a place to play, Marshall hired Lud Wray as head coach and gave him full responsibility for recruiting a team. Wray, who had played for the Buffalo All-Americans and the Rochester Jeffersons in the NFL in the early twenties, and had coached at his alma mater, the University of Pennsylvania, set about the task with enthusiasm.

"How do you go about assembling a brand-new football team?" James J. Haggerty asked in his book *Hail to the Redskins* in 1964:

> **In 1932, it wasn't all that difficult. The college draft had not yet been invented so the entire collegiate pool was available and there were only eight NFL teams bidding. In addition, the folding of three teams after the previous season had sent some 60 experienced pros scurrying for another chance.**
>
> **Wray signed up 40 players, and another 30 or more willing to pay their own expenses to Boston for a tryout came in over the transom. To save travel money, Marshall rented a bus on the West Coast. Albert Glen "Turk" Edwards, a very large tackle from Washington State, drove the bus cross-country, picking up the signees at various stops.**

The biggest find was Marshall's, however, and it was one of pure serendipity. The youngster was Cliff "Gip" Battles from the obscure college of West Virginia Wesleyan. A fleet halfback who could also pass and kick, Battles had starred in a game the year before in Washington against Georgetown, which Marshall had just happened to attend. Now that he had a team, Marshall wanted Gip Battles on it; and, as was soon to become evident, Marshall usually got what he wanted. He sent a scout down to West Virginia to sign him. The scout allegedly asked, "What if he won't sign?" "Then just keep on going," Marshall is said to have told him. Battles was signed by Boston; it helped, of course, that few other NFL teams had heard of him down at tiny West Virginia Wesleyan.

Other major acquisitions besides Battles and Turk Edwards, both of whom would eventually represent the Redskins in the Pro Football Hall of Fame, were two gifted backs from Southern Cal: Erny Pinckert, an exceptional blocking back, and Jim Musick, a punishing fullback.

The best players, however, were spread among three teams. The Green Bay Packers, coached by Curly Lambeau, had won three straight NFL titles. They had a balanced offense that featured the speed and pass-catching abilities of half-back Johnny "Blood" McNally; the league's top passer, tailback Arnie Herber; and the bruising power of fullback Clarke Hinkle. In addition, they boasted a pair of linemen destined for the Hall of Fame: tackle Cal Hubbard and guard "Iron" Mike Michalske.

Redskin back Erny Pinckert intercepts a Chicago Cardinals pass in the 1933 meeting between the two teams. Washington won that day, 10-0.

There was also Green Bay's stalwart rival, the Chicago Bears, whose backfield showcased a pair of football legends: halfback Red Grange and fullback Bronko Nagurski. The Portsmouth Spartans were a factor too, guided on the field by All-Pro tailback Dutch Clark and augmented by two other exceptional backs, Ace Gutowsky and Father Lumpkin.

So it was in the autumn of 1932 that George Preston Marshall brought his brand-new Braves to confront the Depression, the Packers, the Bears, the Spartans, and the whims of Boston's sports fans.

• • •

The Braves made their Massachusetts debut not in Boston but in nearby Quincy, in an exhibition game against the semipro Quincy Trojans at a place called Fore River Field. About 3,000 fans turned out for the game that late September Sunday afternoon. Boston, which according to a local sportswriter of the day, Arthur Sampson, was "displaying its All-America-studded cast of

THE FIRST STARTING LINEUP, 1932

		HGT.	WGT.	COLLEGE
E	Paul Collins	6'1"	195	Pittsburgh
E	George Kenneally	6'	190	St. Bonaventure
T	Turk Edwards	6'2"	230	Washington State
T	Jim MacMurdo	6'1"	205	Pittsburgh
G	Joe Kresky	6'	210	Wisconsin
G	George Hurley	6'	200	Washington State
C	Mickey Erickson	6'2"	210	Northwestern
B	"Honolulu" Hughes	5'10"	195	Oregon State
HB	Cliff Battles	6'1"	190	West Virginia Wesleyan
HB	Erny Pinckert	6'	200	Southern California
FB	Jim Musick	5'11"	205	Southern California
Coach	Lud Wray			

former intercollegiate stars," had little trouble dispatching the Quincy men, winning 25–0. Fullback Musick contributed two touchdowns, and Tony Plansky and Reggie Rust accounted for the other two. But it was hardly a lesson in "slick-smooth" football; according to Sampson in his game wrap-up: "Frequent penalties, sloppy handling of the ball, indecisive blocking, and missed assignments cropped out often enough to prevent either team from many sustained marches."

The Braves opened the 1932 regular season at their own ballpark before a crowd of about 6,000 on Sunday, October 2, playing host to the Brooklyn Dodgers. The Dodgers were led by one of the game's best passing quarterbacks, Benny Friedman, although passing was still only a minor part of each team's

FIRST YEAR, 1932: 4-4-2

Braves	0	Brooklyn Dodgers	14	Home
Braves	14	New York Giants	6	Home
Braves	0	Chicago Cardinals	9	Home
Braves	0	New York Giants	0	Away
Braves	7	Chicago Bears	7	Home
Braves	19	Staten Island Stapletons	6	Home
Braves	0	Green Bay Packers	21	Home
Braves	0	Portsmouth Spartans	10	Away
Braves	8	Chicago Cardinals	6	Away
Braves	7	Brooklyn Dodgers	0	Away

offensive game plan. Friedman and an impenetrable Brooklyn defense managed to blank the Braves in their premiere performance in Boston, 14–0. George Preston Marshall made his presence known not only with his sartorial splendor as he sat in his box, but also on the sideline from time to time as he passed on a variety of opinions regarding strategy, substitutions, and other such tips to Coach Wray.

The following Sunday, Marshall's Braves posted their first regular-season victory. It was also staged at Braves Field and it involved another New York team, Tim Mara's Giants, who were captained and coached by tackle Steve Owen. The Giants also featured such future Hall of Famers as center Mel Hein and ends Ray Flaherty and Red Badgro, as well as a pair of electrifying backs, Chris Cagle and "Shipwreck" Kelly. But behind the tailbacking of Cliff Battles, and an impressive 55-yard return of an intercepted lateral by defensive back Algy Clark for a touchdown, the Braves prevailed, 14–6.

The rest of the season seesawed. The Braves found they could not beat the Bears, Packers, or Spartans, but they handled themselves respectably against all the other teams in the league. At season's end, the Braves, with a record of 4–4–2,

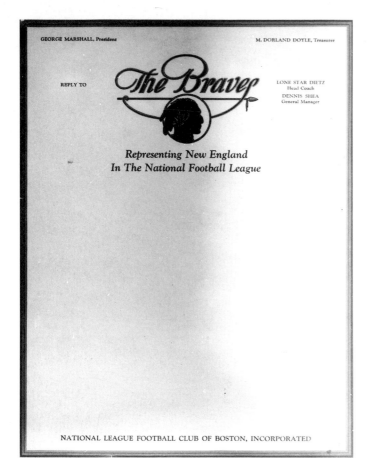

were in fourth place in the NFL behind, unsurprisingly, the Bears, Packers, and Spartans. Cliff Battles had the honor of leading the league in rushing, with 576 yards on 148 carries, gaining more yards than such illustrious backs as the Bears' Bronko Nagurski, the Stapletons' Ken Strong, Green Bay's Clarke Hinkle, and Portsmouth's Dutch Clark.

Although the Braves played some good football and showcased some exciting players, Bostonians interested themselves in other Sunday activities for the most part, and the team ended the season with a loss of about $46,000. It was enough to induce Marshall's three partners to look for a safer investment; but the laundryman was hooked on pro football. He announced he was in it to stay and was gearing all his efforts to making it "not only a treat for the people of Boston but also a profitable venture, without stinting on hiring the best players that money can buy."

There were to be major changes, however. Lud Wray had felt Marshall's dissatisfaction. At the same time, the coach had begun to harbor similar sentiments toward his meddling boss, who had spent a major part of the season personally delivering or sending messages to Wray on the sideline or in the locker room—most of which the coach had ignored. Before Marshall could fire Wray, however, Wray quit to coach the Philadelphia Eagles, who had just joined the NFL.

Wray was replaced by William "Lone Star" Dietz, a full-blooded Native American who had played alongside the legendary Jim Thorpe at Carlisle and had coached the Indian team at Haskell Institute. Dietz was an appropriate selection because Marshall, who had just changed the team's name to the Redskins, had decided that he was going to exploit the "Indian motif," as he called it, to the fullest. To set the tone, he now had his Redskins players pose with war paint on their faces and wearing feathers. Their new coach was also known to appear from

The Big Chief himself, George Preston Marshall, has his ceremonial headdress adjusted by his wife, former movie star Corinne Griffith.

In the thirties, we would, at the urging of George [Preston Marshall], put on war paint before a game and do a little Indian dance to entertain the paying customers. None of us liked that very much.

time to time in a full headdress. Marshall then moved the team from Braves Field to Fenway Park, home of the Boston Red Sox.

Pro football itself had undergone some changes when the Redskins took the field in 1933. Some of the changes were the result of the efforts of Marshall. He was a veritable novice in the league compared to Halas, Lambeau, and Mara, but Marshall, with the backing of those stalwarts, persuaded the other owners to restructure the league into two divisions, with a championship game between the division winners at the season's end. There was also a slew of new rules pushed through by Marshall and Halas to make the game more offense-oriented and thus higher-scoring. Forward passing was now permitted from anywhere behind the line of scrimmage (previously it had only been allowed from five yards or more behind the line), and lateral passes could be made anywhere on the field. For the next play after plays that ended out of bounds or near the sideline, the ball was brought 10 yards in from the sideline; in addition, the goal posts were moved from the end line to the goal line, and a new, slimmer football, which was more advantageous for passing, was introduced.

The Redskins were slotted in the NFL East along with the New York Giants, the Brooklyn Dodgers, the Philadelphia Eagles, and the Pittsburgh Pirates. Both the Eagles, founded by Bert Bell, and the Pirates (later to become the Steelers), launched by Art Rooney, were newcomers to the NFL. The year before, the Redskins had finished higher in the league standings than the other three teams now in the NFL East. If a favorite to win the division had been picked before the season, it would have been Marshall's Redskins. But it was not to be. Losses to the Bears and the Portsmouth Spartans and a tie with Green Bay in their first five games effectively kept the Redskins out of the running. The rejuvenated New York Giants, who had added triple-threat All-Pro Ken Strong to their backfield, marched through the division to an 11–3–0 season.

Despite the best running attack in the entire NFL, the Redskins of 1933 were still unable to break the .500 barrier, winning five, losing five, and tying two—a finish that was only good enough for third place in the NFL East. The Redskins did have the two top rushers in the league, however, with Jim Musick grinding out 809 yards on 173 carries and Cliff Battles sprinting for 737 on 146 carries. Both Battles and tackle Turk Edwards were named to the NFL's All-Pro team.

The move to Fenway Park, however, didn't entice more fans than Braves Field had the year before. The team was again in the red at the end of the year; money was so tight that during home games, the story has often been told, Marshall would personally go in after balls kicked into the stands and demand that they be returned.

The Redskins added several impressive rookies in 1934, most notably a 6'4" end from Texas A&M, Charley Malone, and halfback Pug Rentner from

Northwestern University. On the downside, however, Marshall could not come to terms with league-leading rusher Jim Musick, and the fullback decided to sit out the season.

Once again the Redskins struggled in the first part of the season. Losses to the Dodgers, the Giants, and the Detroit Lions (formerly the Portsmouth Spartans) in the first five games of the 1934 season almost prevented them from attaining a second-place finish and moving a step closer to the division-winning Giants (8–5–0). The Redskins lost both of their encounters with the Giants.

Battles gained 511 yards rushing, but was omitted from that season's All-Pro squad—it was the year that the Bears' Beattie Feathers, behind the blocking of Bronko Nagurski, became the first NFL rusher to gain more than 1,000 yards (1,004, a 9.4-yard average). Rookie Charley Malone made his presence felt by leading the team in pass receptions with 11 for 121 yards—the fourth most in the NFL that year, illustrating how run-oriented the game was in the 1930s.

BOSTON POST, MONDAY, OCTOBER 16, 1933

Unable to produce a winning season in two tries, Lone Star Dietz was expelled from the tribe, and Marshall replaced him with a hometown favorite, Eddie Casey. For the four previous years Casey had been the head coach at neighboring Harvard, and back in 1919 he had won All-America honors as a halfback at that institution. Casey was well known around Boston and respected for his football leadership, and Marshall felt he had landed both a winning coach and a local hero sure to attract additional fans to Fenway Park.

The Redskins acquired a fine pair of rookies in 1935: Bill Shepherd, an all-around back from Western Maryland, and Jim Barber, a tackle out of San Francisco University. Shepherd led the team in rushing and passing in 1935 but did not complete the season in Boston. He was sent to Detroit in a trade because he could not get along with Coach Casey.

Marshall, on the other hand, seemed to like Casey a lot. He sat on the bench next to him at almost every game, offering plays, strategies, and other bits of football advice. He liked him, at least, through the season opener. After two preseason romps over semipro teams, the Redskins defeated the Brooklyn Dodgers, 7–3, to open the 1935 season on a winning note. Unfortunately, it was the only victory they would post until the next to last game of the year. With a record of 2–8–1 and a fourth-place finish, Casey lost his seat next to Marshall on the sideline.

The new coach for 1936, the Redskins' fourth in their five-year history, was Ray Flaherty, an often-honored All-Pro end who had retired from the Giants at the end of the 1935 season. Flaherty had a keen eye for football talent, and in that first year of the collegiate draft he focused it well. In the first round, the Redskins selected All-America tailback Riley Smith of Alabama, known to be a fine passer,

League Standing (Nov. 26)

Eastern Division	Won	Lost	Tied	Per.	Western Division	Won	Lost	Tied	Per.
New York	7	4	0	.636	Chicago Bears	11	0	0	1.000
BOSTON	5	6	0	.454	Detroit	10	1	0	.909
Brooklyn	4	5	0	.444	Green Bay	6	5	0	.545
Philadelphia	3	7	0	.300	Chicago Cards	4	6	0	.400
Pittsburgh	2	10	0	.166	St. Louis	1	9	0	.100

CAPTAIN ERNY PINCKERT with the faithful "Snooks," Mascot

☞ *ORDER YOUR 1935 SEASON TICKETS IN ADVANCE*

Team captain Erny Pinckert poses with the Washington mascot (named "Snooks") in 1934. A fullback out of Southern Cal, Pinckert was a stalwart on Redskins teams throughout the thirties.

MARSHALL'S CODE OF CONDUCT

In the thirties, George Preston Marshall, as fastidious as he was stubborn, published a Code of Conduct for his players and distributed it:

You will be expected to conduct yourselves in such a manner as to always be a credit to the game and your club.

Violation of publicly accepted and traditional training rules for athletes—rowdiness, boisterousness and ungentlemanly conduct of any and every sort—will not be tolerated.

In hotel lobbies, dining rooms and restaurants, and at all public functions where the team appears as a unit, shirts, ties and coats are to be worn unless otherwise instructed.

Night clubs, bars, cocktail lounges and gambling spots are definitely out of bounds.

something Marshall's team had lacked in its first four years. To give Smith a top-notch receiver to throw to, Boston acquired All-America end Wayne Millner from Notre Dame in the eighth round. A fine receiver, but also an exceptional blocker and defensive player, Millner would perform well enough in six seasons with the Redskins to earn entry into the Pro Football Hall of Fame. Two other acquisitions for the backfield were Eddie Britt of Holy Cross and Ed Justice of Gonzaga.

In his first year, Flaherty not only added a plethora of talent to the Redskins team, he also did what no other Boston coach had been able to do: he got Marshall off the sideline and into the grandstands. Flaherty demanded autonomy in running the team, and Marshall, perhaps still feeling the awful pain of a 2–8–1 season, conceded.

With full field control, Flaherty sailed into the 1936 season with what the Boston sports press considered a leaky ship patched with new but still unproven timbers. Coach Flaherty, however, ignored the preseason prognostications. He continued to ignore them even after the Skins were shut out in the opener at Pittsburgh, 10-0, by a team that had posted a paltry 4–8–0 record the year before.

Battles reversed the momentum the following week, however, when he once again asserted his team leadership on the field and led the Redskins to a 26–3 victory over the Philadelphia Eagles. The following week he contributed a 65-yard touchdown run to another win, 14–3, over the Brooklyn Dodgers.

From that point on, the Redskins joined a season-long title battle with the divisional champion Giants and the Pittsburgh Pirates.

With just two games remaining in their regular season, the Redskins were essentially tied for first place, with a record of 5–5–0. The Giants and Pirates were also in the running, with respective records of 4–5–1 and 6–5–0. (The Pirates had only one game remaining in those days of convenience scheduling.) Those were the two teams Flaherty's contenders had to face.

Pittsburgh came to Fenway Park for the Redskins' last home game of 1936, hoping to wrest first place from Boston with a victory. But the Skins were ready and destroyed any lingering hope Pittsburgh had for a divisional title with a 30–0 triumph, then the second-highest margin of victory in Redskins history (they had defeated the Pirates 39–0 in 1934).

Marshall was enthralled with the overwhelming performance of his team that Sunday, but he was appalled at the sparsely filled stadium— only a few more than 4,800 had turned out to see the crucial contest. One reason many stayed away, however, was the fact that Marshall had suddenly raised ticket prices on the day of the game. More than a few disgruntled fans had turned their backs on the box office and sought Sunday entertainment elsewhere.

Marshall's disenchantment with the lack of paying customers and the indifference of the city's sports scribes had exceeded his threshold of patience. After the game, he announced that he was through with the city. "I'm licked, so far as Boston is concerned," he said:

> **Fans in paying quantities don't seem to want us. Maybe they don't want me. Whatever it is, five years of trying and $100,000 [his estimated losses over that period] in money is enough to spend in one place when you can't get anywhere. We'll stay in the game, but it will be somewhere else.**

With that in mind, Marshall and Flaherty took the Redskins down to New York to face the Giants at the Polo Grounds in a game that would decide that year's NFL East title. The Redskins were 6–5–0 and the Giants, who had defeated the Dodgers while Boston was mauling the Pirates, had a record of 5–5–1. (The Pirates had ended their season with a record of 6–6–0 and were mathematically eliminated from the race.)

G eorge Preston Marshall was never known for throwing nickels around with abandon during his three decades of running the Redskins. He set the standard, so to speak, from the very beginning. These are the salaries of the highest-paid members of the Boston Redskins the year they reached their first NFL championship game:

		SALARY PER GAME
HB	Cliff Battles	$210
QB	Riley Smith	$200
FB	Erny Pinckert	$165
T	Turk Edwards	$165
E	Wayne Millner	$165
HB	Jim Musick	$165
FB	Pug Rentner	$150
HB	Eddie Britt	$140
C	Larry Siemering	$140
HB	Ed Justice	$135
HB	Ed Smith	$135

Most of the other players earned about $100 a game. Head Coach Ray Flaherty received $450 a game, more than twice his highest-paid player. Total expenses for the Redskins (according to the organization's accounting sheets) for 26 players, two coaches, one trainer, and the office staff, were less than $45,000 for the eastern division champions that year.

A heavy rain earlier in the day had made the field a mud hole, and an intermittent cold drizzle throughout the game did not make for the best of conditions. Still, more than 18,000 stalwart fans passed through the turnstiles at the Polo Grounds, a fact that did not go unnoticed by Marshall.

The Redskins managed to march to the New York 1-yard line after Battles snagged a short pass and ran 20 yards with it. From there fullback Don Irwin, who had just been acquired the week before, bulled in for a touchdown. In the second half, the fleet Battles, seemingly unfazed by the semiswamp in which he was playing, darted and dodged, slipped and slid 75 yards for another touchdown. It was all the scoring that would take place that rain-swept afternoon, giving the Redskins a 14–0 triumph and their first divisional crown.

The NFL East winner was scheduled to host the 1936 championship game, so it was in Boston that Lambeau's Green Bay Packers, triumphant in the NFL West, were scheduled to do battle for the NFL title. But Marshall, who felt that Boston had abandoned him and his team, decided to abandon Boston. Remembering the 18,000 who had braved the rain and cold in New York to watch a football game and the 4,800 who had shown up in Boston, he announced that the 1936 title game would be played at the Polo Grounds in New York.

The divisional champs met on that neutral site on December 13, 1936. There the now-homeless Redskins fell to a favored Green Bay Packer team, 21–6.

A week after the game, George Preston Marshall announced that in 1937 the Boston Redskins would be known as the Washington Redskins and would play their games at Griffith Stadium, home of baseball's Washington Senators, in the nation's capital and at the hub of his laundry empire.

Shirley Povich, in an article for the *Washington Post*, once accurately and insightfully described the Redskins' founding father in a single sentence:

> **The supreme authority of the Washington Redskins was George Preston Marshall, as dashing a figure as ever strode the American sports scene, and sometimes as notorious and unloved as he was famous and admired for his innovations.**

He was known as the Big Chief, and from its inception in 1932 until poor health forced him to step down in 1962, no one ever doubted that he ruled the tribe like a true autocrat. He made all the business decisions, as well as many of those regarding football strategy; he hired and discarded coaches as if they came from a temporary-help agency; and he was an outspoken and highly active leader in league affairs. Always the showman, the personification of pizzazz, he also introduced to the National Football League the marching band and halftime entertainment, appropriately billed as extravaganzas. In his hometown of Washington he became a legend of sorts. As Jack Walsh of the Washington Post observed:

> **Whether having a shampoo in the Statler-Hilton barber shop, dining at Duke Zeibert's, or holding court on the Shoreham [hotel] terrace, Marshall considered it a lost opportunity were he not the center of attention.**

To the chagrin of his parade of coaches, Marshall was notorious for giving his opinions on everything from game plans to player personnel, not to mention specific plays during the course of a game. He telephoned instructions from his private box to the bandstand to dictate songs and the specifics of halftime entertainment by his beloved band. One Washington reporter even noted, "He [Marshall] never obtained a license to drive an auto, but he always sat beside his chauffeur giving directions and instructions."

His contributions to the National Football League and the football fans of Washington, however, were profound enough to gain him charter membership in the Pro Football Hall of Fame. His innovations on and off the field—from rule changes to a team fight song—were instrumental in forming the professional football league we know today and in popularizing the sport.

In 1932, Marshall and three partners purchased the franchise designated for Boston and named his team the Boston Braves. It was reported that he put up only $1,500 for the franchise and posted another $1,500 as a guarantee. Later he claimed he never paid a single penny for the franchise itself. After a dismal year at the box office, a mediocre season on the field (4–4–2), and a net loss of $46,000, Marshall lost his three partners but hung on to the team.

In 1933, his second year in the NFL, Marshall and his friend and archrival George Halas of the Chicago Bears were the guiding forces behind a league reorganization and the adoption of a variety of new rules. Generally regarded as the dawn of the "modern NFL," these Marshall/Halas innovations included forming two separate divisions with a championship game between the winners of each, allowing forward passes from anywhere behind the line of scrimmage, instituting hash marks, and moving the goal posts from the end line to the goal line. The result was a more open, high-scoring game, and a much more dramatic season finale.

Show business had always been part of Marshall's life. After graduating from Randolph-Macon College in Virginia, he aspired to be an actor. He landed a few small parts in shows in Washington and New York but finally admitted, "I wasn't much of an actor." Then he quickly added, to counter the negative:

I once brought the house down delivering just a single line. It was at the Walker Theater in Winnipeg, Canada, in 1917. The stage manager asked me to go out at intermission and make an announcement. I stepped out in front of the curtain and said: "The United States has just declared war on Germany." And those Canadians went crazy.

Marshall had inherited the Palace Laundry in Washington, D.C., from his father back in 1918, and over the next three decades he built it into a booming business that eventually had 57 outlets (thus the nickname "Wet Wash King" Marshall, by which he was known in certain corners of the NFL). It was Marshall's flair for promotion that turned an otherwise run-down laundry shop into an extremely profitable business.

In the later twenties, Marshall sponsored a semipro basketball team and named them the Palace Big Five. It was through that organization that he met then–NFL President Joe Carr and Chicago Bears owner and coach George Halas, both of whom were associated with the basketball league in football's off-season. It was at their urging that he took on the NFL's Boston franchise in 1932.

The city of Boston and George Preston Marshall, however, did not exactly embrace each other with fervor. As Shirley Povich once observed in the *Washington Post*:

> **Certain habits of Boston people had outraged Marshall. First it was their custom of not attending his team's games in great numbers. Second, it was the low priority given his team in the sports pages, with the city's sports editors allotting more importance to traditional Boston favorites such as Harvard and Boston College football and its two big league baseball teams, the Red Sox and Braves. Marshall's pique peaked on one game day when Boston's leading newspaper gave more prominence to the Radcliffe girls hockey team than to his precious football lads.**

When Marshall raised ticket prices during the 1936 season, even more fans otherwise occupied themselves on Sunday afternoons. The newspapers finally gave him some attention, but it was to berate him for the ticket-price increase.

So Marshall gathered up all the players, shoulder pads, helmets, uniforms, and other assorted paraphernalia and left town. He did it in true Marshall fashion. His team had won the NFL Eastern Division title in 1936, earning them the right to face the Green Bay Packers for the league championship. Marshall talked the league into staging the contest for the crown—scheduled to be played in Boston—in New York City instead. And after the game, he kept right on going south until he reached the nation's capital and the hub of his laundry business.

Marshall engaged the Washington football fans immediately, first by bringing them rookie superstar Sammy Baugh and second by giving them an NFL championship his first year in town. The love affair that developed during that 1937 season between the city and the Redskins never wilted, despite frustrating times and an unholy 35-year drought between two championship eras.

With an excellent team and personally designed theatrics, Marshall filled the 29,000 seats of Griffith Stadium, then added 6,000 more to accommodate the crowds, which were much more enthusiastic than those encountered in Boston. Tickets ranged from $4.40 down to $3.60, and they were hard to obtain.

Awash in the popularity of his team, Marshall extended it by setting up a radio network that broadcast the Redskins games throughout the mid-Atlantic and Southern states. As a result, the team became the NFL's first to build a large following outside its own metropolitan area.

Marshall was also the first NFL owner to publicly announce that he wanted to attract women to his ballgames. Said Marshall:

> **For the women, football alone is not enough. I always try to present halftime entertainment to give them something to look forward to—a little music, dancing, color, something they can understand and enjoy.**

He also added that if he got women to come out to the games, he would get that many more men to come out.

Those he did not encourage to come were blacks, at least in the uniform of his team. The Redskins, under Marshall, were the last team in the NFL to add a black player to their roster. They did not do so until 1962, long after the other teams had easily (and very effectively) integrated their squads. When criticized for his nonemployment of blacks, Marshall responded, "I'll start using Negroes when the Harlem Globetrotters start using white basketball players." But in 1961, Secretary of the Interior Stewart Udall threatened to oust the team from the new and metropolitan-controlled D.C. Stadium if it did not begin hiring blacks.

So, in 1962, Marshall finally integrated the team by signing Bobby Mitchell—who would prove to be one of the finest receivers in the history of the NFL and who would merit enshrinement in the Pro Football Hall of Fame—as well as three other blacks.

It was the same year that failing health forced the 65-year-old Marshall to give up managerial control of the team and the marching band he loved so well.

George Preston Marshall died in 1969, bequeathing not only the Redskins to the world of professional football, but a long list of innovations and unique contributions to the sport.

In eulogy, John F. Steadman, then sports editor of the *Baltimore News-American*, captured the essence of the flamboyant and complex founder of the Washington Redskins:

George Preston Marshall was involved in every facet of the game, which meant improving the product.

He was also a strong-willed, unbending, non-compromising man with the strength of his convictions in all matters, be it in the area of politics, sports, religion or racial relations.

We heard him express himself on the question of integration and watched as he fought against hiring a Negro player for his Washington Redskins—a team that so much reflected the Marshall personality because of the way he operated it.

Suffice to say that George Preston Marshall was not a hypocrite. Whether you liked him or found him repulsive, you knew the stand he had taken because he let the world know it.

Marshall rarely backed away. He would arrive at a position and there was no changing him. Logic and reasoning and even the facts weren't going to influence Marshall's opinion on anything.

He was dictatorial in how he lived and tried to make others live. Marshall never allowed any of his employees with the Redskins to wish him a happy birthday because he wasn't cognizant of age and, in his world, he was going to live forever. . . .

It was Marshall's unfortunate belief he was infallible. Equipped with this kind of a personality meant that he made enemies at almost every turn. But he cared not, or at least it appeared that way.

Marshall would take an unpopular position and hold it—regardless of how much fire he had to face. If ever a man was his own man it was this tall, articulate, flamboyant figure who dominated the football scene for almost three decades. . . .

George Preston Marshall died at age 72 after a lingering, painful illness. He was proud and he was vain. Maybe now he might possibly admit that death is going to come to us all since he found out that even George Preston Marshall wasn't to be excluded.

The dapper laundryman turned sportsman: Redskins owner George Preston Marshall.

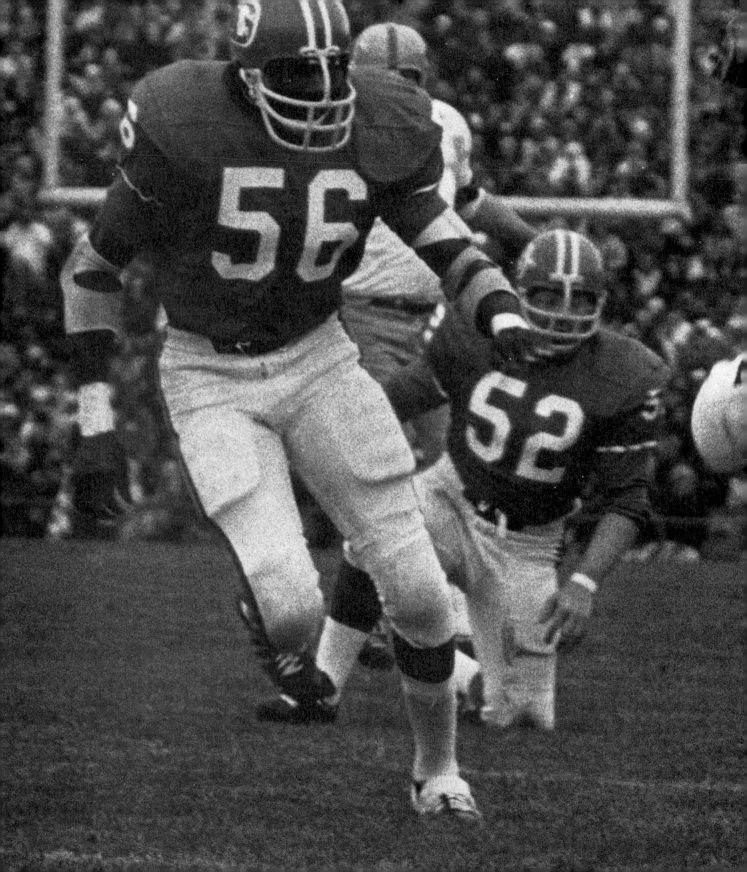

2
The Great Runners

Over the years, the Redskins have had a number of certifiably great runners carrying the ball for them. The first was Hall of Famer Cliff Battles, who debuted in their initial season in 1932, when the Redskins were the Braves and their hometown was Boston. Next came another Hall of Fame honoree, "Bullet" Bill Dudley, who joined the Skins in 1950. In 1969, Larry Brown came aboard and made his presence felt throughout the defenses of the NFC. Mike Thomas arrived in 1975. The following year the raucous John Riggins began his career in Washington. And in 1985 Heisman Trophy–winner George Rogers came from New Orleans to give the Skins a much-needed running game.

The most productive rusher ever to wear the burgundy and gold was John Riggins. In his nine years with the Redskins, Riggins gained 7,472 yards, almost 1,600 yards more than Larry Brown, who ate up 5,875 yards during his eight years in Washington. Only eight Redskins have gained more than 1,000 yards in a single season: Riggins (four times); Larry Brown, George Rogers, Earnest Byner, Terry Allen, and Stephen Davis (twice each); and Mike Thomas and Reggie Brooks (once each). Brown and Thomas did it in 14-game seasons.

Davis holds the top season total (1,405 in 1999). The mark for most yards gained in a single game was set in 1989 when Gerald Riggs gained 221 yards on 29 attempts against the Eagles. Cliff Battles gained 215 yards on 16 carries in 1933, an average of more than 13 yards per carry, in a game against the Giants. It was not until 1985 that another Redskins runner broke the 200-yard mark: George Rogers, when he gained 206 against the St. Louis Cardinals. The only other Washington rusher to top 200 yards in a game is Timmy Smith, who dazzled the football world with 204 yards gained during Super Bowl XXII in January 1988.

The longest run from scrimmage belongs to Billy Wells, who scampered 88 yards for a touchdown against the Chicago

Cardinals in 1954. Reggie Brooks ran 85 yards to score against Philadelphia in 1993. In 1950, Rob Goode accounted for the third longest run when he raced 80 yards for a score in a game with the Packers. And both Cliff Battles and Wilbur Moore have 75-yard touchdown runs to their credit, the former against the Giants in 1937 and the latter through the Chicago Cardinal defense of 1944.

Larry Jones holds the record for the longest kickoff return, 102 yards for a touchdown against the Eagles in 1974. The longest punt return, 96 yards, was logged by Bill Dudley in 1950, resulting in another touchdown during a game with the Steelers.

There have been other fine ball carriers over the almost seven decades of Redskins football, less renowned perhaps than those mentioned above, but certainly worthy of note. In the late thirties and forties there were Jim Musick, Pug Rentner, Andy Farkas, and Dick Todd. The best of the fifties included Rob Goode and Don Bosseler, and there was some brief but outstanding running from Charlie "Choo Choo" Justice, Billy Wells, and Vic Janowicz. The sixties, a much leaner

Fullback Andy Farkas makes a one-handed stab for a pass from Sammy Baugh in this game in the late thirties. Farkas was a mainstay on the Redskins from 1938 through 1944. He led the team in rushing four times; his most productive year was 1939, when he gained 547 yards and scored six touchdowns.

Running back Joe Washington struggles to hold onto the football after catching a pass from Joe Theismann in a 1983 game against the Oakland Raiders. Washington played for the Skins from 1981 through 1984 and led the team in rushing in 1981 with 916 yards.

decade in terms of rushing yardage, had some memorable days provided by Dick James, Charley Taylor, and A. D. Whitfield. In the seventies, an era dominated by the greats Brown, Thomas, and Riggins, Washington also got considerable yardage from Charlie Harraway. In the eighties, there were memorable performances from Joe Washington, Kelvin Bryant, and Timmy Smith, and in the nineties and beyond, Earnest Byner, Terry Allen, and Stephen Davis.

From these fine runners have come some of the most exciting moments in Washington Redskins history, from dazzling breakaway runs to 200-yard rushing days to game-winning touchdowns.

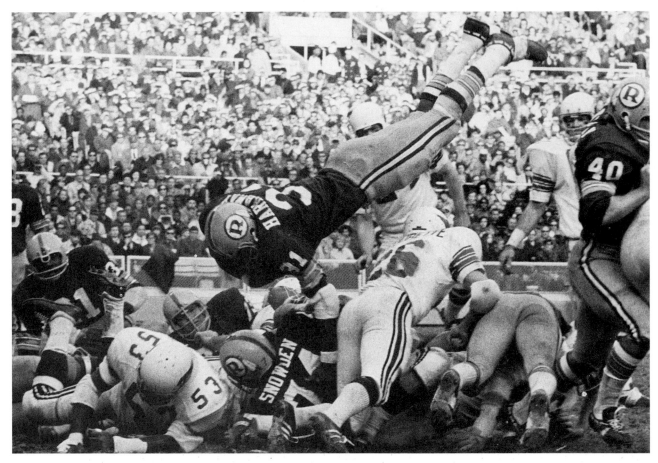

Fullback Charlie Harraway dives for a touchdown against the Cardinals in 1970. The Skins won that day, 28–27. Identifiable blockers are tackle Jim Snowden (on the ground) and halfback Dave Kopay (No. 40).

CLIFF BATTLES

Cliff "Gip" Battles was a 6'1", 190-pound tailback from West Virginia Wesleyan. George Preston Marshall discovered Battles himself—at least that's the way the Big Chief liked to tell the story. Marshall had seen him play in Washington in a game against Georgetown in 1931 and had been very impressed.

Marshall was not alone in his judgment of Battles. The New York Giants and the Portsmouth Spartans were also aware of him and offered contracts, but Battles chose to go with the Boston Braves in 1932 because they were the only team that actually sent someone to personally see him in West Virginia. And so he joined the fledgling Braves in their very first season in the National Football League.

Battles was the highest-paid player on Marshall's new ballclub, signed for a reported salary of $175 a game, with the stipulation that he would not be required to play more than two games in any one week. Almost all the other players on that maiden team were paid $100 a game or less. As Battles wryly observed later, "Our game checks were so small we were able to cash them on the bus after the game."

The Gip, as he was called, had been a magnificent runner in college; in one game against Salem, Battles gained 378 yards rushing and another 85 on punt returns. Had he played for a larger college, he surely would have won All-America honors.

Battles proved his worth from the very start. The Braves were a mediocre team in 1932, winning four games, losing four, and tying the other two. But Battles gained 576 yards rushing, the most in the league that year—more than Red Grange, Bronko Nagurski, Johnny "Blood" McNally, Dutch Clark, Ken Strong, and Clarke Hinkle, among others.

The following year, working out of a new double-wing formation installed by new Coach Lone Star Dietz for the renamed Redskins, Battles gained 737 yards, second in the NFL only to his fullback, Jim Musick, a rookie who ground out 809 for the Redskins. As he had the year before, Battles won All-Pro honors.

Battles was the star attraction through the next two seasons, but they were unexciting ones (6–6–0, 2–8–1). In 1936, however, he was able to lead the Skins to their first NFL divisional title. Leading the team in rushing yardage, with 614 yards, and in scoring, with 42 points, he was again named All-Pro.

In 1937, Battles moved with the Redskins to Washington and became one prong of the best two-pronged offense up to that time in NFL history. Marshall had signed "Slingin'" Sammy Baugh to pass for the Redskins while Battles, now a 201-pound fullback, would run the ball for them. The tandem did their jobs so well that each led the league that year—Baugh with 81 completions and 1,127 yards passing and Battles with 874 yards rushing (at the time the second most in NFL history). They also brought Washington its first NFL championship.

To get to the championship game that year, however, the Redskins had to win their last game of the season against the always difficult Giants in the always hostile Polo Grounds. They did it on the legs of Battles, who turned in one of the finest single-game performances of his illustrious football career. He scored two touchdowns and set up two more with a 75-yard run from scrimmage and a 76-yard interception return. When the afternoon was over, Battles had gained 170 yards rushing (an average of seven yards per carry) and the Redskins were on top of a 49–14 score.

Cliff Battles, from West Virginia Wesleyan, was the first great running back to wear a Braves (and then a Redskins) uniform, starring from 1932 through 1937. He was inducted into the Pro Football Hall of Fame in 1968. *Photo copyright the* Washington Post; *reprinted by permission of the Washington, D.C., Public Library.*

In the championship game against the Chicago Bears, which would prove to be the last pro football game of Battles's career, he gained 51 yards rushing and another 82 catching Baugh passes to help lead the Redskins to a 28–21 triumph.

A Phi Beta Kappa scholar in college, Battles was also an astute businessman. When Marshall refused to raise the fullback's yearly salary above $3,000 after his electrifying All-Pro season of 1937, the 28-year-old Battles quit and took a job coaching at Columbia University for $4,000 a year.

When he left, Battles had gained more yards rushing than any player in NFL history: 3,622. An All-Pro in three of his six years in the NFL, Cliff Battles was inducted into the Pro Football Hall of Fame in 1968.

BILL DUDLEY

"Bullet" Bill Dudley came to the Redskins in 1950 as an established star, having shone for six years on the fields of the Pittsburgh Steelers and the Detroit Lions. A true triple-threat back, although just a mere 5'10" and 175 pounds, he had been an All-America halfback at the University of Virginia and an All-Pro in the National Football League.

The nickname "Bullet" was not altogether appropriate, since Dudley was never known for having great speed. But he was renowned for his elusiveness when carrying the ball, which enabled him to provide some spectacular runs. He was an accomplished passer even though he threw the ball sidearm. He had the most unorthodox place-kicking style in the game (he never used an approach step), but he was consistent and effective. Dudley was also one of pro football's most feared punt-return specialists.

Dudley was, as they say, in the autumn of his career when he came to Washington. He had been traded to the Redskins by the Detroit Lions. When he sat down to discuss his contract with Washington Coach Herman Ball, they could not come to terms. Afterward, Dudley recalled:

> **George Preston Marshall . . . called me and asked me to meet him for lunch at this Greek restaurant. [He] came in wearing this very expensive suit. He was impeccable, very impressive. He said, "Bill, you're going to be playing for the first time for a football team that knows what it's doing."**

After some haggling and Marshall's discovery that Dudley was as intractable in negotiation as he was elusive on the football field, the laundryman hit the table with his fist and said, "All right, go tell Herman to give it to you." The "it" was a one-year salary of $12,500.

To show his appreciation, Dudley gave Marshall what the Big Chief later said was "one of the most exciting things I've ever seen on a football field." The Bullet fielded a punt in a 1950 game against the Pittsburgh Steelers at his own 4-yard line and wove his way back 96 yards for a touchdown. At the time it was the second-longest punt return in NFL history.

Dudley played for the Redskins in 1950 and 1951, left for a year to coach the backfield at Yale, and then returned to Washington for his last season in 1953. Dudley carried the ball, passed it, caught passes, kicked field goals and extra points, punted, and played defensive halfback.

"Bullet" Bill Dudley, who played his college ball at Virginia, was an outstanding halfback for the Redskins in 1950, 1951, and 1953. He was enshrined in the Pro Football Hall of Fame in 1966.

Dudley's days in Washington were only one segment of a pro football career rich enough to gain admittance to the Hall of Fame, an honor that was bestowed on him in 1966. During those years in the early fifties, he brought many people out to Griffith Stadium to watch his wily runs and flat-footed kicking style.

When the collective statistics were compiled for his nine-year NFL career, Bullet Bill Dudley had rushed for 3,057 yards (an average of four yards per carry); caught 123 passes for 1,383 yards; scored 19 touchdowns on runs and 18 on pass receptions; kicked 33 field goals and 121 extra points; gained 1,743 yards returning kickoffs and another 1,515 bringing back punts; intercepted 23 passes (returning two for touchdowns); and scored a total of 484 points.

Halfback Bill Dudley shows a little of his running style. Dudley made a name for himself not only with the Redskins but also with the Pittsburgh Steelers and the Detroit Lions before he came to Washington in 1950. He was also an excellent kickoff and punt returner as well as a fine defensive back in those days of the 60-minute men. *Photo courtesy of the Washington, D.C., Public Library, Washingtoniana Division.*

LARRY BROWN

Vince Lombardi, in his first and only year as head coach of the Redskins, knew his team desperately needed to develop a running game if it was to be a contender in the NFL East. He found his solution in the eighth round of the 1969 draft: 21-year-old running back Larry Brown from Kansas State. The legendary Lombardi saw Brown as the perfect counterpart in the Redskins backfield to the Hall of Fame passing combination of Sonny Jurgensen and Charley Taylor.

Lombardi not only fused the 5'11", 204-pound rookie into his starting backfield, but in the preseason took care of a hearing problem that was making it difficult for Brown to hear signals when he lined up to the left of the quarterback. "I picked up my helmet one day and there it was," Brown said, "a hearing aid attached inside."

Brown responded by gaining 888 yards rushing that first season, the second most in club annals at the time (Rob Goode had ground out 951 in 1951). It was the fourth-highest rushing total that year in the NFL, behind Gale Sayers of the Bears, Calvin Hill of the Cowboys, and Tom Matte of the Colts. Brown added another 302 yards on pass receptions, earned an invitation to the Pro Bowl, and was runner-up to Calvin Hill for NFL Rookie of the Year.

The following year Brown became the first Washington running back to gain more than 1,000 yards in a season. The 1,125 yards he churned out, with an average of 4.7 per carry, was the most in the NFL, and he was named All-Pro for his performance. He also rushed for more than 100 yards in six games.

Brown's finest year came in 1972. In the first 11 games of that season, Brown scored 12 touchdowns, including an electrifying 88-yard run after a 1-yard pass from Billy Kilmer in a game against the New York Jets. In a game against the New York Giants, he ran for 191 yards—a team record that eclipsed the 190 rushing yards Johnny Olszewski logged against the Cleveland Browns in 1959. The 1,216 yards Brown gained in the 14-game 1972 season, another club standard (which stood until John Riggins broke it in 16 games in 1983), was the most in the NFC and only 35 yards fewer than league-leader O. J. Simpson of the Buffalo Bills. In the playoffs that year, Brown helped the Skins win over the Packers and Cowboys by rushing for 101 and 88 yards, respectively. After the Redskins eliminated the Cowboys from the 1972 playoffs, Dallas Coach Tom Landry shook his head and said, "Larry Brown is the catalyst of the Redskins. He's what makes them go."

Running back Larry Brown takes off behind the block of tight end Jerry Smith in a 1971 game against the St. Louis Cardinals. Brown, who played for Washington from 1969 through 1976, is the second leading rusher in Redskins history with 5,875 yards.

After five years with Washington, Brown had gained 5,467 yards rushing. He was only the third player in NFL history to average over 1,000 yards a season for five consecutive years, joining the illustrious company of Jim Brown of the Browns and Jim Taylor of the Packers.

When Larry Brown called it a career after the 1976 season, he stood as the Redskins' all-time leading rusher, with a total of 5,875 yards and a then-record nineteen 100-yard games. He had earned another 2,485 yards on pass receptions. His total of 330 points scored came from 35 rushing touchdowns and 20 on-pass plays. The four trips he made to the Pro Bowl are the most of any running back in Redskins history.

Larry Brown (No. 43), turned around here in the end zone, scores for the Redskins in a 1976 preseason game against the New York Jets. Brown led the Redskins in rushing during five consecutive years (1969–1973), breaking the 1,000-yard mark twice, with 1,125 in 1970 and 1,216 in 1972.

MIKE THOMAS

By pro football standards, Mike Thomas, at 5'11" and 190 pounds, could be described as diminutive. He was also not the fastest of backs, admitting himself, "I have always survived not because of speed but because of my quickness." He more than survived for four fine years with the Redskins and proved to be a worthy successor to Larry Brown as the ball carrier for the Washington offensive game plan.

Coach George Allen had the highest regard for Thomas going into the 1975 draft, but had to hope that the feisty halfback, who had gained more than 3,000 yards and scored 40 touchdowns at the University of Nevada at Las Vegas, would last into the fifth round. Under the Allen philosophy of "the future is now," the first four Washington draft picks had already been traded.

Thomas was there and Allen grabbed him, to the surprise of many, since the Redskins already had a veteran backfield that included Larry Brown, Duane Thomas, Moses Denson, and Bob Brunet. Allen had so much faith in the rookie (something alien to the coach's veteran-loving nature) that he shifted Brown to fullback and slotted Thomas as halfback.

Mike Thomas not only earned a starting role in the Redskins backfield as a rookie, but ended up leading the team in rushing with 919 yards, then the fifth most in Redskins history. Thomas was known for gaining yards the hard way. As former Redskins great and then–Washington scouting director Bobby Mitchell noted:

> **He really runs better inside than outside, and there's a reason for that. He runs with a quick shuffle of the feet, so he can change direction very fast. When he goes inside, it doesn't take much for him to change directions and spurt.**

His first 100-yard performance came in the fourth game of the regular season against the St. Louis Cardinals, and it was actually a "100-yard half," because he had sat out the entire first half of the game. Thomas also gained 483 yards on 40 receptions that year, which was enough for him to win the NFL's Offensive Rookie of the Year award for 1975.

The following year Thomas became only the second rusher in Washington history to gain more than 1,000 yards in a season, joining Larry Brown as the only Redskin with that distinction. His 1,101 yards gained was fifth best in the

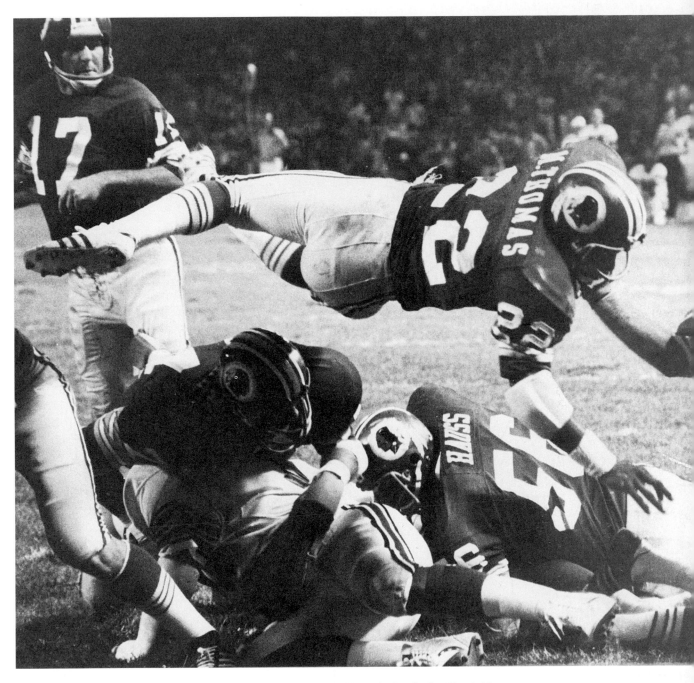

Mike Thomas dives for crucial yardage in a contest against the St. Louis Cardinals after taking a handoff from Billy Kilmer (No. 17).

One of the most controversial running backs to play for Washington, the former Dallas Cowboy Duane Thomas gains a few yards here against the San Francisco 49ers at RFK Stadium in 1973. The Skins won that day, 33–9. Thomas played only two seasons in Washington, 1973 and 1974.

NFC. His most memorable performance that year, and also his career best, came when he gained 195 yards rushing, a club record, in a game against the St. Louis Cardinals.

The tenure of Mike Thomas came to an end in Washington after the 1978 season, when he was traded to the San Diego Chargers. Upon his departure, only Larry Brown had gained more yards rushing for the Redskins than Thomas' 3,360. He caught 131 passes for 1,405 yards and scored 15 touchdowns rushing and 11 on pass receptions.

Mike Thomas was the key running back for the Redskins from 1975 to 1979. He led the team in rushing for three consecutive years, 1975–1977, and is the fifth most productive ball carrier in franchise history with 3,360 yards.

JOHN RIGGINS

John Riggins can lay claim to two Washington Redskins titles: he was the most productive and certainly the most flamboyant running back in team history. He carried the ball more often, gained more yards, scored more touchdowns rushing, and toted up more 100-yard games than any Redskins running back ever. He also once sported a mohawk haircut, painted his toenails green, attended a contract signing stripped to the waist and wearing a derby with a feather stuck in it, and created a camouflage clothes craze in Washington.

The tempestuous and talented Riggins, out of the University of Kansas, was a first-round draft choice of the New York Jets in 1971. After a fine five years in the backfield there, the 6'2", 240-pound fullback signed with the Redskins as a free agent in 1976. At first Riggins was not happy there. He was the up back in George Allen's I formation and was used mainly to block for Mike Thomas. He later expressed his disenchantment in public:

> George Allen's idea of offense was, "Don't lose the game with it and the defense
> will win for you." It was a joke, my being there, a waste of my time and their
> money.

It was not until 1978, under new Head Coach Jack Pardee, that Riggins was properly appreciated in the Redskins backfield. That year he became the third Washington running back in history to churn out more than 1,000 yards in a season (1,014). The next year he became the first Skin to post back-to-back 1,000-yard seasons when he gained 1,153 yards. It was in the last game of that season that he ripped off the longest run of his career, a 66-yard jaunt for a touchdown against Dallas.

The following year the irrepressible Riggins asked for a new contract and a raise to $500,000 a year. He did not get it, and sat out the year back in Lawrence, Kansas. But in 1981, the then-32-year-old Big John was back in the Washington camp and ready to show the Redskins' new coach, Joe Gibbs, that he was still a force to be reckoned with. His only comment to the press was, "I'm bored, I'm broke, and I'm back."

He was indeed back, leading the team in rushing. In 1982, he became football's Reggie Jackson, illuminating the postseason for the Redskins and carrying his team to its first Super Bowl championship. In the wild-card game against the

All-time leading Redskins rusher John Riggins. Playing from 1976 through 1985, the running back from the University of Kansas gained 7,472 yards for the Redskins. He also holds team records for the most rushing touchdowns (79), most 100-plus-yard games (19), and the most carries (1,988).

John Riggins vaults over a Chicago Bear in this 1976 game at Chicago's Soldier Field. The Redskins lost to the Bears that day, 33–7.

Lions, Riggins romped for 119 yards. A week later, in the playoff game against the Vikings, he gained 185 yards rushing, still a Redskins playoff standard. Then, in the 1982 NFC title battle with the Cowboys, he chalked up another 140 yards and two touchdowns. Finally, in Super Bowl XVII, he rushed for 166 yards, including a 43-yard run for the touchdown that put the Skins ahead of the Miami Dolphins for good. As a reward, Riggins was named the game's Most Valuable Player.

Riggins added 1,000-yard seasons in 1983 and 1984. It was also in 1983 that Big John scored 24 touchdowns rushing, an NFL record, and was the recipient of the Bert Bell Award as NFL Player of the Year.

After the 1985 season, Riggins retired. Of his 13 years in the NFL, he spent eight of them in Washington and became one of the town's most recognizable celebrities. His iconoclastic behavior off the field was as well known as his sterling performances on it. "Riggo," as he came to be known around the nation's capital, left football with practically every team rushing record: most yards gained (7,472); most in a season (1,347 in 1983—since broken by Terry Allen and Stephen Davis); most carries (1,988); most carries in a season (375 in 1983); most carries in a game (38 against the Dolphins in Super Bowl XVII—since broken by Jamie Morris and Earnest Byner); most 100-yard games (25); most touchdowns rushing (79); and most touchdowns rushing in a season (24). He is the tenth-leading rusher in NFL history with a total of 11,352 yards. He was inducted into the Pro Football Hall of Fame in 1992.

And, he was an honorary member of the Hogs, the only non-lineman to be so slopped.

GEORGE ROGERS

George Rogers had gained more than 5,000 yards in five years with the New Orleans Saints before being traded to the Redskins in 1985. Washington had to give up a first-round draft choice for him, but Joe Gibbs knew he needed a top-flight back to fuel the running game since John Riggins, at 36, had slowed perceptibly.

The 1980 Heisman Trophy winner from South Carolina, Rogers quickly became Washington's premier ball carrier, but he labored through much of the 1985 season. Before game 14 he had gained just 642 yards, noticeably below his output in New Orleans. The press did not quite believe him when he announced before that game, "I know I can still get 1,000." They should have. He went out that afternoon and ran for 150 yards. The following week it was 95, including a game-winning touchdown run of 34 yards against the Cincinnati Bengals. Then, in the last game of the season, Rogers raced for 206 yards against the St. Louis Cardinals, the most ever in a single game by a Redskins runner. At season's end, he had finished with 1,093 rushing yards.

The next year, Rogers became only the second Redskins back to post consecutive 1,000-yard seasons (John Riggins had done it twice) when he rumbled for 1,203. He also turned in five 100-yard games that year and scored a league-high 18 touchdowns rushing (second only to John Riggins' 24 in 1983).

Bothered by a toe injury early in the 1987 season, Rogers was unable to gain his previous form and his yardage was limited to 613.

George Rogers was the Redskins' premier running back from 1985 through 1987.

With the promise shown by rookie running back Timmy Smith, the Redskins decided to release Rogers after the 1987 season. In his three years with the Redskins, Rogers gained enough yards to become the team's ninth all-time rusher (2,909). Only Riggins and Brown turned in more 100-yard games than Rogers' 12, and only those two scored more touchdowns rushing than his 31. When he left the Redskins, Rogers ranked 15th among all-time rushers in the NFL, with a total of 7,176 yards.

Having made a football name for himself at the University of South Carolina and with the New Orleans Saints before coming to Washington, George Rogers ranks eighth on the all-time Redskins rushing list with 2,909 yards. *Photo reprinted courtesy of Bruce Bennett Studios.*

TERRY ALLEN

Terry Allen played his college ball at Clemson and came to Washington in 1995 after several years with the Minnesota Vikings. During his first year with the Redskins, Allen gained 1,309 yards rushing. In 1996 he upped that output to 1,353 yards, a Redskins record at the time; he also scored 21 touchdowns, second only to the 24 John Riggins recorded in 1983. Allen was released after the 1998 season, and stands as the third most productive rusher in Redskins history with 4,086 yards; his 37 rushing touchdowns is second to Riggins' 79.

Running back Timmy Smith picks up a few yards for the Redskins in a 1987 game at RFK stadium. A rookie that year, out of Texas Tech, Smith was picked to start in the playoffs over George Rogers and showed his appreciation by rushing for 204 yards in Super Bowl XXII.

Redskin Terry Allen faces down a Philadelphia Eagle. *Photo reprinted by permission Peter Read Miller / TimePix.*

3
The Great
Passers

In the early days of the Redskins' history, when the team worked out of the single-wing formation, the passer and backfield focal point was not the quarterback, but the tailback. He handled the snap, initiated the play, and was the principal passer. In the first five years of the team's existence, however, the Redskins rarely threw the football. It was not until the franchise moved to Washington and "Slingin'" Sammy Baugh came up from Texas Christian in 1937 that aerial warfare became an integral part of the team's battle plan. Ever since, passing has become one of the Redskins' essential assault weapons.

During the almost five decades since the immortal Baugh threw his last pass, the Redskins have showcased some of the most memorable and colorful quarterbacks in NFL lore. Tiny Eddie LeBaron replaced Baugh in 1952, Norm Snead made an appearance in the early sixties, and portly Sonny Jurgensen and middle-aged Billy Kilmer followed. Joe Theismann left an indelible mark in the seventies and the first part of the eighties, and Jay Schroeder, Doug Williams, Mark Rypien, Brad Johnson, and Jeff George provided the aerial excitement after him.

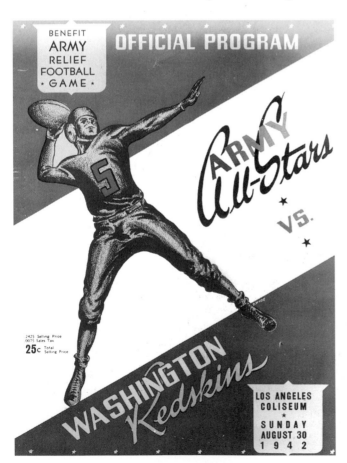

In between that roster of rifle arms, there were a few cameo appearances lasting a year, maybe two, made by Frank Filchock, Harry Gilmer, Jack Scarbath, Al Dorow, and Ralph Guglielmi.

Most of Washington's career passing records belong to Joe Theismann, who threw the most completions (2,044), gained the most yards passing (25,206), and threw the most passes (3,602). But Sonny Jurgensen maintains the highest overall quarterback rating (85.0), and Sammy Baugh was named All-Pro the most (five times). Jurgensen also had the best completion percentage (58.0 percent), and Baugh threw the most touchdown passes (187). Only one quarterback has ever exceeded a rating of 100 in a season: Sammy Baugh, with 109.7 in 1945. Jay Schroeder and Brad Johnson are the sole Redskins to gain more than 4,000 yards passing in a season, with 4,109 in 1986 and 4,005 in 1999, respectively.

Since 1937, Washington football fans have been treated to a grand series of spiraling footballs sent over the fields of Griffith, RFK, and FedEx stadiums by some very gifted arms.

SAMMY BAUGH

When George Preston Marshall brought his football caravan to Washington in 1937, he decided that he needed a showcase-caliber player who would bring the fans out in droves. So he decided to put a cowboy on his Redskins team, a long, lean Texan named Samuel Adrian Baugh. The year before, "Slingin'" Sammy Baugh, as he had come to be known due to his passing prowess, played his last season at Texas Christian, where he was a unanimous All-America selection at tailback. Passer, punter, team leader, he had all the basic requisites.

Baugh, who had been raised in the small railroad switching town of Sweetwater, Texas, was the young man Marshall believed was destined to capture the hearts and minds of Washingtonians. So Marshall acquired him in the first round of the 1937 draft and signed him on as the team's highest-paid player, with a salary of $8,000. Some did not share Marshall's enthusiasm, and felt that Baugh's reedy frame (6'2", 180 pounds) might be too brittle for any kind of extended NFL career. "If you get him [Baugh]," famed sportswriter Grantland Rice said to Marshall one day, "you better have his right arm insured for a million dollars, because the pros will break it off."

Yet Baugh's throwing arm survived his rookie year and 15 more thereafter, and it proved to be one of the most spectacular limbs ever wielded in a backfield in the National Football League. After his first day in training camp, his passing accuracy was never again questioned. It was on that day, the story has often been told, that Coach Ray Flaherty wanted a look at his new passer's form. He told end Wayne Millner that he wanted him to run a simple buttonhook pattern over the middle, then turned to Baugh and said, "I want you to hit him square in the eye with the ball." Baugh lined up at his tailback position, waiting for the snap, looked over his shoulder at Flaherty, and said, "One thing, Coach. Which eye?"

No one broke off Baugh's leg either, which he used with whiplash ferocity to set two NFL punting records that still stand today, averaging 51.4 yards a punt during the 1940 season and 45.1 yards over his 16-year career.

Injured and dejected, the great Sammy Baugh (middle figure, with his hood raised) sits on the bench during the 19- NFL championship game against the Chicago Bears. Although he suffered a concussion in the first half, Baugh returned to the game later; but the Ski still lost that day, 41–21. One of the NF all-time great quarterbacks and punter Baugh was a Redskin from 1937 through 1952, and was inducted as a charter member of the Pro Football Hall of Fam in 1963.

SAMMY BAUGH

[As a boy] I used to practice by throwing a football at a tire hung from a tree in our backyard, but as I think about it now that probably didn't help all that much. You really need to throw it to somebody who is moving, not just some tire swinging back and forth. If you could get a tire to move as fast as a man running down the field it might work, I guess, otherwise the tire doesn't do a damn bit of good. But I did spend a lot of time throwing at one when I was a boy.

Working as tailback out of the single wing, Baugh led the league in passing during his first year as a pro with 81 completions out of 171 attempts for 1,127 yards and eight touchdowns, becoming only the second back in pro football history to pass for more than 1,000 yards in a season. (Arnie Herber of the Green Bay Packers had set the mark the year before with 1,239 yards.) Baugh also brought Washington its first NFL championship that maiden year, and earned for himself All-Pro honors. In the title game against the Chicago Bears, it was almost a one-man show, with Slingin' Sammy completing 18 of 33 passes for 335 yards. Three of them were for touchdowns as the Redskins downed the Bears, 28–21.

His winning ways and down-home, droll Texas wit made Sammy Baugh an instant hero with the newly established Redskins fans. Joe F. Carr, NFL president from 1921 through 1939, wrote of Baugh's rookie season, "In one short season, his first as a professional, he became football's greatest thrill." Baugh's on-field brilliance helped the Redskins establish the support they had found sorely lacking in Boston. The fact that fans in the nation's capital are among the most ardently loyal in the league can be traced directly to the

Redskin Big Chiefs Hold Powwow
(Associated Press Wirefoto)

Among Redskins gathered in the Nation's Capital to bring downfall to Chicago's Bears in pro football's "World Series" tomorrow are the potent warriors above. Left to right, Sammy Baugh, Dick Todd, Frank Filchock and Andy Farkas. A sellout is expected at Griffith Stadium which seats some 36,000.

arrival of Slingin' Sam, cowboy hat and all, back in Washington's first season in the NFL.

Winning and Washington would become synonymous during Baugh's first nine years in the league (1937–1945). The rangy Texan quarterbacked the Redskins to 68 wins during that period against only 24 losses and 5 ties. Washington had five championship game appearances, winning two of them (1937 and 1942), but bowing in the other three (1940, 1943, and 1945).

Baugh was certainly one of the game's most versatile stars. Besides passing and punting, he was also an outstanding defensive back. Said Baugh:

I actually liked to play defense. Hell, when I'd punt a ball I'd be about the third or fourth man down the field to make the tackle. You see, they couldn't touch the punter, so I could just kick the ball and get the hell down the field while all the others were blocking each other.

An example of his great versatility was a feat in 1943 that will never be matched in this age of football specialization. That year, Baugh led the NFL in passing (133 completions for 1,754 yards and 23 touchdowns), punting (45.9-yard average), and interceptions by a defender (11).

COMPLETING A POPULAR PASS.   —By JIM BERRYMAN.

Baugh was also an unquestioned team leader. There was a common belief among his teammates that the more nervous he got before a game, the better he was going to be and consequently the better they would fare that day. "The tip-off was the number of times he went to the john during the time he was getting suited up," said former teammate and fullback Jim Castiglia. "If he went more than three times, we knew we were going to have a hell of a day. You can book it."

As great a year as Baugh had in 1937, Washington came close to losing him to major league baseball. After college he had signed a contract to play for the St. Louis Cardinals, beginning in the spring of 1938. Following the Redskins' championship season, however, Baugh injured his breastbone in a postseason exhibition game. It had not properly healed by the time he reported to the Cardinals for spring training. In camp, he was shifted from third base to shortstop, but his performance was hampered by the injury and he made a less than auspicious debut. The Cardinals gave him an ultimatum: they wanted him to give up football completely and concentrate solely on baseball. Baugh gave it a good deal of thought:

> I always loved baseball more than anything I had ever done, but I knew I had a better future in football. So I gave up baseball and never regretted it one bit. I had trouble hitting the change-up pitch and the curve and, besides, Marty Marion was also in the farm system. I knew he was going to be the shortstop at St. Louis pretty soon, not me.

So Slingin' Sammy stayed with football, determined to stay healthy and leave his mark on the game:

> One thing I especially remember from when I first started with the pros was that there wasn't a lot of protection for the passer. I did all our passing and I know it sure was hell. Passers took a terrible beating. That's one rule Mr. Marshall finally got changed. I remember he called me in and asked me if it would help if he could get a rule through that would protect passers. I said, "Heck, yes, it would probably let me play 10 years longer."

Marshall did get the rule passed, and Baugh went on to set the record for number of seasons played in the NFL.

Sammy Baugh used the forward pass as a potent weapon. Never the possessor of great speed, he made up for it with an uncanny knack for evading oncoming defenders, a consistent ability to find open receivers, and one of the quickest releases in the history of the game. As Baugh later explained:

> The way to make a passer is to let him make every mistake in the book, and find out for himself how to correct them. If I went out to quarterback a team now, I doubt I'd do things much different than I did before. My theory, the way I was taught by Dutch Meyer [his coach] at TCU, was you try to beat a defense. They're going to let you have a weak spot, so you find it and pick on it. You keep going to a weakness until they adjust to cover it. Then they leave themselves open somewhere else and you go to that.

SAMMY BAUGH

I liked Mr. Marshall a lot. I thought he was a real fine businessman. And he did a lot for the league, he and Mr. Halas from Chicago. . . . They got a lot of the rules changed for the better of the game. Mr. Marshall was also quite a showman. I especially remember how he'd always bring a Santa Claus at halftime of the game just before Christmas. He'd do it a dang different way every year. Once it was on a sleigh. Another time he was going to parachute one in, but the wind was blowing so much that the Santa Claus missed the stadium and landed on a house about a block away.

Another deadly weapon Baugh used from his position at tailback was the quick kick. Many opponents expecting a pass on third down were surprised and embarrassed to see a thundering punt from Baugh soar over their heads and bounce unattended downfield until a Redskin downed it.

In 1944, however, Baugh moved to a new position. In that year, the Redskins adopted the T formation, which George Halas and his converted tailback-to-quarterback Sid Luckman had been using so successfully for the Chicago Bears. "When I switched from a single-wing tailback to a T-formation quarterback in '44, it was the most difficult thing I'd ever had to do in my football career," Baugh admitted. By 1947, he had mastered the position better than anyone who had ever played it before. That season he had the best passing year of his career, setting two NFL records by completing 210 passes for 2,938 yards, both of which would remain league standards until the sixties. Said Baugh:

Actually, the T was good for me. I'd played 10 or 11 years of single-wing ball, counting college, and I figured I only could go maybe another year or two as tailback. Hell, I was getting beat up and hurt all the time and my shoulders and knees were getting pretty bad by that

Sammy Baugh is honored in Washington in 1947. As part of "Sammy Baugh Day," he was given a brand-new car.

time. But with the T formation I didn't take such a beating and that enabled me to play another seven or eight years.

When Baugh, at age 38, retired from professional football after the 1952 season, he had thrown more passes (2,995), completed more passes (1,693), gained more yardage passing (21,886, or approximately 13 miles), and passed for more touchdowns (187) than any previous passer in NFL history. He led the league in passing six times and in number of pass completions five times, two league records that still stand today. His passing, punting, defensive skills, and team leadership combined to earn Baugh the honor of being one of the 17 charter members enshrined in the Pro Football Hall of Fame.

EDDIE LEBARON

He was called "the Little General," and the press release announcing that Eddie LeBaron was joining the Redskins in 1950 referred to him as "a pint-size package of dynamite." Pint-size because, coming out of the College of the Pacific that year, he stood at 5'9" and weighed somewhere in the vicinity of 160 pounds, which afforded him the distinction of being the smallest quarterback in Redskins history.

LeBaron, Washington's 10th-round draft choice that year, played in only two preseason games before joining the marines to serve in the Korean conflict, where he was wounded twice. He returned in 1952 to take up the quarterbacking chores that were being abandoned by Sammy Baugh in the last year of his pro career. He proved an able replacement, passing for 1,420 yards and 14 touchdowns. In one game against the Giants, he threw four touchdown passes. He was subsequently named the NFL Rookie of the Year.

After another year in Washington, the Little General, who did not get along with his defense-emphasizing coach, Curly Lambeau, defected to the Canadian Football League; but he returned to the Skins in 1955 when Joe Kuharich took over from Lambeau. LeBaron led the team on the field for the next five years, although for only part of the season in 1956, when he was benched with an injury.

The most memorable game of LeBaron's career in Washington was the opener of his first season back from Canada. The Skins went to Cleveland to take on the Browns, a team they hadn't beaten in nine previous encounters. The Browns had

Two former college All-Americans show off their form: Eddie LeBaron (No. 14) from College of the Pacific and Jack Scarbath out of Maryland. LeBaron was the starting quarterback for the Redskins in 1952, 1955, and 1957-1959; Scarbath quarterbacked the team in 1953 and 1954. LeBaron's best year was 1957, when he completed 99 passes for 1,508 yards and 11 touchdowns. Scarbath's best was 1953, when he completed 45 passes for 862 yards and 9 touchdowns.

annihilated them the year before by a score of 62–3, which remains today their worst regular-season defeat. As LeBaron tells it:

> It was exciting going into Cleveland that day. It wasn't hard for me to get pumped up with the anticipation of playing against a guy like [Otto] Graham. And they were also the NFL defending champs.

The Little General turned the tide on the Browns that day, throwing passes for two touchdowns and running 20 yards for another to lead the Skins to a 27–17 victory. "It got the momentum going and we went on to have our best season while I was in Washington [8–4–0]."

LeBaron's own best season was in 1957, when he completed 99 passes for 1,508 yards and received a quarterback rating of 88.6. His most impressive individual performance, although not the most personally memorable, was the day in 1958 when he tossed five touchdown passes in a 45–31 triumph over the Chicago Cardinals.

In 1960, after announcing his retirement, LeBaron decided to return to the game when Tom Landry of the newly enfranchised Dallas Cowboys selected him in the expansion draft. LeBaron played for another four years. In his overall pro career of 11 years, the Little General gained 13,399 yards with his passing.

Chief Joseph - Nez Perce

REDSKINS vs. CLEVELAND BROWNS
October 16, 1955   Price 50c Incl. Tax

NORM SNEAD

Norm Snead could legitimately say that he surfaced in the wrong place at the wrong time when he signed with the Redskins in 1961 after a notable college career at Wake Forest. He had been Washington's first-round draft choice that year, but it was a team that had won only one game the season before, had ended up in last place in the NFL East, and was sorely in need of a quarterback.

Norm Snead, out of Wake Forest, was drafted by Washington in the first round in 1961. He quarterbacked the Redskins through the 1963 season. His best year was 1963, when he became the first Redskin to pass for more than 3,000 yards in a season (3,043). The following year he was traded to the Eagles for Sonny Jurgensen.

At 6'4" and 215 pounds, Snead was a gargantuan replacement for the diminutive LeBaron and the unproductive Guglielmi, who had called the signals for the Skins the year before. The rookie had little trouble landing the starting job, which he quickly learned was hazardous to his health. Besieged by seemingly undeterred pass rushers from the first game of 1961, which Washington lost to the San Francisco 49ers, 35–3, until the last game of the season, Snead went a long time without the sweet smell of victory. In one game against the Giants, he was tackled in the end zone twice for safeties, contributing four points to New York's 53–0 win. Snead's calm appraisal of it all: "That first year I really learned to throw under pressure."

Finally, however, in the last game of the season, things changed. With the Skins' record at 0–12–1, most of the fans came out to D.C. Stadium, according to one sportswriter, "to watch the wingding Christmas show that Marshall traditionally stages during the intermission of the final game." They and Norm Snead were surprised, however, to find that suddenly the quarterback had some time to throw the ball. Snead not only moved the Redskins, but also helped them defeat the Dallas Cowboys, 34–24. (It was their first win since they beat the Cowboys 24 games earlier, 26–14 in Washington, October 9, 1960.)

When the stats were in, Snead had completed 172 passes for 2,337 yards and 11 touchdowns, all records at the time for a rookie in the NFL—not bad for a quarterback who had spent most of the season scrambling for his life. After the season, Coach Bill McPeak said, "It'll take about three years, but Snead is going to be a great one."

The Redskins were definitely better the following year (5–7–2), and so were Snead's stats. He was helped enormously by the addition of Washington's first black player, a remarkable flanker named Bobby Mitchell who would lead the league that year in pass receptions and receiving yardage. Snead completed 184 passes for 2,926 yards (only 12 yards shy of the club record set by Sammy Baugh in 1947) and 22 touchdowns.

In 1963, Snead continued to demonstrate his propensity for throwing the football—especially to Mitchell. The Redskins won only 3 of their 14 games that year, but Snead set a club record by gaining 3,043 yards passing, the first NFL quarterback ever to broach the 3,000-yard mark.

After the season, however, Snead was traded to the Eagles for their quarterback, the rather rotund but well-seasoned Sonny Jurgensen. Snead played 10 more

Frank Filchock and Andy Farkas teamed up to set an NFL record in 1939 for the longest pass play in NFL history. Against the Pittsburgh Steelers, and with the ball on the Washington 1-yard line, Filchock threw a little two-yard pass to Farkas, who raced 97 more yards with it for a touchdown.

Since then, only seven other 99-yard pass plays have joined it in the record book, and two of them were carried off by the Redskins. In 1963, George Izo tossed a 45-yard pass to Bobby Mitchell, who raced an additional 54 yards for a score in a game against the Cleveland Browns. Five years later, Sonny Jurgensen unloaded another 45-yard pass, which was caught by Gerry Allen, who sprinted the remaining 54 yards for a touchdown against the Chicago Bears. The Redskins were the victims of a 99-yard pass play by the Los Angeles Raiders, from Jim Plunkett to Cliff Branch, in 1983.

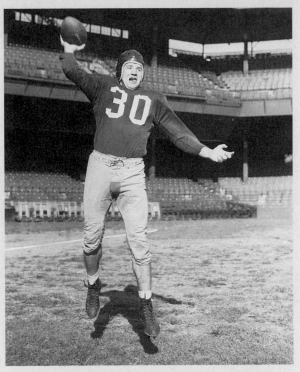

Frank Filchock played for the Redskins from 1938 to 1941 and in 1944 and 1945.

years in the NFL, with Philadelphia, the Vikings, the Giants, and the 49ers, turning in career totals of 2,076 completions for 30,797 yards and 196 touchdowns.

SONNY JURGENSEN

Ron Reid, writing for *Sports Illustrated*, summed up Sonny Jurgensen delicately but well: "A free spirit for whom training rules have, at times, been just too vexing." He also noted, however, that the sometimes-stout quarterback was "without peer in the art of throwing a football."

Born Christian Adolph Jurgensen III in Wilmington, North Carolina, Sonny was a quarterback at Duke, where he threw only six passes in three years before matriculating to the pros. A fourth-round draft choice of the Philadelphia Eagles in 1957, he was then a relatively solid 5'11", 200-pound would-be quarterback who was slated to be a backup to the aging Bobby Thomason. The next year he played the subordinate role to veteran Norm Van Brocklin, who had been brought in to replace the retiring Thomason.

It was not until 1961 that Jurgensen got his chance to show what he could do tossing a football. Van Brocklin, after 12 memorable seasons in the NFL, retired, and Jurgensen was given the job. He took to it like Mozart to music. In that first full season, he set three NFL passing records when he completed 235 passes for 3,723 yards and 32 touchdowns, and he easily earned All-Pro honors.

From the start, Jurgensen was defined as a pocket passer, and after that first year more than one observer noted that he had the quickest release in pro football. "I never thought it necessary," he once said, "to run around or hang around too long in one's own backfield." He also built an off-field reputation for roistering that would make him acceptable company for the likes of Johnny Blood McNally, Shipwreck Kelly, Bobby Layne, Art Donovan, Paul Hornung, and Doug Atkins, among other notorious NFL rowdies. As *Sports Illustrated's* Ron Reid pegged him, "The guy whose identifying mark was a six-pack gut . . . rumor has it, paid enough fines to meet the taxi squad's payroll and sneaked out of camp so often that his room in the players' dorm came with a sublease."

Washington was the beneficiary in 1964 when Jurgensen was traded to the Redskins for Snead. Jurgensen turned 30 that year and really was just in the prime of his passing career. McPeak was then the head coach of a definitely lackluster Redskins team. They had the exceptional Mitchell at flanker and a promising rookie halfback and future wide receiver named Charley Taylor, but overall they were destined to be losers. Jurgensen completed 207 passes for 2,934 yards and 24 touchdowns, all three stats among the top few in club history, but Washington still could manage only six wins against eight losses.

In 1966, Jurgensen broke just about every team passing record. His 254 completions demolished the standard of 210 set by Baugh back in 1947. His 3,209 yards passing eclipsed Snead's 3,043 of 1963, and his 28 touchdown tosses exceeded Baugh's 25 of 1947.

The following year he not only reset all those club marks but established three NFL records as well. Throwing mostly to Taylor, Mitchell, and Jerry Smith, Jurgensen hurled more passes (508) and completed more passes (288) for more yards (3,747) than any passer up to that time in NFL history. His total of 31 touchdown passes still stands as the all-time Redskins standard. Despite all that, Johnny Unitas was chosen as an All-Pro ahead of him.

Sonny Jurgensen holds the highest career quarterback rating of any player in Redskins history, 85.0, as well as the highest completion percentage, 58 percent. Only Joe Theismann has completed more passes than Jurgensen's 1,831, and gained more yardage passing than his 22,585. Jurgensen played for the Redskins from 1964 through 1974 and was inducted into the Pro Football Hall of Fame in 1983.

Jurgensen remained the starting quarterback through the 1969 season, which he played at age 35 under Vince Lombardi, his third coach since coming to Washington. "I'm a good trivia question," Jurgensen once said. "Name all my coaches." Actually, with the Redskins, he played under five altogether: Bill McPeak, Otto Graham, Lombardi, Bill Austin, and George Allen.

During his reign with the Redskins, Jurgensen had some very memorable games. There was that day in 1965 when he threw for 411 yards and beat the dreaded Cowboys, 34–31. Then in 1967, against the Cleveland Browns, he set the still-standing club mark of 32 completions, picking up 418 yards with them. And what Skins fan could forget the little surprise he laid on the Chicago Bears when

A shook-up Sonny Jurgensen gets a few words of encouragement from Dallas Cowboys quarterback "Dandy" Don Meredith (No. 17).

he connected with Gerry Allen on a 99-yard touchdown pass, giving him a share of that NFL record.

A shoulder injury in the last game of the 1971 preseason precipitated the replacement of Jurgensen with newly acquired, but veteran, Billy Kilmer. Out for most of that season, Jurgensen was back for 1972. There was indeed controversy when George Allen opted to stay with Kilmer and keep a healthy, although 38-year-old, Jurgensen on the sidelines.

But Jurgensen was far from through. He came off the bench when needed and threw the ball as he had in his heyday. In 1974, Jurgensen, as adroit a reliever as there was in the game despite the fact that he was 40 years old, showed that he

Sonny Jurgensen in the rain. One of the greatest Washington quarterbacks, Jurgensen, who played for Duke in college, came to the Redskins from the Philadelphia Eagles in a 1964 trade.

still had it. Against the Miami Dolphins, winner of the previous season's Super Bowl, Jurgensen, who, in *Sports Illustrated* writer Dan Jenkins's words, had to "scrape off the rust from a carcass that, in its day, has had legs, shoulders, ribs, elbows, ankles, and knees—to say nothing of pride—bent in all kinds of ways," was there to rally his Redskins to a last-second 20–17 victory. The following week, he took on the Giants in lieu of Kilmer and pitched touchdowns to Roy Jefferson, Larry Brown, and Moses Denson in a 24–3 romp. That year, 1974, his last in the pros, he led the entire NFL with a completion percentage of 64.1, hitting receivers with 107 of his 167 tosses.

As a Redskin, Sonny Jurgensen ranks second behind Theismann in best career stats. He threw 3,155 passes, completing 1,831 for 22,585 yards and 179

In the locker room with Sonny Jurgensen (left) and Billy Kilmer in the early seventies.

touchdowns (second to Baugh). He has the highest career quarterback rating of any Redskin in history, 85.0, as well as the highest completion percentage, 58.0.

During his 18-year NFL career, Jurgensen threw 4,262 passes, completing 2,433 of them for 32,224 yards (that's 18.3 miles) and 255 touchdowns, against only 189 interceptions. He led the league in passing yardage five times, tied with Dan Marino for the most of any quarterback in NFL history.

Jurgensen, who a teammate once said "looks more like a Wednesday night bowler than a football player," was deservedly inducted into the Pro Football Hall of Fame in 1983.

BILLY KILMER

When Billy Kilmer arrived in Washington in 1971 as a charter member of George Allen's "Over-the-Hill Gang," it was a surprise to many who read his press packet that the ambling 31-year-old had been a feared running back during the days when he starred for UCLA in the late fifties. Since then he had become a quarterback and, over 10 years, had played for the San Francisco 49ers and the New Orleans Saints before Allen acquired him.

There was one thing, however, for which no press release was necessary. Kilmer came with the reputation of being the gutsiest, most never-say-die quarterback in the game since Bobby Layne had called it quits a decade earlier. He may have been known to throw some wobbly passes, but there was no denying his fearless stands in the face of charging defenders. As Coach Allen aptly characterized him, "Billy is a winner, a competitor, and a leader. He gets the job done, no matter what." No matter how battered, bleeding, or pain-filled he was, Kilmer could be counted on to get up and go back to the battle.

Billy Kilmer provided a brave and sturdy bridge in Washington quarterbacking between the eras of Jurgensen and Theismann. Jurgensen was 37 years old when Kilmer arrived, and an injury to the NFL's dean of quarterbacks thrust Kilmer into the starting role his first year there, one that he would handle memorably for most of the next seven years.

Kilmer led the Redskins to a second-place finish in the NFL East, with a record of 9–4–1, during his first year in a burgundy and gold uniform, and to a berth in the playoffs. It was the most victories Redskins fans had seen in 29 seasons. Kilmer completed 166 passes for 2,221 yards. He threw two touchdown passes in the playoff game against the 49ers, but the Skins still fell to San Francisco, 24–20.

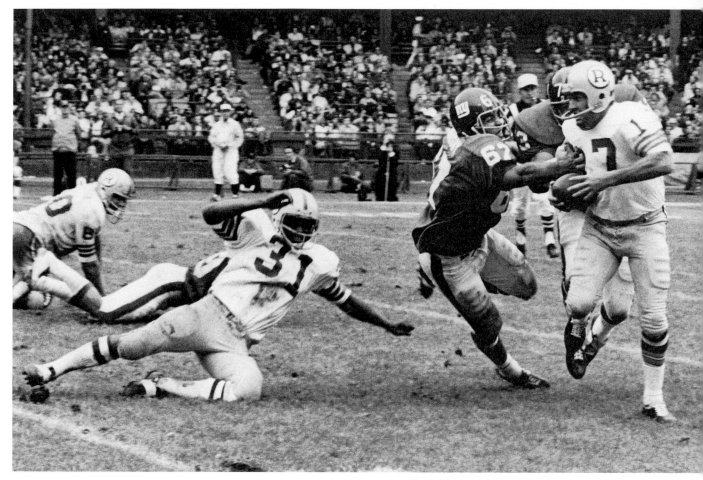

Billy Kilmer, never known for his speed, scrambles here in a 1971 game against the New York Giants. Kilmer took over the quarterbacking duties that year and remained with the Redskins through the 1978 season. Kilmer ranks fifth in the Redskins record book for passing yardage (12,352) and pass completions (953), and fourth in touchdown passes (103).

In the ensuing years, Kilmer had his favorite receivers, such notables as Charley Taylor, Roy Jefferson, Larry Brown, and Jerry Smith. He had his highs and lows with the fans (coming on to replace Jurgensen, who was still in uniform, did not endear him to many Washington fans), endured the boos, and enjoyed the cheers.

The most cheers came his second year, when the Redskins—behind the passing of Kilmer, the running of Brown, and a steel-gate defense—went to their first NFL championship game since 1945. Kilmer had thrown 19 touchdown passes during the regular season and posted an 84.6 quarterback rating. In the contest to

The headline in the Christmas Day 1971 edition of *Pro Football Weekly* read: Kilmer Leaves Jail to Rally. Following it was columnist Dave Brady's incisive look into a story of true dedication.

Kilmer had been called upon to replace the heralded Sonny Jurgensen and lead the Redskins through the 1971 regular season after Jurgensen suffered a fractured shoulder in the final preseason game that year. He had risen to the occasion admirably by piloting the Redskins to five consecutive wins at the outset of the season and keeping them in first place until the 10th game that year. With the glint of a playoff berth twinkling about RFK Stadium, nothing was going to keep him from his appointed rounds—not even jail.

Here is how Dave Brady described the incident, which occurred late in the season:

> The first report of his altercation in an Arlington, Va., coffee shop knocked the India-Pakistan war off page one in the city's afternoon tabloid newspaper.
>
> All he did was have a few drinks, stop for some eggs and coffee, and have the misfortune to have only a hundred-dollar bill to pay the check in a spot where he was not at all famous.
>
> A guy with deep conviction, as he is in the huddle, Kilmer argued his case with a no-nonsense waitress, even offering to leave the C note with her, along with his name and address. The fuss attracted a policeman who was unacquainted with Kilmer. Kilmer thought he was so right that he told the copper, "If you think I am in the wrong, put me in jail."
>
> The policeman took the hint, Kilmer briefly was caged, but was released after officials at the pokey were able to make change for another C note so he could post $15 in collateral.
>
> The next day he forfeited the collateral, showed up at the Redskins headquarters to sweat out the night before in a sauna, watch game films at 8:30 A.M., and all at once every guy in town who ever celebrated too enthusiastically identified with Kilmer.
>
> The quarterback was the most popular Redskin in town by the time he disclosed that he had suffered a jammed neck the day before and was trying to ease the pain. He arranged for the waitress to keep the disputed $100, and said in jest, "Pete Rozelle probably will put that whole chain of coffee houses off limits."

determine the NFC title against hated Dallas, he tossed two TD passes to spark a 26–3 victory.

In 1974, injuries hampered him much of the season and he was forced to share the spotlight with the then 40-year-old Jurgensen. But the following year, despite some nagging injuries, Kilmer again guided Washington's attack and was rewarded with the George Halas Award for most courageous player in the NFL.

Kilmer gave up the starting job of quarterback to Theismann in 1978. He was 38 years old, scarred and aching, but still there, ready and willing to relieve, to get back into the fray. At season's end he retired. Kilmer is the fifth-ranking passer in Redskins history in terms of completions (953), passing yardage (12,352), and completion percentage (53.2 percent). His quarterback rating of 77.0 trails only Jurgensen, Mark Rypien, and Theismann.

Billy Kilmer is snagged here by Dallas defensive end Jethro Pugh. Kilmer, a certified member of George Allen's "Over-the-Hill Gang," was a 10-year NFL veteran when he came to Washington in 1971. In his college days he was a star quarterback for UCLA.

In overall statistics during his 16-year pro career, Kilmer completed 1,585 passes for 20,495 yards and 152 touchdowns, with a lifetime completion percentage of 53.12. As his predecessor in Washington, Jurgensen, said of him:

Something has to go wrong for him to get all fired up—boos, a cheap shot, some pain. That's when he comes out and gets the job done. It may not be pretty, but he makes the big play or gets the ball across the goal line.

JOE THEISMANN

It took Joe Theismann eight long and frustrating years before he became a regular starter in the NFL. A bright star in Notre Dame's long line of great quarterbacks, he was runner-up to Jim Plunkett for the Heisman Trophy in 1970 and was then drafted in the fourth round the following year by the Miami Dolphins. With a youthful Bob Griese entrenched at quarterback, Theismann feared he would never get a chance to play. He spurned the NFL and signed with the Toronto Argonauts in the Canadian Football League.

After three years north of the border, George Allen acquired Theismann for the Redskins, and the young quarterback returned, anticipating that the less-than-youthful Jurgensen and Kilmer, 40 and 34 respectively, would not be around that much longer. But as he later observed:

I figured I'd spend a season or two learning from them and then get my shot. Little did I know that when they went out drinking, they were partaking of the fountain of youth.

With George Allen's predilection for aging veterans, Theismann remained in relative obscurity in Washington from 1974 to 1978, relieving here and there, starting a few games, but inevitably existing in Kilmer's shadow. It was not easy for Theismann, who was never known for a lack of self-confidence or self-esteem. When Jack Pardee replaced Allen in 1978, however, Theismann got the job full-time.

Everything was coming up cherry blossoms in Washington that first year— through the first six games, anyway, all of which they won, their best start since the Baugh-led Redskins of 1940 won their first seven. Unfortunately, they won only two of their remaining 10 games, and confidence in the new quarterback

Better known for his passing skills, Joe Theismann gets ready to hand off here in a game against the New York Jets. After a stint with and the Toronto Argonauts (of the Canadian Football League), Theismann was brought into the Redskins' fold in 1974. At Notre Dame, he was a runner-up for the Heisman Trophy in 1970.

was, as they say, on the wane. Still, in his first year Theismann completed 187 passes for 2,593 yards, the most productive aerial performance by a Redskin since Jurgensen was starting in 1970.

Confidence was restored with gusto the following year as Theismann, supplemented by the running of John Riggins, brought the Redskins a 10–6–0 season and just a point-differential tiebreaker away from the playoffs. The Skins amassed 348 points in 1979, the second most in their then-48-year history. (In 1966, Coach Graham's offense had scored 351.) Theismann impressed even the previous year's most skeptical observers, completing 233 passes for 2,797 yards and

JOE THEISMANN

I don't *necessarily* play football for George Allen. I also play for my family and myself. I respect him as a great football coach and I've enjoyed playing for him—when I've had a chance to play. I don't like the fact that he favors veteran players.

20 touchdowns. His quarterback rating of 84.0 was the second best in the NFL, and his colleagues voted him the team's Most Valuable Player. In the words of the last of the "Over-the-Hill Gang," defensive tackle Diron Talbert:

> Theismann has really become a great team leader. He's become one of the guys, a brother. Still, Joe has stayed Joe. . . . If you're a cocky kid, be a cocky kid. Be yourself. He's the Redskins' franchise.

In 1981, Theismann set a new team standard (since broken by Brad Johnson) with 293 successful passes, breaking the completion record of 288 set by Jurgensen in 1967. He amassed 3,566 yards passing that year, then the second most in team history. He also turned in his best single-game performance up to that time when he passed for 388 yards and four touchdowns in a game against the St. Louis Cardinals.

The most successful year for a Theismann-directed Washington team, however, was 1982. Shortened by a players' strike, it turned into a Super Bowl season and simply a super season for Theismann. With a rating of 91.3, he was the top-rated quarterback in the NFC. He completed 63.9 percent of his passes, the third-best percentage ever in Washington (Baugh had 70.3 in 1945 and Jurgensen 64.1 in 1974). In the first playoff game that year, Theismann completed 14 of 19 passes for 210 yards and three touchdowns (Washington 31, Detroit 7). The following week, he was 17 of 23 for 213 yards and two TDs (Washington 21, Minnesota 7). Then, in the third game of that elongated playoff schedule, Theismann hit on 12 of 20 for 150 yards and a touchdown (Washington 31, Dallas 17). In Super Bowl XVII, Theismann went 15 of 23 for 143 yards and two TDs (Washington 27, Miami 17). Joe Theismann finally had a Super Bowl ring.

Behind Theismann, the Redskins, with a 14–2–0 regular-season record in 1983, returned to the Super Bowl but could not repeat the championship. With Theismann winging 29 touchdown passes that year (the second most ever in

Joe Theismann lofts a pass here against the St. Louis Cardinals in 1983. During his 12-year Redskins career, Theismann set most of the team's all-time passing records. No one has thrown more completions than his 2,044, nor gained more passing yardage than his 25,206. He also has the third-best career quarterback rating, 77.4.

Washington after Jurgensen's 31 in 1967), the Skins set an NFL regular-season record by scoring a grand total of 541 points. The 29 TDs, 3,714 yards gained passing, and 97.0 rating in 1983 were all career highs for Theismann, and he had the special honor of being named the NFL's Most Valuable Player.

Joe Theismann's professional football career came to an end on Monday night, November 18, 1985, before an aghast national TV audience, when he suffered a compound leg fracture and was wheeled off the field before a deadly silent crowd at RFK Stadium. In his 12-year career with Washington, he had thrown more passes (3,602), completed more passes (2,044), and gained more yards with them (25,206) than any player in Redskins history. His career rating of 77.4 is third behind only Jurgensen's 85.0 and Rypien's 80.2.

Jay Schroeder runs out of the pocket in a game against the Philadelphia Eagles. Feared more for his passing than his running, Schroeder led the Redskins' offensive attack much of the time from 1985 to 1987, although he was plagued by injuries during those years. In 1986, Schroeder set two all-time, single-season team passing records when he completed 541 passes for 4,109 yards; both records still stand today.

JAY SCHROEDER

After the 1983 season, Coach Gibbs knew he needed a backup quarterback for Theismann; he traded for veteran Jim Hart of the Cardinals and signed 6'4", 215-pound Jay Schroeder, a third-round draft choice out of UCLA.

Schroeder did not get his first real chance until Monday night, November 18, 1985, that fateful game against the Giants in which Theismann suffered a career-ending broken leg. Coming off the sideline, Schroeder had thrown only eight passes in NFL competition. The fans in RFK Stadium that evening looked on with collective despair at the damage done to Theismann and the dim prospects offered by the unknown and untested Schroeder.

The despair disappeared into the night with Schroeder's second pass, however, a 44-yard completion to Art Monk that set up a touchdown. With 12 more completions to follow, including a 14-yard game winner to Clint Didier, he rallied the Skins to a 23–21 win. Schroeder then quarterbacked the Redskins to four more victories in the next five games. (Even in the game they lost, he passed for 348 yards.)

Jay Schroeder on the telephone on the sideline. Schroeder was a third-round draft choice out of UCLA in 1984.

Schroeder quickly made it known that the bomb, or the big play, was part of his portfolio. As former Steeler great Terry Bradshaw noted, "Schroeder's got a real cannon on his shoulder, one of the most awesome weapons I've seen in the league." He also had the receivers to break the big one in All-Pros Art Monk and Gary Clark.

In 1986 Schroeder posted the two most productive games of his career, back-to-back against the Giants and Minnesota. In New York he threw for 420 yards (22 completions), and at RFK he gained 378 (24 completions) in a win over the Vikings. That was, of course, the year Schroeder broke the Redskins' passing-yardage record of 3,747, set by Jurgensen in

1967, and also became the first Washington passer to break the 4,000-yard mark (4,109).

Joe Gibbs was duly impressed:

What I like about Jay is he has a lot of poise for a young guy. Nothing seems to disrupt him. When they [the pass rushers] come after him, it's his reaction just to stand in there till he finds the open man.

With the fabled Hogs in front of him, Schroeder usually had an extra second or two to zero in on an open receiver.

A shoulder separation in the opening game of 1987 benched Schroeder, and he was replaced by veteran Doug Williams. Schroeder did not make it back until the sixth game of that strike-shortened season. But from that point forward, the quarterbacking role became a revolving one between Schroeder and Williams. For the playoffs, into which Schroeder, Williams, and the strike-replacement Skins had earned their way with an 11–4–0 record, the coach's call went to Williams.

Unable to regain the starting quarterback job in 1988, Schroeder asked for a trade and was sent to the Los Angeles Raiders. Despite the brevity of his career in Washington, Schroeder still accumulated 7,445 yards on 517 completions.

DOUG WILLIAMS

Practically all of Doug Williams' accomplishments as a football player have been modified in the nation's press by the adjective *black*. In 1977, his last year at Grambling, he became the first black quarterback to be named to the Associated Press All-America team. When Tampa Bay selected him in 1978, he became the first black quarterback ever to be chosen in the first round of the NFL draft. In January 1988, Williams was heralded, or at least touted, as the first black man to start at quarterback in the Super Bowl. He shrugs it off:

It's always been that way, as far back as I can remember in my athletic career. It makes no difference. What matters is if I do what I need to do right.

And he certainly did do things right as a quarterback; the millions who watched Super Bowl XXII in January of 1988 can testify to that fact.

Doug Williams (No. 17) throws from the pocket in a 1988 game at RFK Stadium. Williams took over the starting job at quarterback in 1987 after Jay Schroeder was injured. He went on to lead the Skins to a championship season; in Super Bowl XXII he set four records, threw four touchdown passes, and was named the game's MVP. Coming out of Grambling in 1977, Williams played for the Tampa Bay Buccaneers for five years, then two in the short-lived USFL, before coming to the Redskins in 1986.

Williams played five years with the Tampa Bay Buccaneers, then left after a salary dispute and spent two seasons in the USFL before that league folded. Out of work in the summer of 1986, he received a telephone call from Gibbs, who told him he dearly needed a seasoned backup quarterback. No one else called, so Williams became a Redskin.

In 1987, when Schroeder was injured early in the opener against the Eagles, Williams took over and led the Skins to a 34–24 win. Later in the season, with Schroeder blundering in a game against the Lions in which the Skins were trailing 13–3 and going nowhere, Williams came on in relief again and tossed two touchdown passes to give Washington a come-from-behind 20–13 victory. And again in the season finale at Minnesota Williams was called on to revitalize a faltering Washington offense. He responded with two touchdown passes to Ricky Sanders that sent the game into overtime, during which he marched the team into field-goal range and a 27–24 triumph.

After that comeback, Gibbs decided that Williams was his quarterback for the playoffs. He threw for 207 yards and a touchdown to lead the Redskins to a 21–17 win over the Bears at hostile Soldier Field in Chicago. Then, back home at RFK Stadium, he tossed the game-winning touchdown to tight end Clint Didier in the fourth quarter of the NFC title match to give Washington a 17–10 victory over the Minnesota Vikings. Super Bowl XXII was next on the postseason agenda. At that spectacle of spectacles in the football world, with the Redskins trailing Denver 10–0 at the end of the first quarter, Williams made NFL history, leaving spectators, viewers, listeners, and especially the Broncos thunderstruck by his performance. He threw four touchdown passes in the second period—80 yards to Ricky Sanders, 27 to Gary Clark, 50 to Sanders, and 8 to Didier. It blew the game open and led the way to a 42–10 romp over the Broncos. At game's end Williams was the holder of four new all-time Super Bowl records: 340 yards gained passing, 228 yards on passes in one quarter, four touchdown passes, and the longest completion ever in a Super Bowl (at that time), his 80-yarder to Sanders.

An emergency appendectomy sidelined Williams for part of the 1988 season. In his nine-year pro career, he completed 1,240 passes for 16,998 yards and 100 touchdowns.

MARK RYPIEN

In high school in Spokane, Washington, it was unclear which way Mark Rypien might go to make his mark in the sports world: as a senior he was All-State in baseball, basketball, and football. One of his fonder memories of that time was, in fact, from the basketball court rather than the football field: in four games he guarded John Stockton, who went on to fame with the Utah Jazz. Although Stockton averaged 35 points in those four games, Rypien's team still won all four.

At Washington State, however, he concentrated on football and earned All-Pac-10 honors as a quarterback.

But success in the NFL seemed unlikely for Mark Rypien based on his first two years with the Redskins. The strapping 6"4", 234-pound quarterback was a sixth-round draft choice in 1986. A knee injury kept him on injured reserve his rookie year; the following year it was his back that placed him on injured reserve the entire season.

The 1988 season was a different story, however. In training camp, Ryp, as he was known to his teammates, beat out an aging Jay Schroeder for the No. 2 slot on the quarterback depth chart. In the fourth game of the regular season he took over as starter after Doug Williams was struck with appendicitis.

By 1989 Rypien was the undisputed starting quarterback, a job he would not relinquish until 1994. Behind Rypien's passing, the Skins ended up 10–6, winning their last five games in a row. The 3,768 yards Rypien passed for in 1989 was, at the time, second in Redskins history only to the 4,109 Schroeder had accumulated in 1986, and the 280 passes he completed was third in the Redskins record book behind Joe Theismann's 293 (1981) and Sonny Jurgensen's 288 (1967). He had the third-highest quarterback rating in the NFC that year, 88.1.

Rypien missed six games in 1990 with a sprained left knee but came back to lead the Skins to victory in the last five games of the season and to secure a berth in the playoffs. As a wild card, Washington met the Eagles in the first round; Rypien passed for two touchdowns and the Skins triumphed 20–7, only to lose to the 49ers the following week.

The 1991 playoffs were a different story. They were also the capstone of Rypien's professional football career. With Rypien passing to Art Monk, Gary Clark, and Ricky Sanders, and Earnest Byner running with the ball, Washington marched through the regular season, winning fourteen and losing only two games. Rypien led the NFC in passing yardage and was second in the NFL with 3,564. He had the same conference and league ranking in touchdown passes, and his 28 remains second in Redskins history to the 31 touchdown passes Sonny Jurgensen threw in 1967.

In the postseason, Rypien guided the Skins through easy victories over Atlanta, 24–7, and Detroit, 41–10. In Super Bowl XXVI, against the Buffalo Bills, he engineered drive after drive, capping two with touchdown passes to Earnest Byner and Gary Clark, and guided the Redskins to a decisive win that day in the

Quarterback Mark Rypien makes a play against the New York Giants. *Photo reprinted by permission Damian Strohmeyer / TimePix.*

Minneapolis Metrodome, 37–24. Rypien had completed 18 of 33 passes for 292 yards and was named the Super Bowl MVP.

When his career with the Redskins came to an end after the 1993 season, Mark Rypien took his place in the record book along with the team's other illustrious quarterbacks. In franchise history, he ranks fourth in pass completions (1,244), passing yardage (15,928), passes attempted (2,207), and completion percentage (56.4 percent). His Washington career quarterback rating of 80.2 is second only to Sonny Jurgensen's 85.0, while his career interception percentage of 3.4 percent is the best in team history.

4 The Great Receivers

The Redskins have showcased some of the greatest pass receivers in NFL history. Since Sammy Baugh began slinging the football back in the late thirties, the passing game has been a crucial part of the Washington offensive game plan. To make it work the team has had to have receivers who were fast and elusive, sure-handed, and able to run with the ball after they caught it. They found a number of men with just those skills.

Three Redskins receivers have already been inducted into the Pro Football Hall of Fame: Wayne Millner, who played in the thirties; Bobby Mitchell, a hero of the sixties; and Charley Taylor, who toiled in both the sixties and seventies. There have been many other great receivers who also played instrumental roles in the success of the Washington passing game. They include Charley Malone and Hugh "Bones"

Two of the finest wide receivers in Redskins history, Ricky Sanders (No. 83) and Gary Clark (No. 84), on the Washington sideline in 1987. They had a lot to smile about: the Redskins went to super Bowl XXII and beat the Denver Broncos, 42–10. Sanders' career with the Redskins spanned the years 1986–1993 and Clark's 1985–1992.

Taylor, whose passes came mainly from the arms of Baugh, and then later Roy Jefferson, Art Monk, and Gary Clark.

In the earlier days of the league, receivers were not nearly as swift or as productive as today's wide receivers. (Don Hutson of the Green Bay Packers is the notable exception on both counts.) The reason was, of course, that they were not specialists then. When the ball was turned over to an opponent, they did not trot off the field. Instead they lined up at end or linebacker or in the secondary to play defense. In addition, blocking for the running game was equally important as catching passes back in those grind-it-out days of pro football. By the fourth quarter, it was indeed a lung-bursting, leg-numbed end who took off down the field for a Baugh bomb.

Besides the greats, Washington has provided a home to many other noteworthy receivers. During the Baugh era there was Dick Todd, Bob Masterson, Wilbur Moore, and Steve Bagarus; in the fifties, they had Johnny Carson and Joe Walton; and more recently, Joe Washington, Clint Didier, Ricky Sanders, Henry Ellard, and Michael Westbrook have worn the burgundy and gold.

Charley Taylor was Washington's most productive pass catcher eight times, four times in the sixties and four times in the seventies. His namesake (though no relation), Bones Taylor, was tops six consecutive years, 1949–1954, while Bobby Mitchell took the honors in four straight years, 1962–1965. Art Monk claims most career pass-reception marks, with 888 catches for 12,026 yards and the team record for receptions in a season with 106 in 1984. His 65 touchdowns are second to Charley Taylor's 79. Bobby Mitchell accounted for the most yards gained on receptions in a single season, collecting 1,436 in 1963.

WAYNE MILLNER

An All-America end from Notre Dame, Wayne Millner, at 6'1" and 190 pounds, joined the Boston Redskins in 1936. His coach, Ray Flaherty, also in his first year with the team, was so elated at signing him that he sent boss George Preston Marshall a one-sentence wire: "With that Yankee playing end, please accept my resignation if the Redskins do not win the championship this year."

Millner could not only catch the ball well, he was also an outstanding defensive player, difficult to block and a ferocious tackler. He was also an excellent blocker. His teammate and fellow Hall of Famer Cliff Battles said of Millner:

I always knew if I could get out in the open, Wayne would be there to throw a block for me. It was Wayne's blocks that determined whether or not I would get away for a long run.

During his seven-year career with the Redskins, Millner played in four NFL title games (1936, 1937, 1940, and 1945). He missed the 1942 championship match, as well as the next two years, because he was serving in the U.S. Navy. When asked about his most memorable game, Millner said, "Has to be the 1937 championship against the Bears." Millner made it memorable for all Washington football fans. With the Skins trailing Chicago in the third quarter, 14–7, he grabbed a 20-yard pass over the middle from Baugh and raced another 35 yards for a touchdown. Later that same period, with Washington now down 21–14, Millner again teamed with Baugh. Slingin' Sam dropped back from his own 22-yard line and rifled it to Millner at midfield, who carried it 50 yards into the end zone. Having been burned twice in the same quarter, the Bears were all over Millner; so, Baugh then used him as a decoy and tossed another touchdown pass to Ed Justice. At day's end, Millner had caught nine passes for 179 yards, and the Redskins were victorious, 28–21. To this day only Monk has caught more passes in a playoff game (10, in divisional playoff games against the Bears in 1984 and the 49ers in 1991).

The most passes Millner caught in a single season were the 22 he gathered in during the 1940 season; the most yardage he chalked up was 294 in 1939. His career stats with the Skins: 124 receptions, 1,578 yards, 12 touchdowns.

Wayne Millner joined the Redskins in Boston in 1936 and stayed with the team through the 1941 season. After a stint in the U.S. Navy during World War II, he returned for the 1945 season. Millner was inducted into the Pro Football Hall of Fame in 1968.

End Wayne Millner (No. 40) in action. Millner, an All-American out of Notre Dame, was recognized as one of the finest 60-minute men in the late thirties. A top pass receiver, he was also a feared blocker and an outstanding defensive player. In the 1937 NFL title game he caught two touchdown passes of 78 and 55 yards to help the Skins to a 28–21 victory.

As a result of his exceptional play on offense and defense, Wayne Millner was elected to the Pro Football Hall of Fame in 1968.

CHARLEY MALONE

Marshall went all the way down to Texas A&M to get a rather large end in 1934. He was Charley Malone, and he stood 6'4" tall and weighed in the vicinity of 200 pounds.

Malone moved right into the starting lineup that rookie year and immediately became the principal receiver—which in those days meant he caught an incidental 11 passes for 121 yards and two touchdowns. In 1935, however, with the addition of tailback Bill Shepherd, who was not a bad passer, and an invigorated emphasis on passing from new Coach Eddie Casey, Malone doubled his catches with 22. The 433 yards he gained on them were the most in the NFL that year.

With the arrival of Millner in 1936, the Redskins could boast the most solid and dangerous flanks in football, although they were still a year away from obtaining a passer worthy of the two receivers. That, of course, was Baugh; in Slingin' Sam's rookie year, 1937, Malone became his favorite target. He caught 28 passes for 419 yards; only Don Hutson of the Packers, Bill Hewitt of the Eagles, and Gaynell Tinsley of the Chicago Cardinals scored more than Malone's four touchdowns on pass receptions.

Malone again led the Redskins in the receiving department in 1938, this time with 24 catches for 257 yards. He stayed with the Redskins through the 1942 season, although he missed 1941. When he retired, Charley Malone had caught a total of 137 passes for the Redskins for 1,922 yards and 13 touchdowns. His mark of 433 yards on receptions in 1935 stood until Bagarus broke it in 1945 with 637.

HUGH "BONES" TAYLOR

Arriving in Washington as a free agent in 1947, Hugh Taylor was a gangly 6'4", 198-pound end from Oklahoma City University who brought with him the appropriate nickname of "Bones." Rawboned and wiry, with craggy features, he seemed to be almost an extension of Baugh. The long-legged, long-striding Taylor was soon to become Baugh's favorite target. As Baugh later said of him, "Bones had the body of a basketball player, but a pair of hands that just naturally belonged around a football."

The walk-on Taylor not only made the team but won a starting position in 1947. He was the third most productive pass receiver (the most productive end) after halfbacks Eddie Saenz and Bob Nussbaumer—Baugh had taken a liking to throwing to them coming out of the backfield. However, Taylor led the team in TD catches with six, then the second most in club history.

By 1949, it was clear that Bones Taylor was the premier receiver on the Redskins. During that year he set two Washington records when he gained 781 yards on receptions, demolishing the mark of 637 set by Bagarus in 1945, and scored nine touchdowns to take the honor from Joe Aguirre, who had caught seven touchdown passes in 1943. That was the first of six consecutive years in which Taylor would lead the team in pass receptions.

Taylor broke his own reception-yardage record the following year with 833 and tied the TD mark with another nine. His finest year, however, was 1952, a

Steve Bagarus, a halfback out of Notre Dame, is corralled here after catching a pass from Sammy Baugh in a game against the Pittsburgh Steelers in 1946. Bagarus played for the Skins in 1945, 1946, and 1948.

season during which he was catching passes from a quarterback who could walk under his outstretched arm without ducking: Eddie LeBaron. That year Bones set two auspicious records. He caught 12 touchdown passes, a standard that remains the all-time high today (Charley Taylor tied it in 1966, as did Jerry Smith in 1967 and Ricky Sanders in 1988), and gained 961 yards on his catches, a mark that would stand until Mitchell ran off 1,384 in 1962. His average of 23.4 yards per reception that year was the highest in the NFL.

When Bones Taylor retired after the 1954 season, he had rewritten the Redskins' record book for career pass receiving. Bones had pulled in 272 passes, which stands today as the seventh most in club history. He gained a total of

End Hugh "Bones" Taylor goes high in the air for a pass in this sparsely attended game. The lanky, rawboned Taylor was the favorite receiver of three Washington quarterbacks: Sammy Baugh, Eddie LeBaron, and Jack Scarbath.

5,233 yards, again ranked seventh. His 58 touchdown receptions have only been exceeded by Charley Taylor (79), Art Monk (65), and Jerry Smith (60). In his eight years with the Skins, Bones Taylor was credited with 348 points scored, the eighth most in club annals.

BOBBY MITCHELL

Bobby Mitchell was already an established star when he came to the Redskins in 1962. He had played four years in the Cleveland Browns backfield with the legendary Jim Brown and was considered one of the most explosive runners in the game.

The Redskins wanted him badly. In fact, they traded their first-round draft choice and the first pick in that year's draft—Heisman Trophy–winner Ernie Davis of Syracuse—to the Browns for Mitchell and running back Leroy Jackson, the first two black players ever to wear Washington Redskins uniforms. In his column in the *Washington Post*, Shirley Povich nailed it down:

Hugh "Bones" Taylor was Washington's top receiver for five consecutive years, 1949–1954. From Oklahoma City University, he joined the Redskins in 1947 and set two Skins records in 1949 with his 781 yards on receptions and 9 for touchdowns. He retired after the 1954 season.

> The Redskins' fascination for Mitchell, to the point of giving up the most publicized number one draft choice of the decade, is understandable. In the period since Mitchell abandoned his Olympic sprint ambitions and came into the league from U. of Illinois, he has wrecked the Washington team. The Redskins have scouted him mostly from the rear.

Proof of that particular pudding came early during one of Mitchell's first encounters with the Redskins, during his rookie year of 1958: he rushed for 232 yards that day and added another 20 on pass catches.

At 6'0" and 195 pounds, Mitchell was graced with three exceptional talents: speed (he ran the 100-yard dash in 9.7 seconds in college), an uncanny faking ability, and perfect balance. Combining them, he became a pure hellion on the football field.

Washington Coach Bill McPeak announced that Mitchell would be slotted as a flanker instead of a running back, a move that would prove to be both wise and heartily welcomed by Mitchell (he had wanted to play flanker at Cleveland). In his first game against the Browns, with their Coach, Paul Brown, very aware of what Mitchell could do on a football field, he was double-teamed, which proved effective . . . until the last two minutes of the game, when a stymied, frustrated Mitchell bounced off one defender into another, somehow got his hands on a Norm Snead pass at the 50-yard line, broke a tackle, put moves on several other would-be tacklers, and streaked into the end zone for the game-winning touchdown. He gave further testimony of the sagacity of the conversion to flanker that first year in Washington when, on the receiving end of Snead's passes, he led the NFL in receptions and found a place in the Redskins record book with 72 catches for 1,384 yards, becoming the first Skin to break the 1,000-yard receiving mark. Also devastating on kickoff returns, Mitchell was a unanimous choice for All-Pro.

The following year was equally dazzling. Although he caught three fewer passes, he gained 1,436 yards with them, the NFL high and a Washington record that has yet to be matched. Ninety-nine of those yards came on an NFL record-tying touchdown pass from George Izo in another contest with his former employer, the Browns. In a game against the Steelers, Mitchell gained 218 yards on pass catches, the fourth most in Washington history.

A simple fact that Mitchell proved beyond a doubt in his first two years at flanker was that an opponent's troubles were just beginning *after* Mitchell caught a pass—he was recognized as the most difficult receiver in the league to corral and ground once he got his hands on the ball. He had his own philosophy:

> **You've got to go out there with confidence. If you come hesitating, that defenseman has you in his back pocket. You got to aim at him with authority and make him worry about *you*, and not you worry about *him*.**

As it turned out, Mitchell, in his seven years with the Skins, gave defenders a great deal to worry about. He was forever a threat to break the big play: a 60-yard touchdown here, a 45-yarder there, leaving a defender flat-footed with a move, breaking away from the pack with an explosive burst of speed, inevitably gobbling up great chunks of yardage.

Mitchell retired from the game after the 1968 season, but his Redskins career did not end there. He moved into the front office, where he has served in a variety of capacities, from director of pro scouting to assistant general manager.

As a player with the Redskins, Mitchell ranks sixth in pass receptions (393) and fourth in yards gained receiving (6,491). He maintains the highest average

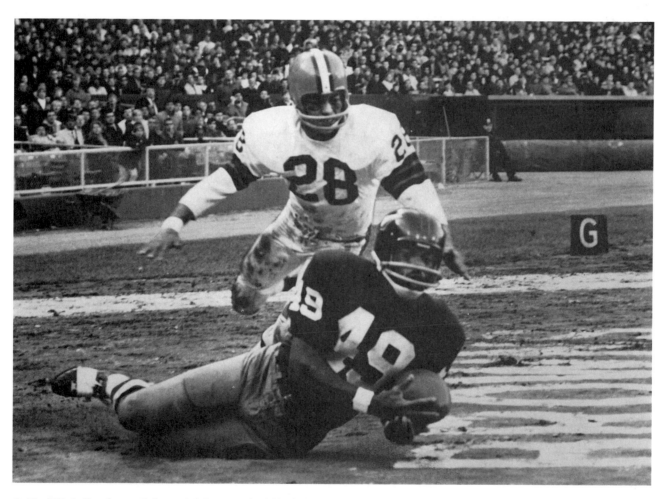

Bobby Mitchell makes a diving catch here against his former team, the Cleveland Browns. Traded to Washington in 1962, he was switched from running back to flanker and played through the 1968 season. Among his fondest memories is the second regular-season game he played for Washington; he scored the game-winning touchdown against his former employer from Cleveland.

kickoff return in club annals (28.5). His combined net yards gained of 8,162 ranks seventh in the Redskins record book.

In 11 seasons in the NFL, Bobby Mitchell rushed for 2,735 yards and gained 7,954 yards on pass receptions, 2,690 on kickoff returns, and 699 on punt returns. He scored a total of 91 touchdowns (65 on receptions, 18 rushing, 5 on kickoff returns, and 3 on punt returns). In 1983, he was inducted into the Pro Football Hall of Fame.

CHARLEY TAYLOR

The Redskins and Coach Bill McPeak had no reservations about who their first-round draft pick would be in 1964. It was the 6'3", 210-pound speedster from Arizona State named Charley Taylor. The question kicked around backstage in Washington, however, was where to play him—at running back, where he had excelled in college, or, as some lobbied, at defensive cornerback. No one, at the time, was thinking wide receiver.

The running back advocates prevailed. He was thrust into the backfield his rookie year and became the running game to augment the passing game of Sonny Jurgensen, another first-year Redskin in 1964. Taylor responded, exhilarating the Washington fans by turning in the most exciting and productive season by a Redskins ball carrier in a decade and a half. He not only churned out 755 yards rushing—the most since Rob Goode set the team standard of 951 in 1950—but also caught 53 passes for 814 yards, only a whisper behind flanker Mitchell in both categories. He contributed 10 touchdowns, 5 running and 5 catching the ball. For all that, he was named the NFL Rookie of the Year.

Taylor also led the Skins in rushing during the following year, but in 1966 a coaching change put Otto Graham, one of the game's greatest quarterbacks in his day, at the helm and increased the emphasis on passing in the Redskins' offensive scheme. Graham looked at Taylor and came to certain conclusions:

> Charley was poetry in motion, but he couldn't gear his speed to his interference. More often than not he'd be out in front of the guard who should have been leading the running play, or climbing up the back of a slow tackle. He was devastating once he had room to run, so we kept asking ourselves what was the best way to get Taylor out into the open field. The answer was obvious: put him outside as a receiver.

A familiar sight: Charley Taylor about to haul in a pass for the Redskins. In his 14 years with Washington, Taylor set team records for most receptions (649), which was also an NFL record at the time, and most yardage gained on pass catches (9,140), since surpassed by Art Monk. Taylor still holds the record for most touchdown receptions (79). He was inducted into the Pro Football Hall of Fame in 1984.

That shrewd decision changed Taylor's life and eventually inked a new name and new figures in the NFL record book. In the second half of the 1966 regular season, Taylor ceased to be the Skins' leading ground gainer and began a stint as top receiver that would span the next 11 years in Washington. In his first effort split out at end, during a game against the Baltimore Colts, he hauled in eight passes for 111 yards; the following week against Dallas, he tied Mitchell's team record of 11 receptions in a game. After one of those catches he shook off three would-be tacklers and raced to a 78-yard touchdown. Taylor ended the 1966 season with 72 receptions, the most in the NFL that year, which also tied the team record set by Mitchell four years earlier. Of the 72, 54 of those receptions came in the six games he lined up as a wide receiver. His 12 touchdowns on pass catches also tied the club record, set by Bones Taylor in 1952.

Three of the finest Redskins performers pose for the camera: wide receiver Charley Taylor (No. 42), linebacker Chris Hanburger (No. 55), and tight end Jerry Smith (No. 87). Taylor, from Arizona State, played for Washington from 1964 to 1977; Hanburger, out of North Carolina, from 1965 to 1978; Smith, also from Arizona State, was a Redskin from 1965 to 1977.

George Allen came on the scene in 1971 and brought along a raft of veterans, dismantling the lineup almost completely in the process. One post he had no desire to tamper with, however, was wide receiver. He had a definite fondness for Charley Taylor; later, when he wrote a book about the greatest pro football players, he ranked Taylor as the fourth-best receiver of all time, behind Don Hutson, Lenny Moore, and "Crazylegs" Hirsch. Said Allen:

> **Charley was very disciplined. He had good moves, and ran perfect routes. He could catch the ball long or short. He could make the tough catch over the middle. He had sure hands and could catch the ball one-handed. He was also a tremendous blocker.**

Taylor missed much of the 1971 season and all of 1976 because of injuries. Other than those years he was always at or near the top of the NFL receiving charts. He endeared himself to Redskins fans by consistently being at his best in games against the abhorred Cowboys. In the 1972 NFC title game against Dallas, for example, he grabbed seven passes and scored the game's only two touchdowns, on passes of 15 and 45 yards, to ensure a 26–3 Washington victory. Charlie Waters, the Cowboys' All-Pro safety who spent much of his career chasing Taylor, said of him:

> **I hate to say it, but I sure wasn't crying when Charley couldn't play. . . . He's a hell of a competitor, and his competence is overwhelming. We'll jaw back and forth at each other; he's always trying to psych me out. He's one guy who talks a good game and can also back it up.**

When Charley Taylor ended his pro foot-ball career after the 1977 season, he was the NFL all-time leading pass catcher, having gathered in 649 passes.

Taylor owned all Washington career pass-catching records until Art Monk came along. The 649 he snared (second to Monk) accounted for 9,140 yards (also second to Monk) and 79 touchdowns, a team record. He teamed with Sonny Jurgensen to produce three of the longest pass plays in team history, an 88-yarder against the Dallas Cowboys in 1969, and two for 86 yards against the Atlanta Falcons in 1966 and the Los Angeles Rams in 1967. His total of 90 touchdowns is the most ever by a Redskin, and the 540 points Taylor scored is third behind the 1,204 amassed by kicker Mark Moseley and 787 by another kicker, Chip Lohmiller.

Charley Taylor snagging one of his record 79 touchdown receptions, this one against the archrival Dallas Cowboys. Taylor went to the Pro Bowl eight times during his 14 years with the Redskins.

Charley Taylor earned his way to the Pro Bowl eight times and into the Pro Football Hall of Fame in 1984.

ROY JEFFERSON

In his first year as head coach in 1971, George Allen went after veteran wide receiver Roy Jefferson before he realized how desperately he would need him. The 6'2", 195-pound Jefferson had played with the Pittsburgh Steelers for five years and the Super Bowl–champion Baltimore Colts of 1970 before becoming a member of the "Over-the-Hill Gang" in Washington.

Jefferson, who played his college ball at Utah, was 27 when he donned the burgundy and gold and was anything but over-the-hill. Teaming him at the other

Roy Jefferson (No. 80) cradles a pass from Billy Kilmer in a 1972 game against the Cowboys. Jefferson was acquired from the Baltimore Colts in 1971 and led the team that year in receiving with 49 catches for 701 yards.

end of the line from All-Pro Charley Taylor, Allen envisioned the most threatening double barrel in the NFC. And to complement it, he had the ever-reliable Jerry Smith at tight end. Allen told the press he had "a trio of targets beyond compare" for quarterbacks Jurgensen and Billy Kilmer.

The way they lined up that first season of "The Future Is Now" was with Jefferson and Smith on the strong side and Taylor on the weak side. Unfortunately, it did not stay that way for long; injuries benched both Taylor and Smith for a

Tight end Jerry Smith (No. 87), stepping ahead of a Los Angeles Rams defensive back, is about to collect one of the 421 passes he caught for Washington (fourth highest in Redskins history). Smith played for the Skins for 13 years; the 5,496 yards he gained on receptions ranks sixth in team stats and his touchdown total of 60 is third highest.

On a snowy, cold afternoon at RFK Stadium in 1973, wide receiver Roy Jefferson manages to hold on to a pass from Billy Kilmer. It was the last game of the season, and the Skins won it 38–20, enabling them to secure a wild-card slot in the playoffs.

good part of the season, and Jefferson became the object of attention coming off the line of scrimmage. He carried the burden well and hauled in 47 passes for 701 yards, both team highs that year.

From the time he came to Washington, it became clear that Jefferson was especially dangerous on a quick-post pattern. As he explained it:

> I've made a living off the quick post. Go straight down the field about 10 yards, then cut toward the goalpost on about a 45-degree angle. Of course, I put in a few jukes along the way to get the defender off balance.

The next year, with Kilmer handling most of the quarterbacking chores due to Jurgensen's injuries, the passing game was beautifully balanced, with a healthy Taylor and Smith back to join Jefferson, and Larry Brown coming out of the backfield as well. Among the four of them, they caught 137 passes for 2,849 yards to energize the Redskins as they hurtled toward their first divisional title since 1945. In the regular season, Jefferson, with 35 catches for 550 yards, was the second most productive receiver behind Charley Taylor. In the first playoff game that year, against the Green Bay Packers, Jefferson struck with his favorite quick-post pattern—after a juke, darting across the middle to take a pass from Kilmer for a 32-yard touchdown. Jefferson caught five of Kilmer's seven passes that day for 83 yards as the Skins scalped the Pack, 16–3. Jefferson was also the top receiver for Washington a few weeks later at Super Bowl VII, making five receptions for 50 yards, although the Redskins fell short that day against the Miami Dolphins, 14–7.

After missing all but six games of the 1975 season because of a knee injury, Jefferson came back in 1976, had a credible year, and then retired from the game. He caught 208 passes for the Redskins in his six years in Washington, ranking No. 10 in that category, and gained 3,119 yards, ninth best. During 12 years in the NFL, Roy Jefferson caught a total of 451 passes for 7,539 yards and 52 touchdowns.

ART MONK

The day to remember for Art Monk, Washington's first-round draft choice of 1980 out of Syracuse, was December 16, 1984, at RFK Stadium, the last game of the season, against the St. Louis Cardinals. With the divisional title on the line and the game well into the third quarter, Monk lined up out on the left at the St. Louis 36-yard line while Joe Theismann barked the signals. Suddenly he was racing a fly route down the sideline, then curling to the inside a step ahead of the defender to grab the ball in his sure hands and cross the goal line. A touchdown was signaled, the game was stopped, and the announcement was made: "Art Monk has just caught his 102nd pass this year and broken the NFL record for receptions in a single season." The record, which had been held for the previous 20 years by Charley Hennigan of the Houston Oilers, was further shattered when Monk snared another four passes before the game was over. Besides setting a major pro football record that day (since broken), Monk's 11 receptions for 136 yards and two touchdowns were instrumental in the Skins' 29–27 triumph to earn the NFC East title for 1984.

Art Monk, fresh out of Syracuse, joined the Redskins in 1980, played through the 1992 season, and ended his career with a pair of receiving records that will be difficult to surpass. No one is close to the 888 passes he caught for the Skins nor the 12,026 yards gained on those receptions.

Monk, at 6'3" and 209 pounds, made his presence felt from the very beginning in Washington. Winning a starting role in 1980, he proceeded to wipe out the rookie receiving record of 53 grabs set by Charley Taylor in 1964 with the 58 he caught for 797 yards, both team highs that year. He was honored as the NFL's Offensive Rookie of the Year.

Nicknamed "Money" for his ability to catch clutch passes and pull off the crucial play, Monk led the team in yardage gained on receptions the following year, toting up 894, the most since Charley Taylor earned 990 yards 14 years earlier.

In the strike-torn season of 1982, Monk again led the team in catches, but in the last game he broke his foot and missed the playoffs and Super Bowl XVII. Other injuries plagued him during the first part of the 1983 season, but Monk came back to help the Skins win the eastern divisional title. In the playoff game against the Rams, Monk caught two touchdown passes for 40 and 21 yards as the Skins triumphed, 51–7.

After Monk's record-setting season of 1984, Joe Gibbs said:

I don't think you can ask a football player to do more. He played every down and caught nearly every pass thrown to him, from training camp on.

The totals were surely impressive—106 receptions for 1,372 yards and seven touchdowns. He was a unanimous All-Pro and was voted by his coaches and teammates as the Redskins' Most Valuable Player. Later, the unassuming Monk said of his grand performance:

Last year I did catch more passes . . . and there were a few reasons. The receptions came partly because Charlie Brown [the Redskins' other starting wide receiver] was injured, and partly because when I was open, the ball was coming my way. Lots of times you get open, but the quarterback has already thrown the ball to someone else, or is getting sacked, or just doesn't see you. This past year the ball was always there.

In his 14-year Redskins career, Art Monk caught 888 passes, surpassing Charley Taylor's record of 649 career receptions. He gained 12,026 yards, again topping the mark set by Charley Taylor, who had earned 9,140 in his 13-year Redskins career. Art Monk's most prodigious single game came in December 1985 at RFK Stadium against the Cincinnati Bengals, when he caught 13 passes, a club

Perennial All-Pro wide receiver Art Monk battles for the ball with a Giants defender in this 1981 game. Three years later Monk broke the NFL record for pass catches in a season when he hauled in 106.

record he now shares with Kelvin Bryant, and gained 230 yards, the third most in club annals. He also caught 13 passes for 168 yards in a game against Detroit in November 1990.

GARY CLARK

A featherweight in terms of pro football's weights and measures, Gary Clark was a mere 5'9" and 173 pounds in 1985. A refugee from the USFL, he had been overlooked in the one NFL draft for which he had been eligible. But he was signed by Washington as a free agent that year, mostly on the recommendation of Larry Csonka, former Miami Dolphins fullback and general manager of the Jacksonville Bulls in the USFL, who had had to release Clark because both the franchise and the league were in the process of going bankrupt. Csonka told Coach Joe Gibbs that he thought the elusive, if miniature, Clark might be the perfect complement to Monk in the Redskins' receiving corps. "Quick-footed and filled with an unpredictable array of moves" was one description offered early that first year in a Redskins press release, while a Washington newspaper suggested South American soccer might be a better field for a person of his physical endowments.

Clark, however, did not take long to prove that professional football in the United States was indeed the perfect milieu for him. After breaking into the starting lineup in the fifth game of the regular season, he set about illustrating in dramatic fashion that Csonka indeed had an eye for talent.

Clark, once he got the chance, turned in three 100-yard-plus games that rookie season, including an effort against the New York Giants that netted him 11 receptions and 193 yards. When the regular season came to a close, Clark had pulled in 72 passes, the fifth most in the NFC and the fourth highest in Redskins history. He gained 926 yards for Washington on those receptions and led the team with five touchdowns.

In 1986, Clark hop-skipped, sidestepped, and leaped to the top of the Washington pass-receiving ledger. Two games in particular tell the crux of the story. Against the New York Giants, he shook off all defenders to snatch 11 passes for 241 yards, the latter setting a new club record (Monk had gained 230 yards against the Bengals the year before). Wounded and sidelined the following week, he came back from the bench in overtime to make a game-winning touchdown catch against the Vikings.

When the season was over, Clark led the Redskins in receptions with 74, fifth best in the NFC, and yardage gained (1,265), second in the conference and fourth best in Redskins history.

By the start of the 1987 season, Clark had so established himself that television commentator and former Oakland Raiders coach John Madden said:

Wide receiver Gary Clark makes a diving, fingertip catch—and he holds on to the ball. Clark was signed as a free agent in 1985 and became a starter by the fifth game of that season. At 5'9" and 173 pounds, he was diminutive by NFL standards but mammoth in his performance on the field.

If I was starting a team and had to pick one wide receiver, I'd pick Gary Clark. . . .
He really impresses me. He seems to be one of those guys who keeps his
motor running the whole time. Nobody thinks of him when they think of the best
receivers, but he's always there to make a play when you need it. He's the guy who
keeps the first downs coming, then he'll lull you to sleep and slip behind you for a
deep one. He just knows how to play the game.

Gary Clark played eight years with the Redskins. By the time he departed after the 1992 season, he stood as the third most productive Redskins receiver with 8,742 yards gained on 549 catches. His 58 touchdowns ranks fourth (shared with "Bones" Taylor).

Clark lived up to the accolade that year, ending up with a team-high 56 receptions for 1,066 yards and seven touchdowns. In the NFC championship game of 1987, Clark caught the game-winning touchdown toss from Doug Williams; he then grabbed three for 55 yards and a touchdown in the Skins' victory in Super Bowl XXII.

Gary Clark is well represented in the Washington record book for receiving. In eight years with the Skins, from 1985 to 1992, he caught 549 passes for 8,742 yards and 58 touchdowns.

5

The Great Defenders

One of the game's greatest advocates of defensive football, George Allen, once said—maybe pontificated—that "Great defenses stop great offenses, and win football games." It is a maxim subscribed to by many successful pro football coaches, and its veracity has been corroborated over the years by the list of NFL championship teams who have unmistakably been anchored by fearsome defenses: the Chicago Bears of the thirties and early forties, the New York Giants of the fifties, the Packers of the sixties, the Steelers of the seventies, Tom Landry's flex-defense Cowboys, Minnesota's Purple People Eaters, and every title-bearer of the eighties and nineties.

All-Pro defensive end Dexter Manley in the heat of battle, double-teamed by New York Giants blockers. Manley, one of the Redskins' all-time great defensive linemen, came to Washington in 1981, a fifth-round draft choice out of Oklahoma State, and remained through the 1989 season.

In the good years, the Redskins have fielded exceptional defensive teams with a memorable assortment of All-Pros, from Turk Edwards, who was there in Boston on the very first opening day, to Dexter Manley, who continued to set sack records in the late eighties.

In the early days of the franchise, defensive players were never designated as such because they also played offense—the legendary 60-minute men. Sammy Baugh was not merely a great tailback and quarterback, he was also an outstanding defensive back. Wayne Millner could not only catch passes, he also lined up at defensive end and was known to be a devastating tackler.

Turk Edwards was the first acknowledged great defender to wear the Redskins' burgundy and gold, toiling in the trenches of both Boston and Washington. He was followed by "Wee" Willie Wilkin, who played into the forties. Then there were Al DeMao and Gene Brito. They were all two-way players, battling from both sides of the line of scrimmage each Sunday. With the age of defensive specialists came such luminaries as Chris Hanburger, Ken Houston, Dave Butz, Dexter Manley, Darrell Green, Wilber Marshall, and Ken Harvey—all accurately defined as great.

Defensive statistics were never kept in the early years of pro football. Sacks and interceptions, though, would have been relatively inconsequential because of the dearth of passes thrown by tailbacks or quarterbacks in those days. Since such stats have been collected, Dexter Manley has ravaged the most quarterbacks, collecting 97½ sacks. Darrell Green holds the record for the most career interceptions at 53. The record for most sacks in a season belongs to Manley, who downed quarterbacks 18 times in 1986; the most picked-off passes in one year were snatched by Dan Sandifer, 13 in 1948. Baugh still holds the record for the most interceptions in a game, four in a 1943 contest with the Lions, which Sandifer tied in 1948 against the Boston Yanks. And Diron Talbert can claim most sacks in one contest, accomplished when he scored five against the Giants in 1975, a mark equalled by Manley against those same Giants in 1988.

ALBERT GLEN "TURK" EDWARDS

In an age when behemoths were the exception rather than the rule in pro football, tackle Turk Edwards was known as a monstrosity to all who tried to block him. At 6'2" and 260 pounds in the late thirties, he was truly an immovable object, and when he chose to move he was indeed an irresistible force.

"Turk" Edwards (No. 37) was one of the larger tackles in the game in the thirties (6'2" and 260 pounds). Playing both offense and defense, he was the heart of the Redskins' line throughout the thirties, good enough to earn his way into the Pro Football Hall of Fame, inducted in 1969.

Edwards, who was an All-America lineman for the University of Washington, received offers from the New York Giants, the Portsmouth Spartans, and that new-comer to the league in 1932, the Boston Braves. He chose the latter. "They offered me the most money, $150 a game for 10 games," Edwards explained. "That was a lot of money for a young man in those days."

Turk then began a career that started in Boston and ended in Washington, and one that was illustrious, to say the least. He was named All-Pro four times, in

1932, 1933, 1936, and 1937. As Don Smith wrote for the Pro Football Hall of Fame:

> **Edwards typified overwhelming strength and power, rather than speed. Yet he was agile enough to get the job done as well or better than all but a mere handful who have played the tackle position in pro football.**

Edwards was the typical iron man of the day. In one 15-game season in Boston he was on the field for all but 10 minutes of play during the entire year.

In 1940, after the ceremonial coin toss before a game with the New York Giants, he pivoted to trot off the field and his knee went out on him. It ended Edwards' playing career, but he remained with the Skins as an assistant coach and took on the head-coaching duties from 1946 through 1948. Turk Edwards was inducted into the Pro Football Hall of Fame in 1969.

Other great defenders of the early days include Baugh and Millner, but also less well-known players, such as interior linemen Jim Barber, Dick Farman, and Fred Davis; ends Bob Masterson and Joe Aguirre; linebacker Ki Aldrich; and defensive backs Wilbur Moore, Dick Todd, Dan Sandifer, Dick James, and Jim Steffen.

"WEE" WILLIE WILKIN

His name was Wilbur Byrne Wilkin, but he was known as Wee Willie, as inappropriate a nickname as could be levied—for he was 6'6" and weighed as much as 280 pounds at the height of his career.

Wilkin had played college ball at St. Mary's in California and was signed by the Redskins in 1938. From the very beginning, he was as awesome on the field as he was uncontainable off it. The *Washington Star-News* reported:

> **[In] Wilkin's rookie pro year he was fined $25 nine times for training infractions during the 11-week season, and there was no assurance that he was on his good behavior those other two weeks.**

In battle, he was equally unrestrained. Harry Sheer, writing for the Associated Press, noted:

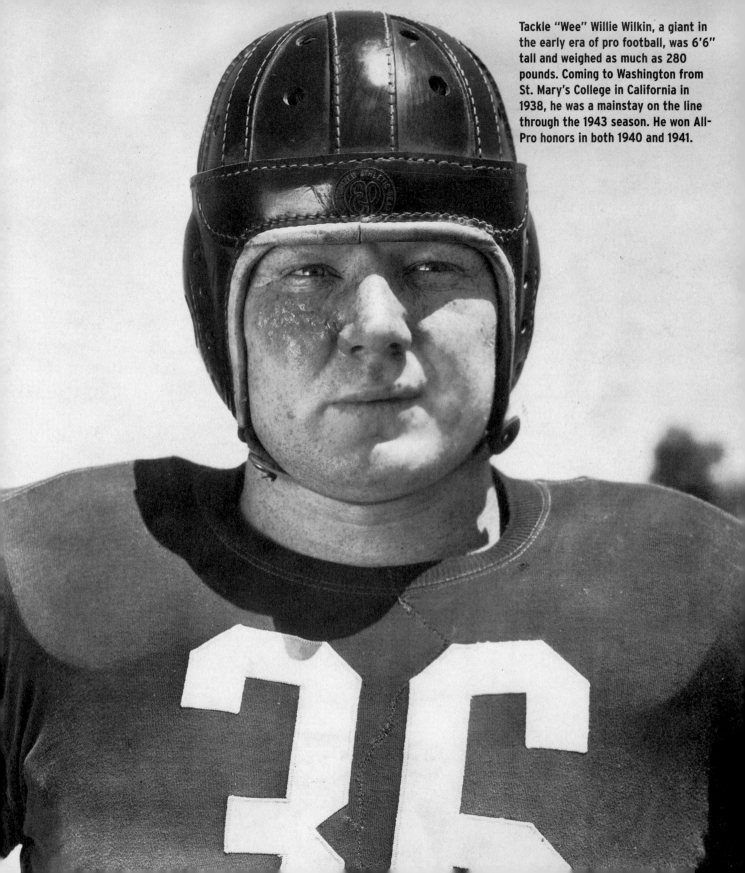

Tackle "Wee" Willie Wilkin, a giant in the early era of pro football, was 6'6" tall and weighed as much as 280 pounds. Coming to Washington from St. Mary's College in California in 1938, he was a mainstay on the line through the 1943 season. He won All-Pro honors in both 1940 and 1941.

> **His first mark of distinction came early, in his second pro game. It was against the Detroit Lions in 1938 and the Redskins were trailing 3–0. The Lions, however, were deep in their own territory and a punt was called. Willie plowed through, picked up the blocker, Ace Gutowsky, and threw him head-on into the kicker. The punt was blocked, a Redskin fell on it for a touchdown, and the Washingtons had won.**

Wilkin was named All-Pro in both 1940 and 1941. Coach Ray Flaherty said that having him on the line in a football game was like having a tank in combat. His ultimate boss, George Preston Marshall, complained that he spent more time bailing Wee Willie out of trouble off the field than he did enjoying his play on the field. Wilkin's NFL career came to an end in Washington after the 1943 season, although he came back and played one last year for the Chicago Rockets in the AAFC in 1946.

AL DEMAO

Al DeMao has the distinction of being the first Redskins lineman ever to have a "Day" held in his honor. It was November 2, 1952, and before then only two Washington ballplayers had ever been so honored: Sammy Baugh and "Bullet" Bill Dudley.

By 1952, DeMao had centered both the offensive and defensive lines for the Redskins for eight years. He had come to the Redskins in 1945 directly from the U.S. Navy, which he had entered after playing a little college ball at Duquesne University. On his "Day," he was described this way:

> **On offense, he is a cunning, bruising blocker; on defense, he has been a shrewd, deadly tackler. And at all times, he has been a true team player.**

At 6'2" and 215 pounds, DeMao was the perfect example of the all-around lineman who lived in relative obscurity for most of his career. It was not until the proverbial twilight of his career that he began to receive the recognition he so richly deserved as a splendid contributor to the Washington Redskins. "Al is fast, strong, and has an absolutely perfect instinct for the game" is the way Curly Lambeau, one of DeMao's six head coaches with the Redskins, put it.

The team and fans honored him that day in 1952. After the following season, DeMao retired, leaving behind an honored career on both sides of the Redskins line.

Al DeMao played center on offense and nose guard on defense for the Redskins from 1945 through 1953. At 6'2" and 215 pounds, he was small for a lineman but made up for it with his quickness and his endurance.

GENE BRITO

When Gene Brito joined the Redskins in 1952, there were 12 ends in camp seeking a job. At the start, Brito, who came out of Loyola of Los Angeles and was drafted in the 18th round, ranked 12th. After the cuts were made, however, the 6'1", 215-pound Brito was still there. During his first two years in Washington, Brito was used mostly on offense, but in 1953 Coach Curly Lambeau decided to play him mostly as a defensive end. The switch worked so well that Brito earned his first of five invitations to the Pro Bowl.

In 1954, along with Redskins quarterback Eddie LeBaron, Brito defected to the Canadian Football League and played for Calgary. The following year, 1955, they were both back in Washington, and Brito, earning All-Pro honors, fully established himself as one of the premier defensive ends in pro football. An opposing player once described him this way:

> You're wasting your time with a delaying block. He's got so many moves he'll leave you flat on your back. The only way to contain him is to go after Gene aggressively— and hope you've got the strength to keep from landing flat on your rear anyhow.

The story has often been told that Ted Marchibroda, when he was quarterbacking for the Pittsburgh Steelers in the mid-fifties, once pulled his tackle from the huddle and said, "I can't take much more of that Brito. I don't care if the ref is looking—if you can't keep him out, hold him."

"You kidding?" the tackle shrugged in reply. "I've *been* holding him."

Gene Brito brightened the Redskins defense through the 1958 season. Besides his 1955 honor, he also earned All-Pro recognition in 1956, 1957, and 1958.

Along with DeMao and Brito, there were many other great Redskins defenders in the fifties, including linebackers the likes of Chuck Drazenovich, LaVern Torgeson, and Sam Huff; quality linemen like Paul Lipscomb, Bob Toneff, Joe Rutgens, and Karl Kammerer; and such great defensive backs as Don Doll and Dick Alban.

CHRIS HANBURGER

The defense-minded George Allen, Chris Hanburger's coach with the Redskins from 1971 through 1977, ranked him among the top 13

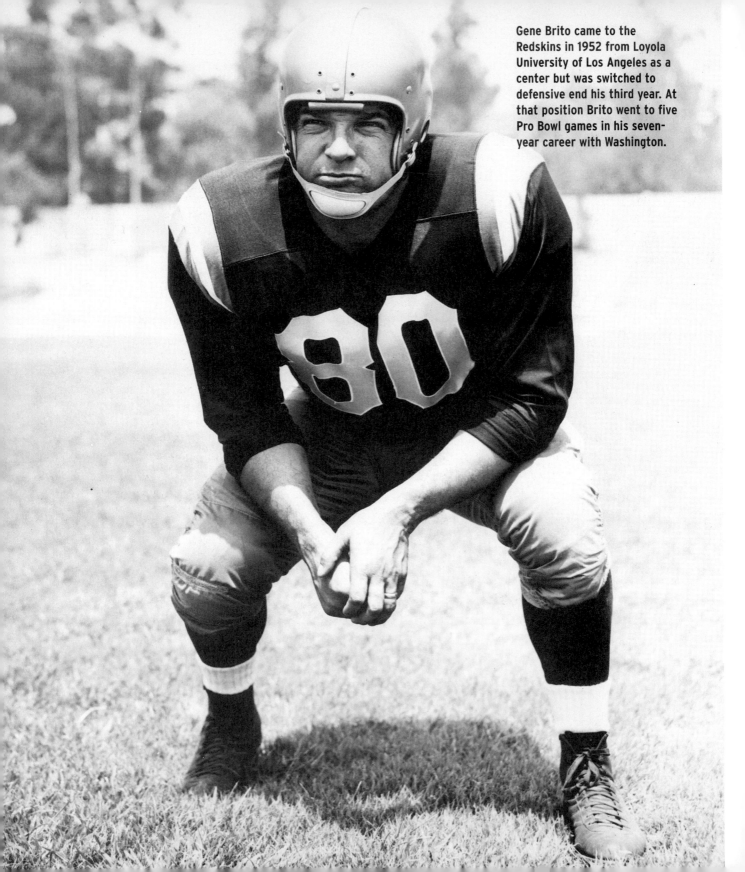

Gene Brito came to the Redskins in 1952 from Loyola University of Los Angeles as a center but was switched to defensive end his third year. At that position Brito went to five Pro Bowl games in his seven-year career with Washington.

Defensive back Dick Alban (No. 42) intercepts a pass thrown by New York Giants quarterback Charlie Conerly in a 1954 game. It was an otherwise dismal season for the Redskins, who ended up 3-9. At the left is the intended receiver, Frank Gifford.

linebackers ever to have played in the NFL, comparing him to the likes of Chuck Bednarik, Dick Butkus, Sam Huff, Ray Nitschke, and Jack Lambert:

> He played the right side as skillfully as almost anyone I ever saw. Chris was a little light for a linebacker [6'2", 218 pounds]. But he was seldom knocked off his feet. He had real good balance and excellent agility. But quickness was his biggest asset. He could really push the passer and he covered a lot of ground on pass defense.

Linebacker Chris Hanburger (No. 55) shirttails Giants quarterback Fran Tarkenton and puts an end to his scrambling on this play. Hanburger was an 18th-round draft choice out of North Carolina in 1965. For 14 years (1965–1978), he remained one of the outstanding outside line-men in pro football.

Hanburger, like All-Pro Brito before him, was almost overlooked by the Redskins and was not drafted until the 18th round in 1965. He broke into the starting lineup at right linebacker in the 10th game that rookie year and remained there through 13 more seasons. The following year he earned a trip to the Pro Bowl, the first of nine such junkets he would make during his late career with the Redskins.

Hanburger was responsible for changing the outcomes of many games for Washington. A player profile from a *GameDay* program in 1973 described him this way:

> Starting from his post as a right linebacker he is liable to turn up anywhere on the
> field, usually hitting harder than anybody in the near vicinity. Unlike the normal
> run of linebackers, Hanburger has a gift for the spectacular play. He stole the ball
> out of Ron Johnson's arms, for instance, to set up a Washington win over New

**York. And in the playoffs [1972], he blitzed the Dallas Cowboys, leaped completely
over a blocker, and landed on Roger Staubach for a crucial sack.**

Hanburger himself shrugged off the assessment. "I don't think of myself as a big-play type. To me every play is important. . . . I just try to keep involved, to be in the middle of the action every time."

And that he was. For 14 years, Hanburger was stopping running backs, sacking quarterbacks, and breaking up pass plays for the Redskins. Only Darrell Green (17), Sammy Baugh (16), and Monte Coleman (16) played more seasons in Washington, and only five Redskins played in more games than Hanburger's 187.

Defensive action from a 1966 game against the St. Louis Cardinals. Chris Hanburger (No. 55) applies a shoulder to a Cardinals ball carrier. Coming in to help is linebacker Sam Huff (No. 70). The Skins won that day in Washington, 26–20.

Chris Hanburger (No. 55) gets a stranglehold on Browns quarterback Frank Ryan in this 1967 game at Municipal Stadium in Cleveland. The Skins lost that day, 42–37.

No Redskin, however, has gone to as many Pro Bowls as the nine attended by Hanburger. He intercepted 19 passes, recovered 12 fumbles, and scored five touchdowns. Three of those five touchdowns were on fumble recoveries, which ranks him second on the all-time NFL list in that category.

Ken Houston in action, intercepting a pass. Houston was invited to the Pro Bowl each of his eight years with the Redskins. *Photo copyright the* Washington Post; *reprinted by permission of the Washington, D.C., Public Library.*

KEN HOUSTON

The Redskins wanted safety Ken Houston so badly that they traded five players to the Houston Oilers for him in 1973. Already an established All-Pro defensive back who shared the NFL record for interceptions returned for touchdowns in a season (four in 1971) and in a game (two against the San Diego

Safety Ken Houston was acquired in a trade with the Houston Oilers in 1973. Houston already had six years of NFL experience when he arrived in Washington. He would stay eight years, retiring after the 1980 season, acknowledged as one of pro football's all-time great defensive backs. He was inducted into the Pro Football Hall of Fame in 1986.

Chargers in 1971), Houston had six pro football seasons behind him when he came to Washington. George Allen, who acquired him, said, "Everyone said I had given too much to get him. Well, he gave me five years the others wouldn't have given me combined." And he gave the Redskins three more than he gave Allen.

At 6'3" and 198 pounds, with speed, strength, and a natural propensity for punishing tackles, Houston had all the natural endowments to become a superb strong safety—which, of course, he did. From Prairie View A&M in Texas, Houston was a late-round draft choice by the Oilers in 1967, but it took him only three games to secure a starting role in their secondary.

Houston had eight super seasons with the Redskins. His value to the team was evinced in many ways, but perhaps one play dramatizes it better than any other. It was October 8, 1973, and the Redskins were locked in a bitter struggle with the Dallas Cowboys, their archrival, at RFK Stadium. Washington led 14–7 with 16 seconds left to play, but the Cowboys had the ball on fourth and goal to go. Craig Morton tossed a short pass to powerful Walt Garrison just outside the goal line. Garrison whirled toward the end zone, but Houston hit him high and wrestled him to the ground less than a yard from a touchdown. "It was the most important tackle I ever made," Houston said after the game. "I knew I had to get him down or it was the ballgame." The play was so important that it won a special place in *The Semi-Official Dallas Cowboys Haters' Handbook*. To the delight of Redskins fans everywhere, Houston consistently came up with big plays against the Cowboys—returning a punt 58 yards for a touchdown to ensure a 28–21 win in 1974, intercepting a Roger Staubach pass in overtime to set up a 30–24 win in 1975, making several key defensive plays to save a 9–5 victory in 1978, among many other plays that tormented Dallas fans during Houston's tenure in Washington.

With Washington, Houston was either All-Pro or All-NFC every year he played. He was invited to 8 consecutive Pro Bowls while a Redskin and 12 straight counting the years with the Oilers.

Houston retired after the 1978 season and still holds the NFL record for the most career touchdowns on interception returns—all nine of them, surprisingly, coming in his six years with the Oilers. During his 12-year NFL career, he intercepted 49 passes, returning them for a net of 898 yards. But in Washington he will probably be best remembered for his bone-jarring tackles and all those things he did to the Cowboys. Ken Houston was elected to the Pro Football Hall of Fame in 1986.

Dave Butz was an All-American tackle at Purdue before joining the NFL. In his 14 years with the Redskins (1975–1988), he established himself as one of the franchise's all-time great defensive linemen. His best year was 1986, when he was credited with 91 tackles. He ranks third on the all-time Redskins list for sacks with 59½, behind only Dexter Manley and Charles Mann.

DAVE BUTZ

Over on Pennsylvania Avenue, Gerald Ford was in the White House when Dave Butz came to Washington in 1975. When the enormous tackle announced his retirement, George H. W. Bush was living there.

At 6'7" and 295 pounds, with a 19½" neck, Butz always captured plenty of attention wherever he went. An All-America defensive tackle from Purdue, he caught the eye of the St. Louis Cardinals, who drafted him in 1973, and he made himself visible enough to NFL official observers to land on that year's NFL All-Rookie team.

After a year on injured reserve in 1974 and an ensuing contract dispute, with his option played out, Butz signed with the Redskins in 1975 for double the salary he had been paid in St. Louis. The league later decided that Washington had to give the Cardinals two first-round and one second-round draft choices in return for Butz, in what was one of the largest compensation deals in NFL history.

Fourteen years later, having watched Butz, "The Master of Intimidation," disassemble offenses, pulverize running backs, terrorize quarterbacks, and display a seemingly endless endurance in Washington's front line, most Redskins fans agreed that he was easily worth the compensation. George Allen loved him for his unsparing devotion to the game of defensive football. Joe Gibbs respected him for his total concentration, dedication, and durability.

In the off-season, Butz liked to sit quietly and carve duck decoys; during the regular season . . . well, as kicker Mark Moseley told it:

> **All season, Dave, Joe Theismann, and I drive to the [home] games together. Dave drives, and he always likes to find some dead animal in the road to run over. It gets him psyched before the games.**

In the Super Bowl season of 1982, Butz led the team with 55 tackles in the regular season and 19 in the playoffs. The following year he led the team with 11½ sacks, forced a team-leading five fumbles, and made 69 tackles. An All-Pro, he was voted Defensive Lineman of the Year by the NFL Alumni Association.

The Redskins' defensive statistics were not logged before 1979, but since then Butz has always been at or near the top of all categories. His best year for tackles was 1986, when he gathered 91, and his 11½ sacks of 1983 was a career high.

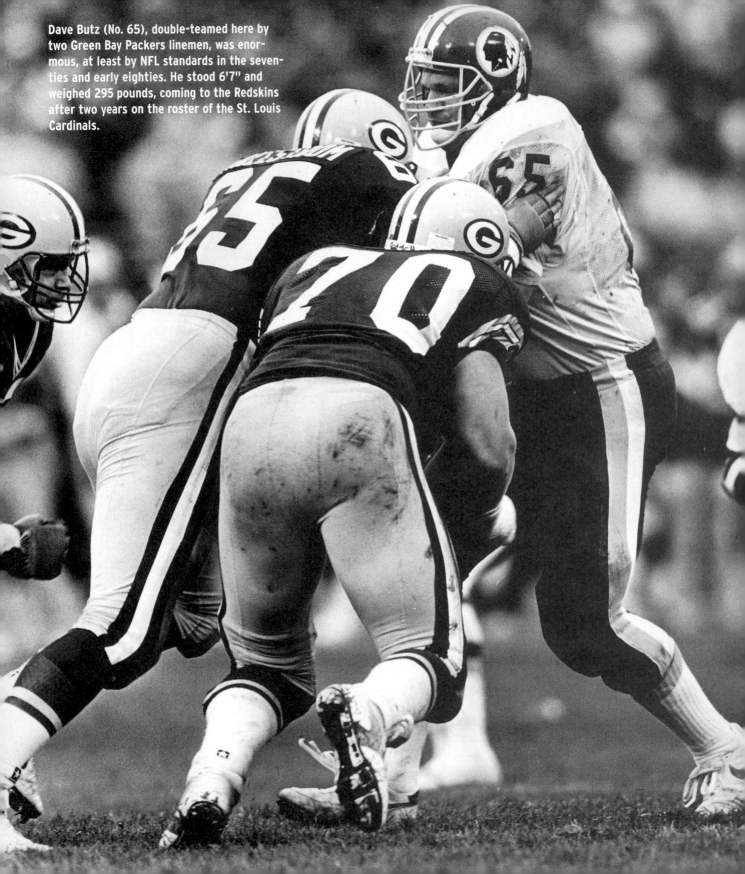

Dave Butz (No. 65), double-teamed here by two Green Bay Packers linemen, was enormous, at least by NFL standards in the seventies and early eighties. He stood 6'7" and weighed 295 pounds, coming to the Redskins after two years on the roster of the St. Louis Cardinals.

Dallas running back Calvin Hill (No. 35) finds an impenetrable wall in this game against the Redskins. Applying a shoulder to Hill is Skins linebacker Myron Pottios (No. 66); moving in is linebacker Chris Hanburger (No. 55).

When Dave Butz retired after the 1988 season, he had recorded (since 1979) 742 tackles and 59½ sacks, recovered 7 fumbles, and forced 15½.

The leaders of the "Over-the-Hill Gang" included many other great defenders of the seventies, including Jack Pardee, Myron Pottios, Verlon Biggs, Diron Talbert, Coy Bacon, Deacon Jones, Rich Petitbon, Ron McDole, and Dave Robinson. Other memorable defenders from the sixties and seventies include Paul Krause, Harold McLinton, Pat Fischer, Bill Brundige, Mike Bass, Brig Owens, Eddie Brown, and Lemar Parrish.

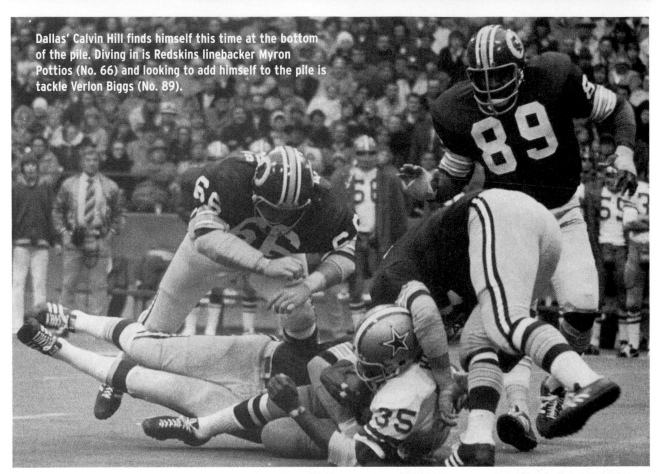

Dallas' Calvin Hill finds himself this time at the bottom of the pile. Diving in is Redskins linebacker Myron Pottios (No. 66) and looking to add himself to the pile is tackle Verlon Biggs (No. 89).

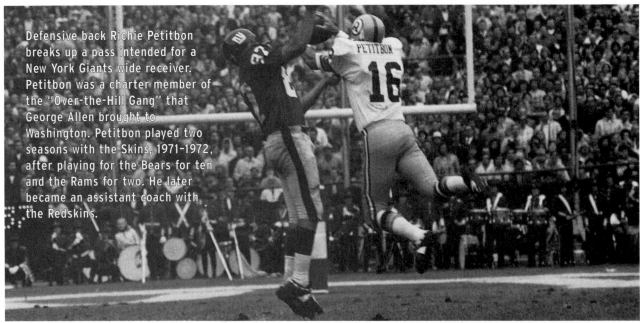

Defensive back Richie Petitbon breaks up a pass intended for a New York Giants wide receiver. Petitbon was a charter member of the "Over-the-Hill Gang" that George Allen brought to Washington. Petitbon played two seasons with the Skins, 1971-1972, after playing for the Bears for ten and the Rams for two. He later became an assistant coach with the Redskins.

In this 1970 game linebacker Harold McLinton (No. 53) pins a Cincinnati Bengals back to the ground. Adding to the crunch is linebacker Marlin McKeever (on top of McLinton). The Skins beat the Bengals that day, 20–0.

DEXTER MANLEY

After Dexter Manley staked a claim as one of the Redskins' defensive ends in 1981, he earned two Super Bowl rings, set the all-time team standard for quarterback sacks, graduated from an alcohol-abuse program, and admitted being a functional illiterate despite having spent four years on a football scholarship at Oklahoma State. He was referred to as the team's "designated talker."

"I like football, I like fun, I like talking," he said before Super Bowl XXII. Charles Mann, the Skins' other defensive end at the time, has said, "Dexter's kind of flamboyant and boisterous." Offensive lineman Raleigh McKenzie mentioned, "Sometimes Dexter likes to let his man know he's there."

The 6'3", 257-pound Manley was a fifth-round draft choice in 1981 and contributed 63 tackles and six sacks during his rookie year. In 1982 he was an integral part of the Super Bowl–champion Redskins, especially during the NFC title

An intense Dexter Manley is captured in this dramatic photo. The All-Pro defensive end, one of the finest pass rushers ever, played for the Redskins from 1981 through 1989. When he finally hung up his cleats, Manley had more tackles credited to him than any Redskins 471, and 97½ sacks, a record that still stands today.

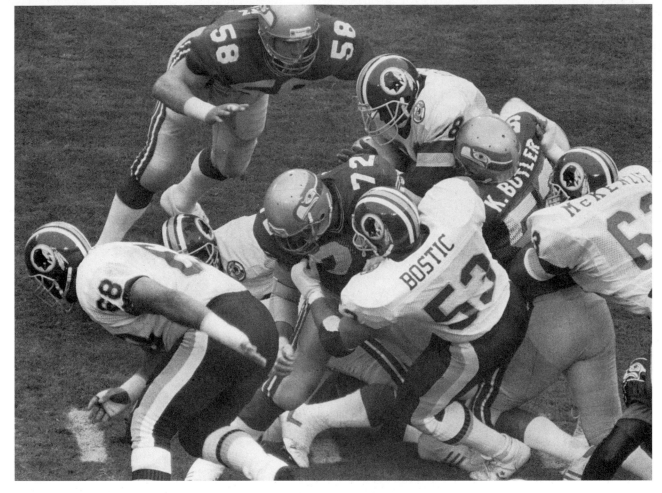

The Redskins offensive line at work here in a game against the Seattle Seahawks. No. 53 is center Jeff Bostic, No. 63 is guard Raleigh McKenzie, and No. 68 is guard Russ Grimm.

game against the Cowboys. First he descended on Dallas quarterback Danny White, leaving him with a concussion. Then, in the fourth quarter, with the Skins trailing 17–14, he tipped a pass from Gary Hogeboom, White's replacement, into the hands of teammate Darryl Grant, who carried it in for the game-winning touchdown.

In 1985, Manley tied the team mark of 15 sacks in a season, set by Coy Bacon back in 1979, and the following year set a new standard with 18, which still stands today.

Along the way, he consistently provided the press with stories and quotes. Before the 1987 playoff game with the Chicago Bears, he called their coach, Mike Ditka, a bum. This prompted Ditka to respond, "Dexter has the IQ of a grapefruit,"

Denver quarterback John Elway (No. 7) is about to meet Washington defensive end Dexter Manley (No. 72). The look on Elway's face illustrates how he feels about the meeting.

which prompted Manley to respond, "Mike Ditka, with that ugly face of his, I got something for him—a case of grapefruit." Grapefruit notwithstanding, Manley and the Redskins eliminated Ditka and the Bears from the playoffs the following Sunday.

Fans will also remember when Manley told reporters during the summit meeting between President Ronald Reagan and the USSR's Mikhail Gorbachev that the Soviet leader should "get the hell out of town and stop drawing attention away from a bigger event," the upcoming Redskins-Cowboys game.

Besides his vocality, Dexter Manley used many other talents to make himself well known around Washington. All-Pro, Pro Bowl, NFL Players Association Defensive Lineman of the Year: the honors kept coming.

Three veteran Washington defenders—tackle Dave Butz (No. 65), linebacker Rich Milot (No. 57), and defensive back Vernon Dean (No. 32)—converge on a Philadelphia Eagles running back.

By the end of the 1989 season he had accounted for 471 total tackles. Manley's 97½ sacks are by far the most in team history. Unfortunately for Manley, the All-Pro defensive end was banned from professional football by the NFL after testing positive for drugs a third time in 1989.

The eighties also featured such other defensive standouts as Mark Murphy, Vernon Dean, Barry Wilburn, Charles Mann, Rich Milot, Neal Olkewicz, Darryl Grant, Monte Coleman, Wilber Marshall, and Alvin Walton.

DARRELL GREEN

Cornerback Barry Wilburn (No. 45) celebrates an interception, which he took in for a touchdown. Wilburn played for the Skins from 1985 through 1987 and holds the record for the longest interception return for a touchdown, 100 yards against the Minnesota Vikings in 1987.

For Washington, 1983 was a very good year. The Redskins got to the Super Bowl that season; they had also made an unforgettable choice on draft day earlier in the year. With the last choice (28th) in the first round, they took cornerback Darrell Green from Texas A&I. Nineteen years later, he would be suiting up for the 2001 season with the distinction of having played more seasons for the Redskins than any player in franchise history.

Green, at 5'8" and 184 pounds, established his level of play during his very first year: he started the first regular-season game, and at the end of the season had the fourth most tackles on a team that won the NFC title. He was a runner-up for the Associated Press honor of Defensive Rookie of the Year and a member of every All-Rookie team. In fact the first time he touched a football in the NFL, he ran back a punt 61 yards for a touchdown; then, in the playoffs against the Los Angeles Rams, he returned an interception 72 yards for a touchdown.

In his second year in the NFL, 1984, a year in which he had five interceptions, Green was selected as a starter in the Pro Bowl. Two of those five interceptions came in a game against archrival Dallas. In the second half and trailing, Green picked off a Cowboy pass and ran it back 32 yards for a touchdown. Later, with

Rookie middle linebacker Neal Olkewicz (No. 52) snags a Cleveland Browns running back in 1979. Olkewicz was a standout on defense throughout the eighties, retiring after the 1989 season.

Dallas threatening, he stopped a drive with an interception in the end zone and Washington won, 30–28.

In 1986 Green again tallied five regular-season interceptions; he gained another in the playoffs, setting up the go-ahead touchdown in the Redskins' upset

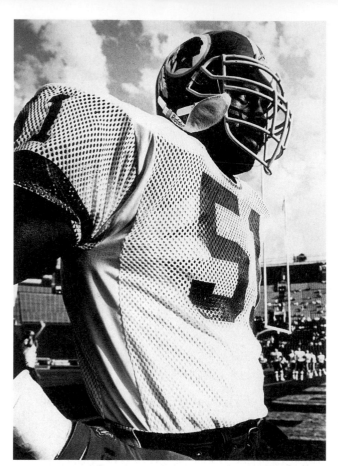

of the NFL defending champion Chicago Bears. In 1987 he picked off three passes in a game against the Lions, a career high; then in the NFC championship game he made a game-saving, fourth-down tackle at the goal line to preserve a 17–10 victory over Minnesota.

Green went to his fourth Pro Bowl in 1990. He began what was to be one of his more memorable years with an interception in each of the first three games (in that third game he almost single-handedly defeated the Cowboys with an interception touchdown and 10 tackles). The following year was even better: a fifth Pro Bowl invitation, five interceptions (one of which led to an overtime victory over

A Giants receiver catches the ball here while Redskins cornerback Darrell Green (No. 28) catches the Giants receiver.

Houston), two interceptions in postseason play, and consensus recognition as one of the key factors in the Redskins' Super Bowl championship season.

By 2001 Green had played in more games than any Redskin, 263 (starting in 250), far ahead of the player with the second most (Monte Coleman with 216). He holds one NFL record: recording at least one interception in 18 straight seasons. He also went to seven Pro Bowls. His 53 interceptions is a Redskins standard, and the 6 interceptions he returned for touchdowns stands as another Washington record.

Darrell Green in action against the Minnesota Vikings in the January 17, 1988, championship game. *Photo reprinted by permission John Iacono / TimePix.*

6
Washington's Championships

THE FIRST CHAMPIONSHIP: 1937

The move to Washington was a smooth one for the Redskins. The Big Chief, George Preston Marshall, had easily secured league approval for the relocation, and skillfully negotiated a beneficial deal for playing home games in Griffith Stadium on Florida Avenue. Clark Griffith, owner of the ballpark and the Washington Senators baseball team, agreed to add removable steel seats that would accommodate an additional 10,000 spectators, and installed a new, modern lighting system, a new public-address system, and a tarpaulin that would cover the entire playing field and keep it dry.

To ensure that the Redskins would get the press coverage that had been nearly nonexistent in Boston, and which meant so much to showman Marshall, the Redskins hired George Washington University's publicity agent, Jack Espey, and gave him the title of general manager.

Marshall also lined up a brass marching band, which soon was expanded to 150 pieces, to entertain before games and at halftime. And he adopted a fight song, with music written by Barnet "Barnee" Breeskin, then the bandleader of the Shoreham Hotel orchestra in Washington. Marshall's wife, silent-film star Corinne Griffith, was given the assignment of writing the lyrics after other professional lyricists had turned down the challenge. She wrote them, and soon the song "Hail to the Redskins" became as much a part of the team as its offense and defense.

What would prove to be the organization's most important addition, however, was a lanky cowboy from Texas who had starred at Texas Christian: "Slingin'" Sammy Baugh, the Redskins' first-round draft choice for 1937. Sports columnist Grantland Rice had touted Baugh to Marshall, suggesting that he was the best passer and punter in the college game. Marshall knew that a passing attack would surely complement the fine running game the Redskins already boasted with such ball carriers as Cliff Battles, Don Irwin, and Erny Pinckert; it would also enliven the game that the Big Chief wanted to dish up to his newfound fans.

Signing Baugh was a difficult matter. Marshall, whose highest-paid player the year before, Cliff Battles, earned $2,100 for the season (plus about $180 for playing in the NFL title game), kept his offer a well-guarded secret. It was said to have been $5,000, which Baugh turned down. It was not until after a lot of haggling and Baugh's threat to devote all his time to baseball—he had signed a contract with the St. Louis Cardinals—and forget about professional football altogether that Marshall cringingly upped his offer to $8,000. Baugh accepted.

Marshall, ever the consummate promoter, arranged to have Baugh brought to Washington to be formally introduced to the city's press and radio corps. The story has often been told that Marshall orchestrated the entire event with his own unique brand of showmanship. But it really never happened the way it was later hyped. As Baugh himself explained:

> Some writer wrote how George Preston Marshall, the owner of the club, called me up down in Texas and asked me if I had cowboy boots and a 10-gallon hat and that I said no. He was supposed to have told me then to go out and buy the things and that he'd pay me back in Washington. Well, hell, that's just a made-up story. I normally wore that kind of stuff. I didn't need him to tell me to wear it and I sure didn't need to go out and buy it. Some writer just made it up and everybody picked it up. Writers like to embellish things like that. After it was written, though, Mr. Marshall got a big kick out of it.

A signed and sealed Baugh was, however, late showing up for training camp because he was in Chicago practicing with the College All-Stars, who were slated to take on the NFL-champion Green Bay Packers to start the 1937 preseason. At that spectacle Baugh gave the first hint of what he was about to bring to the National Football League and the Washington Redskins: his penchant for defeating pro football teams. His 47-yard touchdown pass to Gaynell Tinsley of Louisiana State provided the winning touchdown as the collegians beat the Pack, 6–0.

When tailback Baugh did link up with the Redskins at their training camp in Anacostia, Maryland, that summer, he was quickly assimilated into a single-wing backfield that also featured halfback Cliff Battles, fullback Don Irwin, and quarterback Riley Smith.

Before Baugh had arrived, the Redskins had honed their skills by crushing the American Legion All-Stars at Frederick, Virginia, 50–0. It was an age when preseason schedules were a good deal less defined than they are today.

Baugh was ready for the Redskins' debut in Washington. The New York Giants were in town to launch the 1937 football season and the city's new entry in the NFL. The game was set for Thursday night, September 16. Marshall had hoped for a crowd of about 25,000, but he had to settle for a paid attendance of 19,941. He had also hoped to have President Franklin Delano Roosevelt throw out the first football, but he had to settle instead for Jesse Jones, head of the Reconstruction Finance Corporation.

If the Big Chief did not get exactly what he wanted in the grandstands of Griffith Stadium that opening night, he did get it on the playing field. The Giants were a highly regarded team, picked by many to win the NFL's Eastern Division that year. They showcased one of the best rushers in the game in fullback Tuffy Leemans, who was also very popular in Washington because he had starred in the backfield for George Washington University just two years earlier. But Baugh, passing to ends Charley Malone and Wayne Millner, drove the Redskins into range for two Riley Smith field goals. The Washington defense, spearheaded by monstrous tackle Turk Edwards (6'2", 260 pounds) and defensive back Smith, who picked off a Giants pass and ran it back 60 yards for a touchdown, held New York to just a single field goal all evening. At game's end, the Redskins were on top of a 13–3 score and in possession of the first regular-season victory in their new hometown.

The following week the Redskins played on a Friday night at Griffith Stadium, but this time they were the unhappy possessors of their first defeat in Washington, 21–14. It was a surprise doled out by the mediocre Chicago Cardinals. It was, however, only one of three losses the Redskins would suffer all year. On their way to a climactic showdown with the Giants in the last game of the regular season, they would fall to the Philadelphia Eagles and the Pittsburgh Pirates, as the Steelers were known in those days. But they would prevail twice in games with the Brooklyn Dodgers, as well as beating the Cleveland Rams, the Green Bay Packers (who were the defending NFL champions), the Eagles, and the Pirates.

By December the Redskins were the toast of Washington. With a record of 7–3–0, they barely trailed the Giants, who led the NFL East at 6–2–2. Rookie Sammy Baugh, leading the entire league in passing, and Cliff Battles, the top NFL rusher of 1937, were certified local heroes. They would have to go up to New York and face the Giants, who were favored by the oddsmakers despite the fact that the Redskins had beat them in the season opener, to determine the divisional title on December 5. Washington's support of the Redskins had enthralled Marshall, and it reached a crescendo in the Big Chief's heart when approximately 10,000 fans boarded 15 special trains in Washington's Union Station the day of the game to trek to New York and cheer on their team. Marshall chipped in by bringing along his 150-piece band, replete with full, white-feathered headdresses. Marshall also provided a burgundy feather for each of the hats of the loyal 10,000.

The Redskins band and 10,000 loyal fans march on Manhattan before the last game of the 1937 season, between Washington and the New York Giants. Later that day they were rewarded with a 49-14 Redskins victory.

Marshall and wife Corinne Griffith were on hand to greet the loyalists at Penn Station in New York. As the band and the fans spilled off the trains, Marshall announced, "The Indians have come to reclaim Manhattan Island." Then, with the Big Chief himself in the lead and impeccably attired in a flowing raccoon coat, the throng paraded up Seventh Avenue to the lilting airs of "Hail to the Redskins."

If Marshall had the fans enthusiastic, Coach Ray Flaherty had his players fully inspired. They stormed onto the field at the Polo Grounds and mercilessly destroyed the Giants that Sunday afternoon, 49–14. With Baugh's pinpoint passing to ends Malone and Millner and a bevy of backs, plus the running of Battles (he raced 75 yards from scrimmage on one play and returned an interception 76 yards for a touchdown), there was never any doubt about who controlled that game. An ebullient, exhilarated Marshall led his team, band, and fervent fans back to Washington with the NFL East crown.

When all the stats were in for the regular season, Baugh led the league in pass completions (81) and yards gained passing (1,127). Battles rushed for the most yards in the NFL (874) and scored the most touchdowns rushing (five). In addition, Malone was the league's third-ranked receiver, catching 28 passes for 419 yards. Baugh, Battles, and tackle Turk Edwards were named All-Pro.

Now all they had to do was face the Chicago Bears, victors in the NFL West, to determine which team would wear the NFL crown for 1937.

SAMMY BAUGH

That championship game against the Bears [1937] was something else. It was played on the worst field I've ever played on in my life. The game was at Wrigley Field in Chicago. A week or so before that they had a playoff game there of some kind and it had rained and got real muddy. Hell, they just chewed up that field. Well, when we got on it, it was snowing and the ground had froze up. There were all these little frozen balls of mud, hard and sharp as rocks, all over that damn field. They cut the living hell out of you when you hit the ground. A lot of people got chewed up pretty bad that day. We won the game by a touchdown [28–21]. . . . Despite that damn field I had a pretty good day. Wayne Millner and I teamed up on a couple of long touchdown passes and I got another to Ed Justice. We won it in the [third] quarter—scored two touchdowns and came out on top.

George Halas' Chicago Bears, with a record of 9–1–1, had brutally mauled just about every opponent they faced in the NFL West in 1937. The Bears were a running team, like most others in the NFL during that era. They had the indomitable Bronko Nagurski at fullback, as well as such yardage-gobbling runners as Ray Nolting, Gene Ronzani, Beattie Feathers, and Jack Manders, who was also the top field-goal kicker in the league that year. Blocking for them were three future Hall of Famers: tackle Joe Stydahar and guards Danny Fortmann and George Musso.

The Bears themselves loomed as one obviously measurable obstacle, and so did the weather in Chicago, where the game was to be played at Wrigley Field, home of the Chicago Cubs. A bitter cold front had moved into Chicago the week before the game—not a big surprise in the Windy City in December. By game day

1937 CHAMPIONSHIP LINEUPS

WASHINGTON REDSKINS		CHICAGO BEARS
Wayne Millner	LE	"Eggs" Manske
Turk Edwards	LT	Joe Stydahar
Les Olsson	LG	Danny Fortmann
Ed Kawal	C	Frank Bausch
Jim Karcher	RG	George Musso
Jim Barber	RT	Del Bjork
Charley Malone	RE	George Wilson
Riley Smith	QB	Bernie Masterson
Sammy Baugh	LH	Ray Nolting
Erny Pinckert	RH	Jack Manders
Cliff Battles	FB	Bronko Nagurski
Ray Flaherty	Coach	George Halas

the playing field was frozen solid. Advertisements in the Chicago newspapers announced that there were still 25,000 seats available for the NFL title game.

On Sunday, December 12, at game time, the temperature was 15° above zero and the wind blew at about 12 miles per hour, creating a windchill factor of about 6° below zero. It was enough to keep many of those 25,000 seats at Wrigley Field unoccupied, and only 15,878 well-bundled and hardy fans observed firsthand the combat for the NFL title (about 3,000 of them were Redskins fans who had made the junket from Washington by train). But those who made the sacrifice bore witness to one of the most exciting NFL championship games ever.

The field not only had the solidity of an iceberg, it was also as slippery as one. Both teams, therefore, donned sneakers, having apparently learned from the New

WAYNE MILLNER*

Now we were going to play the Bears in Chicago for the [1937] NFL championship. It was 5° below zero out there all through the week of the game. To make the field playable, the Bears' officials put hay on it. Then the hay was burned. That was supposed to make the ground soft, but it didn't. When we got on the field it was as hard as a brick pile. So we wore sneakers for the game.

On our first play from scrimmage, Sammy gave the Chicago fans an example of what the Eastern writers meant when they said Baugh was opening up the game of football. We were on our 9-yard line and Sam dropped back to punt. Considering the conditions of the field, it was a good call. But when he got the ball, he faked the punt and tossed a pass to Battles. Cliff took it and gained 42 yards on the play. With that good start, we went in for a score with Cliff going seven yards on a reverse. . . .

The Bears were leading us 14–7 in the third quarter when Sammy hit me with a pass on our 47-yard line. I was able to take it the rest of the way for a touchdown.

In the fourth quarter the Bears were ahead again 21 to 14. Once again Sammy hit me with a short pass and I ran about 68 yards for a touchdown. That made it 21 to 21. Late in the game, Sammy called for another pass play. This time I was his decoy. While two men were following me, Ed Justice got loose and Sammy hit him for the touchdown. That won the game and the world championship for us, 28 to 21.

* Excerpted from Pro Football's Rag Days by Bob Curran (Bonanza Books, New York, 1969).

York Giants' use of them on a similarly ice-coated field in the NFL championship game of 1934. At halftime of that game, the New Yorkers had switched to sneakers and turned a 10–3 deficit into a 30–13 victory over the Bears.

Edwards kicked off for the Redskins and the Ice Bowl, as some called it, was under way. Nagurski returned it to the 33. It was not until midway through the first period that a scoring drive was mounted. Directing it was Baugh. Two passes to Riley Smith and another to Erny Pinckert moved the Redskins to the Chicago 10-yard line. Then it was Battles' turn. He gained three yards, and on third down burst through for the remaining seven and a touchdown.

The Bears, however, came right back. Expecting Chicago's patented running attack, the Redskins were stunned by a 51-yard pass play from Bernie Masterson to "Eggs" Manske. Moments later Jack Manders carried it in, and the score was tied, 7–7.

It seemed that the oddsmakers were right about Chicago when George Wilson intercepted a Baugh pass a few plays later and the Bears offense again exploded. This time, Masterson threw a 12-yard pass to Manders at the Washington 25-yard line and the Bears' back shook off a tackler and raced in for another score.

That was the last of the scoring in the first half, but the game was far from over. Baugh, who had missed most of the second quarter after being shaken up, came back, and with him returned the Redskins offense. On their first possession of the second half, Baugh connected with Millner on a 55-yard touchdown pass, and the score was tied at 14 apiece.

The Bears then reverted to their running game, and Nagurski, Nolting, and Manders ground out the yardage, moving the ball all the way to the Washington 4-yard line. There, with fourth down and goal to go, Masterson faked a handoff and then lobbed a jump pass to "Eggs" Manske in the end zone. The Bears had the lead again.

Baugh responded with quick and deadly vengeance. After the kickoff, he went to Millner again. Dropping back from the line of scrimmage at the Washington 22, he threw a perfect strike at the 50 to Millner, who then outran all defenders for a 78-yard touchdown play.

With the score tied at 21, the Redskins' defense tightened. When the team got the ball again, Baugh put on another aerial display to thrill the fans who had accompanied the Redskins to Chicago. Passes to Malone and Millner and finally a 35-yard touchdown toss to Ed Justice put Washington in the lead, 28–21. At the final whistle, the Redskins remained on top.

George Preston Marshall had not only brought professional football to Washington in 1937, he had given the city an NFL championship as well.

The gross gate receipts for the 1937 NFL championship game were less than a single player's winning share of the Super Bowl in the late eighties. The total take of $32,198 in 1937 was almost $4,000 less than the $36,000 earned by each triumphant Super Bowl player in the eighties. Each winning Redskin in 1937 received $225.90 for toiling in that title game, and each losing Bear earned $127.78.

The headline on this December 13, 1937, newspaper says it all.

Protecting Sammy Baugh was the name of the game in the 1937 battle for the NFL championship. Coach Ray Flaherty reminded his team before the game that a healthy Baugh would be a major factor that day and directed all concerned to see that he stayed that way on the field of play.

The reminder was felt necessary because the George Halas–coached Chicago Bears, with certified monsters such as Bronko Nagurski, George Musso, and Joe Stydahar, among others, had a deserved reputation of being tough, nasty, and downright dangerous.

Tackle Turk Edwards took it sincerely to heart and was heard more than once warning opposing defensive linemen that they had better not try any rough stuff with Slingin' Sam or horrendous retribution would be paid. In one overzealous moment, Edwards was so intent on protecting his passer that, in his eagerness to block for Baugh, he backed over him, causing a 15-yard loss.

Later in the game, Chicago end Dick Plasman took special offense at something defensive back Baugh did on a pass play, and he threw a punch at Sammy. Unfortunately for Plasman, it was a short five yards from the Washington bench and, as Shirley Povich later described in the *Washington Post*:

> **Coach Flaherty was the first to leap to his feet and the first to rush to the battle scene. He tackled Plasman high—high around the mouth—with a set of knuckles and put an end to the battle.**

Baugh finished the game in good health, and the Redskins, of course, were triumphant.

THE SECOND CHAMPIONSHIP: 1942

Five years had elapsed since the Redskins had taken home their first NFL trophy. The Great Depression was over and World War II was under way. These had not been uneventful years for the Redskins or their fans, with Washington getting to the championship game once and battling the New York Giants down to the wire for the eastern divisional title in three other years.

WORLD'S CHAMPIONSHIP

NATIONAL FOOTBALL
LEAGUE

DEC. 13, 1942

PLAYERS IN THE

310

ARMED SERVICES

CHAMPIONS
of the West
**CHICAGO
BEARS**

vs.

CHAMPIONS
of the East
**WASHINGTON
REDSKINS**

GRIFFITH STADIUM, WASHINGTON, D. C.

OFFICIAL MAGAZINE   •   PRICE 10c

During their first five years in Washington, the Redskins had yet to experience a losing season, having finished first in the NFL East twice, in second place twice, and in third once. Coach Ray Flaherty had posted an impressive regular-season record of 37–15–3 for Washington's faithful fans.

Now it was time for another championship season.

There were not a lot of players left from the 1937 title winners. Sammy Baugh was still tailbacking at All-Pro level and Ed Justice occasionally carried the ball, but that was about all, the others gone to either retirement or military service. Ray Flaherty still ruled from the sideline but announced that he would be leaving for the U.S. Navy at the end of the season.

Fullback Andy Farkas, who had come to the Redskins from the University of Detroit in 1938, had been the most productive rusher of the previous few years, but the Redskins had Dick Todd, Ray Hare, Bob Seymour, and Dick Poillon as well. Ends Bob Masterson and Ed Cifers and halfback Todd were Baugh's favorite receivers. The line was powerful and the defense would prove to be the best in the league that year, keyed around a behemoth tackle with the inappropriate name of "Wee" Willie Wilkin (6'4", 265 pounds). Other impressive linemen included center/linebacker Ki Aldrich and guards Steve Slivinski and Dick Farman.

The Redskins held training camp in San Diego, California, for the 1942 season, their workouts and scrimmages often providing entertainment for scores of navy men and marines who came over from the nearby San Diego Naval Base. Near the end of camp the Redskins went up to Los Angeles to stage an exhibition game with the Army All-Stars, a team made up of college and pro stars turned soldiers. The military men were guided by Major Wallace Wade, who had made an institution of himself coaching at Alabama in the twenties and at Duke in the thirties. In Southern California, which would not entertain professional football on a regular basis until the Rams moved out there in 1946, the game attracted a fine crowd. Among the 60,000 in attendance were Hollywood celebrities Pat O'Brien, Linda Darnell, George Raft, Ann Sheridan, George Brent, and King Vidor. Washington, on the strength of Baugh's passing, won the contest easily, 26–7, and headed back east.

The Redskins were coming off their poorest season yet in the nation's capital, a 6–5–0 third-place finish in the NFL East in 1941. The reigning divisional champions, the New York Giants, were favored again, but the Pittsburgh Steelers were also formidable, a fact the Redskins learned in their home opener. Pitt had drafted an exceptional multiple-threat back in "Bullet" Bill Dudley out of the University of Virginia, a player whom Marshall coveted but had been unable to obtain. The Redskins got by the Steelers that opening Sunday in 1942, 28–14, but it was the defense that did it. Contributions included a blocked field goal by Ki Aldrich, who snatched the ball from the ground and ran it back 93 yards for a touchdown.

The next week Washington hosted the hated Giants, who had destroyed their dreams so often in the past few years. New York still had future Hall of Famers Tuffy Leemans in the backfield and Mel Hein in the middle of the line. The Redskins defense proved faultless that day except on one play, when Leemans tossed a 30-yard touchdown pass to end Will Walls. The defense was so good, in fact, that it did not give up *one* first down during the entire game. But Leemans' TD toss and the interception of a Dick Poillon hat pass that was returned for another score by Neal Adams were enough to give the New Yorkers a 14–7 triumph.

The Redskins, with a 1–1 record and an offense that had yet to show much potential, hardly appeared to be *the* team of 1942, as Marshall had referred to them in the preseason.

But they were. The next nine regular-season games laid the first paving of proof for Marshall's prognostication. One after the other, the Redskins dispatched the Eagles, Rams, Dodgers, Steelers, Eagles, Cardinals, Giants, Dodgers, and Lions. The defense was overwhelming, limiting the opponents in those nine games to 74 points, an average of just a little over 8 points a game, while Washington, its offense finally accelerating, tallied 192 points.

The team's record of 10–1–0 is today the best won/lost ratio in its history, and it remained the most wins in a single season until George Allen's Super Bowl–bound Redskins of 1972 won 11 of their 14 regular-season games. Second-place Pittsburgh (7–4–0) was clearly outdistanced, and the Giants had collapsed (5–5–1) after five consecutive winning seasons.

Baugh, still working from tailback in the single wing, had the best completion percentage of any passer in the league (59 percent), gaining 1,524 yards on 132 completions, and led the NFL in punting with an average of 46.6 yards per punt. His leading receivers were again Dick Todd (23 for 328 yards) and Bob Masterson (22 for 308 yards). "Handy" Andy Farkas gained the most yards for the Redskins carrying the ball, 468 on 125 jaunts. The Redskins landed only two players on the All-Pro squad that year, however: end Masterson and tackle "Wee" Willie Wilkin.

Just as they had in their two previous visits to the championship classic, the Redskins were to face the abominable Bears, who had wreaked such havoc on them two years earlier in the ignominious 73–0 rout of 1940. This defeat still hovered over Washington, unfettered even by the memory of the Redskins' triumph over the Bears in their first championship appearance in 1937 and their blitzkrieg of a season in 1942.

The Bears were intimidating for reasons besides the awful memory of their last visit to Griffith Stadium. They had virtually rocketed through the 1942 season in the NFL West, easily winning all 11 of their games by a collective score of 376–84. They had held their opponents to 18 points *less* than the vaunted Redskins defense, while outscoring Washington 376 to 227. Besides that perfect season, the Bears now had won 24 consecutive games, including preseason and postseason contests, and had in fact won 39 of their last 40 games. The only loss the Bears had suffered was that of their coach and owner George Halas, who was called to active duty in the U.S. Navy midway through the 1942 season.

Still working out of the T formation behind All-Pro quarterback Sid Luckman, the Bears were truly an intimidating entity. Their line now had four future Hall of Famers tending the trenches—center "Bulldog" Turner, tackle Joe Stydahar, and guards Danny Fortmann and George Musso—as well as tackle Lee Artoe, who had earned All-Pro honors that year. Bruising fullback Gary Famiglietti was their leading ground gainer with 503 yards on 118 carries, and the Bears were well stocked with halfbacks, alternating Hugh Gallarneau, Ray Nolting, Frank Maznicki, Harry Clark, and "Scooter" McLean. McLean was also the team's top receiver; his 571 yards gained on pass receptions was second only to Green Bay's great Don Hutson in the league that year.

The point spread favored the Bears by an overwhelming 22 points. But ever the optimist, Big Chief Marshall could talk only about revenge. Before the game, he entered his team's locker room, without a word walked to the blackboard, chalked on it in large numerals:

73-0

and then left his players and Coach Flaherty to dwell on its grisly significance.

The Washington fans must have shared Marshall's emotions. Despite the war and bitterly cold weather, 36,006 spectators filled Griffith Stadium, the largest crowd to attend a sporting event there since the 1933 World Series. Among the stalwarts in attendance were singer Al Jolson; figure skater Sonja Henie and her husband, Dan Topping, who owned Brooklyn's football Dodgers and would later own the New York Yankees; NFL Commissioner Elmer Layden and coaches "Greasy" Neale of the Eagles, Curly Lambeau of the Packers, Steve Owen of the Giants, and Jimmy Conzelman of the Chicago Cardinals; Senator A. B. "Happy" Chandler, who would later become commissioner of Major League

Sports columnist Bob Considine loved the championship game of 1942 but hated the halftime. As he wrote the next day:

George P. Marshall was so subdued . . . that he didn't make a single call to the bench on the telephone he has in his box. He seems to have some curious idea that Ray Flaherty can coach, which the result did nothing to diminish.

Marshall hit his all-time high and vaudeville suffered another 10-year set-back during the halftime show. First the loudspeaker boomed that the National Football League was extending the wish of a Merry Christmas to our soldiers and sailors, which will come as a great comfort to the boys in foxholes and probably bring Hitler to his knees. Then to cap it all, George's 100-plus-piece Indian band came out on the field with long white beards playing "Jingle Bells." At a late hour last night a war council of the Sioux, Iroquois, Blackfeet, and Choctaw nations was considering secession.

Baseball; and a host of other politicians and brass-laden military officers. Even Lieutenant Commander George Halas had swung a temporary leave from his station at Norman, Oklahoma, to watch his Bears at play.

Another front page that had Redskins fans rejoicing.

The game was broadcast on radio by Harry Wismer and Russ Hodges to 178 stations throughout the country, the most widespread coverage of a pro football game up to that time.

The Bears struck first, led by their defense instead of their heralded offense. Dick Todd fumbled the ball on the 50-yard line and Bears tackle Lee Artoe scooped it up and ambled all the way downfield for a touchdown. But Artoe, perhaps out of breath from his unusual sprint, missed the extra point.

Unlike their play in the 1940 game, however, the Redskins came right back, returning the ensuing kickoff to the Bears' 42-yard line. Three plays

1942 CHAMPIONSHIP LINEUPS

WASHINGTON REDSKINS		CHICAGO BEARS
Bob Masterson	LE	Bob Nowaskey
"Wee" Willie Wilkin	LT	Ed Kolman
Dick Farman	LG	Danny Fortmann
Ki Aldrich	C	"Bulldog" Turner
Steve Slivinski	RG	Ray Bray
Bill Young	RT	Lee Artoe
Ed Cifers	RE	George Wilson
Ray Hare	QB	Sid Luckman
Sammy Baugh	LH	Ray Nolting
Ed Justice	RH	Hugh Gallarneau
Andy Farkas	FB	Gary Famiglietti
Ray Flaherty	Coaches	Hunk Anderson
		Paddy Driscoll
		Luke Johnsos

later, Baugh hit halfback Wilbur Moore with a 38-yard touchdown pass. Bob Masterson's extra point brought the score to 7–6 and the half came to an end.

It appeared the Bears would regain the lead in the third quarter when they marched down the field and Hugh Gallarneau plunged in for a touchdown, but it was nullified because the Bears were penalized, one of their backs having been in motion. The Redskins defense then staged a magnificent goal-line stand and took over the ball.

A Washington drive was more successful. It moved the ball down to the Bears' 1-yard line, where Andy Farkas carried it in for the score. The Redskins' 14–6 lead going into the final period proved to be all that was necessary. There was no scoring in the fourth quarter and, with the final whistle, the Bears' winning streak came to an end in the cold environs of Griffith Stadium. The Washington Redskins had their second NFL title.

SUPER BOWL XVII: 1983

There were more than clouds over the Redskins during the 1982 preseason; they were virtually enshrouded in gloom during the four-game overture. The team, so highly heralded after its resurgence during the second half of the 1981 season, lost all four preseason games, the first time that had happened since 1963 (and that 1963 team had gone on to post a regular-season record of 3–11–0).

Redskins fans, however, were delighted to find that things were not as bad as they seemed. In the opener at Veterans Stadium in Philadelphia, an explosive

TRIVIA

As the decade of the eighties opened, the Redskins public relations office offered some statistics for the numbers-oriented fan:

Since the Redskins were founded in Boston in 1932, the team has produced in its 48 years in the NFL an overall regular-season record of 295–283–26. Since the Redskins moved to Washington in 1937, their posted record was 271–255–21.

Since the Redskins began playing in RFK Stadium in 1961, their record was 80–54–3.

Since 1972, the Redskins had won 77 percent of their games, with a 47–13–1 record.

In the 10-year history of *Monday Night Football*, the Redskins have an overall record of 12–4–0, and have won all eight of their home Monday night games.

match that ended in overtime, the Skins posted their first win of 1982. It was a seesaw game all the way. With just a little more than a minute to play, Eagles quarterback Ron Jaworski hit All-Pro wide receiver Harold Carmichael for a touchdown and Philadelphia gained a 34–31 lead. However, an undaunted Joe Theismann came right back and moved the Skins into Philadelphia territory. Then, with only one second remaining on the clock, Mark Moseley came out and kicked a 48-yard field goal to tie the game. It took just less than five minutes of overtime for Washington to maneuver into Moseley's range again. This time he booted a 26-yarder, and the Redskins won, 37–34.

The next week the Redskins went down to Tampa Bay and easily dominated the Buccaneers, 21–13. Washington was alone in first place in the NFC East with a 2–0–0 record.

And then the season ended, or at least appeared to end, as the players announced they were going on strike. Fans found other things to keep them occupied on Sunday afternoons and Monday nights, and the autumn moved into winter. The strike lasted seven weeks before the players finally capitulated.

The season resumed on Sunday, November 21, with a new schedule that called for seven more games, plus a special playoff arrangement that would involve the top eight teams from each conference.

The Redskins took the field against the Giants and devoured them, then beat the Eagles before succumbing to the Cowboys at RFK Stadium. But that proved to be the only setback of the year for Washington. With the offense functioning perfectly and a defense that allowed only 31 points in the last four games of the 1982 season, Washington was invincible. Its 8–1–0 record was equaled only by the Los Angeles Raiders of the AFC. And so the Redskins were back in postseason play for the first time since 1976.

Besides a volatile offensive unit and a tough defense, the Redskins were aided considerably by the foot of Mark Moseley, who kicked an NFL-record 20 consecutive field goals in a single season and a total of 23 straight including the last three from 1981, another NFL standard at the time. As a result, he earned the honor of being named the NFL's Most Valuable Player.

Because the Redskins had the best record in the NFC, Washington fans were treated to the home-field advantage throughout the playoffs, meaning three games if the Skins continued their winning ways.

The first matchup was with the Detroit Lions, who managed to make the playoffs even though their record was a scant 4–5–0. It was, as many assumed it might be, a blowout, ignited in the first quarter by cornerback Jeris White, who picked off a Detroit pass and returned it 77 yards for a touchdown. A Moseley field goal later in the first period and then two touchdown tosses by Theismann to Alvin Garrett, playing for the injured Art Monk, in the second quarter gave Washington a 24–0 halftime lead. Theismann teamed with Garrett again in the third quarter for another touchdown. An inconsequential touchdown was ceded to the Lions a little later, but they were never in the game, and the final score was Washington 31, Detroit 7.

It had truly been Theismann's day—14 of 19 for 210 yards. And it was Alvin Garrett's as well, as he snared three touchdown passes and three other passes for 110 yards in all. John Riggins picked up 119 yards rushing.

A week later, it was another NFL Central team that traveled to Washington to meet the Redskins. This time it was the divisional runner-up, the Minnesota Vikings, who had won five of their nine regular-season games and then defeated the Atlanta Falcons in the first round of the revamped playoffs of 1982.

It was much the same scenario as the week before, with the same stars shining. Washington got off to a 7–0 lead in the first quarter when Theismann threw a three-yarder to tight end Don Warren in the end zone. Following that, with Riggins tearing the Minnesota defense to shreds as he ground out yard after yard, the Skins marched to the Vikings 2-yard line, where Riggins then banged in for another touchdown.

Minnesota came back with a touchdown in the second period, but Washington responded with one of its own when Theismann threw 18 yards to Garrett. The score was 21–7 at the half, and it never changed. With great ball control, featuring the bruising running of Riggins and a defense that totally shut down the Vikings, the last two quarters were scoreless.

At the final gun, Riggins stood at midfield and bowed to the thunderous ovation of the hometown fans. He had just set a Washington playoff record and his all-time career best, gaining 185 yards rushing, with an average gain of 5 yards per carry. In the locker room afterward, Coach Joe Gibbs shook his head and told the press:

Two weeks ago he [Riggins] came to me and said he was excited about the play-offs. "Just give me the ball," he said. I did, and he was stupendous, remarkable, phenomenal.

Theismann's stats were not shabby either—17 of 23 for 213 yards. And the mighty Redskins defense gave up only 79 yards rushing to the battered Vikes.

It set the stage for the game all Washington wanted. The Cowboys were coming to town, the only team of 1982 to have dealt the Skins a setback. They had easily defeated Tampa Bay and Green Bay in the first two rounds of the playoffs. On the line now was the NFC title and a trip to Super Bowl XVII.

It was perhaps one of the most raucous crowds ever to fill RFK Stadium on January 22, 1983, more than 55,000 strong, and it was truly a revenge-ridden Redskins team that took the field that wintry Sunday afternoon.

Dallas won the coin toss and chose to receive. Then, behind the passing of Danny White and the running of Tony Dorsett, the Cowboys drove 75 yards. At the Washington 20, they were stopped, however, and had to settle for a field goal from Rafael Septien.

The Redskins replied in kind, mounting their own march. It was led by the powerful plunges of Riggins through the holes opened by Washington's superb front line, which had now come to be known as the "Hogs." After moving 65 yards to the Dallas 19-yard line, Theismann took over and tossed a 19-yard touchdown pass to wide receiver Charlie Brown.

In the second period, Dallas' Rod Hill fumbled a punt over to the Skins at the Cowboys' 11-yard line. A few plays later Riggins burst in for the score. Washington's defense was steadfast throughout the quarter—brutal, in fact. Danny White could bear witness to that. Near the end of the second period he was put out of commission by a freight train known as Dexter Manley and went to the sidelines with a concussion. At the half the Redskins had a 14–3 lead.

White's replacement, Gary Hogeboom, got the Cowboys back in the game in the third quarter with a touchdown pass to perennial All-Pro Drew Pearson. But whatever hopes Cowboys fans had of a comeback were punctured on the ensuing kickoff when Mike Nelms broke it for 76 yards to the Dallas 20-yard line. Five plays later the Redskins were at the Dallas 4-yard line, and all they had to do was hand the ball to Riggins. The margin was soon back to 11 points.

Hogeboom, however, countered that with an 84-yard drive that culminated in a 23-yard touchdown pass to Butch Johnson. Going into the final period of play, it was Washington 21, Dallas 17.

The Washington defense then took control in the final period to ensure a victory. First, Redskins linebacker Mel Kaufman snatched a Hogeboom pass, setting up a Moseley field goal of 29 yards. Not long thereafter, Dexter Manley swatted another Hogeboom pass into the hands of defensive tackle Darryl Grant, who lumbered 10 yards with it into the end zone.

That was it for the day's scoring. The final: Washington 31, Dallas 17. Revenge was wreaked by the rushing of Riggins, the dominance of the Hogs in front of him, the clutch passing of Theismann, and the devastating defense of the Skins. But more important, Washington was going to its second Super Bowl, Super Bowl XVII. It was a treat Redskins fans had not savored since 1972, 10 years earlier.

It may have been the shortest regular season in NFL history, but it was also the first time a conference champion had to win three playoff games to get to the league championship match. But the Redskins had done it, bringing with them a composite record of 11–1–0 to face the Miami Dolphins. Coached by Don Shula—who was no stranger to Super Bowls, having taken his Dolphins to three of them in the seventies—Miami had rung up a 7–2–0 record before disposing of New England, San Diego, and the New York Jets in the playoffs.

SUPER BOWL XVII

Site:	The Rose Bowl, Pasadena, California
Date:	January 30, 1983
Weather:	61°, sunny
Attendance:	103,667
Gross receipts:	$19,997,330.86
Player shares:	$36,000 winner, $18,000 loser

STARTING LINEUPS

WASHINGTON REDSKINS	OFFENSE	MIAMI DOLPHINS
Alvin Garrett	WR	Duriel Harris
Joe Jacoby	LT	Jon Giesler
Russ Grimm	LG	Bob Kuechenberg
Jeff Bostic	C	Dwight Stephenson
Fred Dean	RG	Jeff Toews
George Starke	RT	Eric Laasko
Don Warren	TE	Bruce Hardy

Charlie Brown	WR	Jimmy Cefalo
Joe Theismann	QB	David Woodley
Rick Walker	RB	Andra Franklin
John Riggins	FB	Tony Nathan
Mark Moseley	K	Uwe von Schamann

	DEFENSE	
Mat Mendenhall	LE	Doug Betters
Dave Butz	LT/NT	Bob Baumhower
Darryl Grant	RT/RE	Kim Bokamper
Dexter Manley	RE/OLB	Bob Brudzinski
Mel Kaufman	LB/ILB	A. J. Duhe
Neal Olkewicz	MLB/ILB	Earnest Rhone
Rich Milot	LB/OLB	Larry Gordon
Jeris White	CB	Gerald Small
Vernon Dean	CB	Don McNeal
Tony Peters	S	Glenn Blackwood
Mark Murphy	S	Lyle Blackwood
Jeff Hayes	P	Tom Orosz

	COACHES	
Joe Gibbs		Don Shula

SCORING

	1st Qtr	2nd Qtr	3rd Qtr	4th Qtr	Final Score
Redskins	0	10	3	14	27
Dolphins	7	10	0	0	17

All the big names from the earlier Dolphin championship teams were gone—Larry Csonka, Bob Griese, Jim Kiick, Paul Warfield, Howard Twilley, Nick Buoniconti, and the like. Now the team was in the hands of quarterback David Woodley, and its running game depended on the output of Andra Franklin and Tony Nathan. Its defense, which had earned the nickname the "Killer Bees," was considered the best in the AFC in 1982.

The Hogs and the Killer Bees—a confrontation conceived in hell and taking place in the trenches at the Rose Bowl on January 30, 1983. That is the way the matchup was hyped the week before the game (because of the strike-prolonged season and playoff schedule, only one week, instead of the normal two, separated the conference championship games from the Super Bowl).

The Redskins' game plan was a direct one. On offense, it was to establish the running game behind the bulldozing power of John Riggins and to complement it with quick, short passes from Theismann. On defense, the plan was to stop the running game and force Woodley, not considered one of the major throwing threats in the league, to pass more than he normally would.

The plan backfired, at least early in the first quarter. On a second-and-six situation from his own 24-yard line, Woodley dropped back, pump-faked, and then rifled the ball toward the sideline, where wide receiver Jimmy Cefalo grabbed it and outraced all Washington defenders for a 76-yard touchdown. The Redskins moved the ball on the ground during the first period, but they could not manage to score or even get into field position for the deadly toe of MVP Mark Moseley.

The Redskins got a break in the early part of the second quarter when defensive end Dexter Manley broke through to sack Woodley, causing a fumble that was recovered by Dave Butz on the Miami 46-yard line. The Skins reached the 14 before they were stopped and had to settle for a Moseley field goal.

On Miami's next possession, however, Woodley moved all the way to the Washington 3-yard line. There the Washington defense held and escaped with nothing more than a Uwe von Schamann field goal. Then the Hogs began to swat the Killer Bees out of the way as if they were mere annoyances, something they would continue to do for the rest of the afternoon. As a result, Theismann was able to move the Redskins downfield, climaxing the drive with a four-yard touchdown pass to Alvin Garrett, and the score was tied at 10 apiece.

Unfortunately, moments later Washington was once again behind in the game. Miami's Fulton Walker took the kickoff at the 2-yard line and streaked 98 yards for a touchdown, the first kickoff return for a touchdown in Super Bowl

John Madden:

Too bad I didn't bet the ranch on my Friday prediction that the Washington Redskins would win Super Bowl XVII. . . . Riggins plain wore the Miami defense out. After a while, tackling him just wrecks a defense. He gets stronger, you get bruised. With Riggins, it's a lot like boxing. Body punches. He beats on them and beats on them, and suddenly they fall down.

Dave Butz:

I've been in the NFL for 10 years and today is the epitome of everything I've ever wanted. . . . Being No. 1, you can't get any higher. Any feeling any higher and you'd be in heaven.

Mike Downey (Knight-Ridder Newspapers):

It must be hard to sound tough when your football team has a cuddly nickname. Washington fans say stuff like: "Redskins will scalp you." Miami fans probably are stuck making threats like: "Beware Redskins, Dolphins will push you with their noses."

Mickey Richards (a devout fan known as Chief Redskin, dressed for the game in war paint, headdress, beads, and bracelets):

I want people to know I'm a *fan.* I've been waiting 10 years for this day. I'm going to enjoy every minute of it.

Leigh Montville (the *Boston Globe*):

This drunk walked next to me, going down the steps of the Rose Bowl in the final two minutes. He was wearing a full Indian headdress [Ed. note: he was not Chief Redskin]. "Killer bees?" he asked. "Killer bees?" he asked again. "Killer wimps!" he answered as loud as he could.

Joe Gibbs:

I feel like all the people who accomplished what they want to do. I am thrilled, elated, proud, and I feel good for all the people who have been pulling for the Redskins.

Jack Gibbs, Joe's father, in the Redskins' locker room after the game:

That's my boy.

history. That was it for the first half, and Miami took a 17–10 lead into the locker room.

On paper it appeared the Redskins should have been the team with the winning margin at the half, having gained significantly more yardage than the Dolphins, having earned more first downs, and having controlled the ball for most of the first 30 minutes of play. Joe Gibbs told the team during intermission that, if they played the same way in act 2 *and* did not allow any big plays or costly turnovers, they would take home the Vince Lombardi Trophy.

The Redskins took Gibbs' words to heart and continued to dominate the game on offense and defense in the third quarter, but they still had difficulty scoring. All they could muster was a 20-yard field goal from Moseley, set up after Garrett had raced 44 yards on a reverse. The defense, however, completely stifled the Dolphins, allowing no points and almost no net yardage.

Miami might have added a score in the period had it not been for a fine defensive effort by Joe Theismann. Theismann? Indeed. Late in the period, deep in his own territory, Theismann threw over the middle and Dolphin defensive tackle Kim Bokamper slapped the ball up in the air. Bokamper moved under the

THE PRESIDENT HERE

As tradition now has it, the president of the United States treats the Super Bowl with the same regard as a coronation or the death of a head of state. And when its outcome has been determined, he is on the telephone to the victors. President Ronald Reagan was no exception.

When he finally got through to Coach Joe Gibbs in the victorious Redskins' locker room after Super Bowl XVII, he told him:

Last week I was thinking of asking John Riggins to change the spelling of his name, add an *e* and an *a* to it. Now I'm thinking of asking him if he'd mind if I changed the spelling of my name to put an *i* and another *g* in it.

After hearing that, Riggins said: "Ron is the president, but I'm the king." After a pause: "At least for tonight." After another pause: "Aw, I was just joking."

pigskin, arms ready to cradle it, but just as he was about to grab it Theismann lunged and batted it away from him, turning a sure interception into a mere incomplete pass.

In the fourth period, the Redskins finally found the key to the Miami end zone. They entered it first when, on a fourth and one from the Dolphin 43-yard line, Gibbs decided to go for the first down. The Killer Bees swarmed in the trenches, expecting either a Riggins plunge or a Theismann sneak. Instead Theismann handed off to Riggins, who headed around left end and—after confronting only cornerback Don McNeal, whom he virtually ran over—charged down the sidelines and in for a touchdown. It gave Washington its first lead of the day, 20–17.

The Redskins defense remained unyielding throughout the last period of play, and the offense continued to surge. Another drive, with Riggins carrying the ball most of the time, moved Washington down to the Miami 6-yard line. Theismann then sealed the victory by connecting with Charlie Brown in the end zone.

The final score was Washington 27, Miami 17, but it hardly told the story of the way in which the Redskins thoroughly dominated the game on offense and defense. The statistics, of course, revealed that, and it was quite apparent to the more than 103,000 who filled the Rose Bowl that day and the many millions more who watched it on television.

It was Washington's first Super Bowl triumph and the franchise's first NFL title since Sammy Baugh led the Skins over the Chicago Bears back in 1942.

John Riggins, who had gained 166 yards, a Super Bowl record at the time, was a unanimous choice as the game's MVP. His total of 38 carries remains today the Super Bowl standard. Riggins also became the first player in NFL history to gain 100 or more yards in four consecutive postseason games.

The Skins offense gained more than twice the yardage of the Dolphins and chalked up 15 more first downs. There was little question at day's end that the Hogs had neutralized the sting of the Killer Bees, and that the Washington defense had destroyed both the Dolphins' running and passing games.

Joe Gibbs, whose job had appeared to be in jeopardy a season and a half earlier, was now looking forward to a Franklin Delano Roosevelt–type tenure in Washington.

SUPER BOWL XXII: 1988

As the 1987 season approached, the talk of a players' strike was again in the air. The contract between the team owners and the NFL Players Association that had come out of the strike-shortened 1982 season had run its course and the two factions now had to negotiate a new one. Pro football fans everywhere remembered with distaste how the players' strike lopped seven games from the regular season six years earlier, although Washington fans had the euphoric consolation of having marched through the playoffs and then winning the Super Bowl that disrupted season.

The 1987 regular season got off on schedule, however, while representatives of the owners and the union tried to iron out a contract. The Redskins had a few new faces in uniform on opening day, one of whom would play an important role in the team's success later in the season—running back Timmy Smith, Washington's fifth-round draft choice out of Texas Tech.

Opening day at RFK Stadium was a triumphant one, but it was riddled with disasters. Jay Schroeder suffered a shoulder injury on the ninth play of the game and was replaced by Doug Williams. Then place-kicker Jess Atkinson, on his first extra-point try of the regular season, dislocated his left ankle and would not see action again that year. In addition, featured running back George Rogers and All-Pro guard Russ Grimm were sidelined with injuries. Still, the Redskins survived the day and defeated the Eagles, 34–24, helped by a pair of touchdown passes from Doug Williams to Art Monk.

The next week the lowly Atlanta Falcons, who had had losing seasons each year since 1982 and were destined to win only three games in all of 1987, hosted the Skins down at Fulton County Stadium. Ali Haji-Sheikh, a free agent who had set the NFL record for field goals in a season when he booted 35 for the Giants in 1983 (but who had had limited success since), was signed to replace the injured Atkinson. Atlanta seemed unimpressed by the Redskins, who had made it all the way to the NFC title game the year before and were predicted by some to win it all in 1987. And the Skins, unfortunately, took the Falcons for granted. The game went back and forth all the way. Washington had a 20–14 lead in the fourth quarter on touchdown passes from Doug Williams to Kelvin Bryant, Gary Clark, and Art Monk, but it did not last long. The Falcons sustained a drive that resulted in a four-yard touchdown run by Gerald Riggs and a conversion to give them a 21–20 victory and Washington a jolt into reality.

All of professional football received a jolt the next week when the players did indeed walk out on strike. Week three of the regular season saw all games canceled. The players put up a steadfast front, and the owners essentially ignored them and announced that the season would resume in week four with any players who chose to defy the strike plus others whom they would sign up to replace the strikers.

The Redskins fielded a brand-new team for the first replacement game, staged October 4 at RFK Stadium. Quarterbacking them was Ed Rubbert, in his first pro game after playing at Louisville. Another rookie, who was given the assignment of chief rusher, was Lionel Vital from Nicholls State, an NCAA Class 1-AA school down in Thibodaux, Louisiana. Two more seasoned members of the offensive unit were wide receiver Anthony Allen, who'd played three years in the USFL and two with the Atlanta Falcons, and fullback Wayne Wilson, who had carried the ball for the Saints and the Vikings earlier in the decade.

The St. Louis Cardinals arrived with 10 regular players and, as a result, were a definite favorite. But with Allen gathering in three touchdown passes from Rubbert, one an 88-yard play, and another touchdown by Vital, the replacement Skins managed to triumph, 28–21.

The following week the opponent was the replacement New York Giants, who had been massacred the week before by the replacement 49ers, 41–21. However, the world championship Giants, who were now on strike, had not fared any better, losing both of their games before hitting the picket line. Washington had no trouble that Sunday at the Meadowlands. Three touchdowns in the second quarter, two on short runs by Wayne Wilson and one on a 22-yard carry by Lionel Vital, were actually enough, but the replacement Skins added two more in the second half, one on a 64-yard pass from Rubbert to Ted Wilson of Central Florida, and the other on a 14-yard run by Tim Jessie, a rookie from Auburn. The final score was 38–12, Washington.

The Dallas Cowboys, next on the agenda, were another heavy favorite, with veteran quarterback Danny White and a bevy of other starters snubbing the strike. But the upstarts in burgundy and gold were unimpressed. They took the lead in the first quarter on a field goal from Obed Ariri, who had had a brief kicking stint in the USFL, and increased it to 10–0 in the second half when Ted Wilson took a reverse and raced around end 16 yards for a touchdown. Another Ariri field goal and the Redskins had the win, 13–7.

After three salary-less weeks of watching their replacements perform, the regulars decided the strike was not such a good idea after all and voted to return to the playing field. All but a few of the replacements went back to whatever other professions they had been practicing before their brief moments in the NFL sun.

The lost game, it was announced, would not be made up and hence the regular season would be only 15 games. The Redskins had fared well, winning all three of their replacement games, being one of only three NFL teams to do so. With a record of 4–1–0, they were ahead of the pack in the NFC East, with the Cowboys in second place at 3–2–0 and the Super Bowl–champion Giants in a state of total collapse at 0–5–0.

When the Skins reappeared at RFK Stadium, it did not appear that the regulars were going to be as successful as the replacements had been. With a mere 10 minutes remaining in the game against the Jets, they trailed 16–7. Jay Schroeder was back, his shoulder repaired. He finally got a drive mounted, highlighted by three passes to Kelvin Bryant, the last a two-yarder for a touchdown. Ali Haji-Sheikh's conversion brought the Skins to within two points of the Jets with about five minutes remaining. New York came back and moved the ball into field-goal range, but then Dave Butz burst through and sacked New York quarterback Ken O'Brien to take them back out again. After a punt, Schroeder again marched the Skins downfield, the pivotal play being a 39-yard pass to wide receiver Ricky Sanders. Haji-Sheikh came on with 54 seconds left and kicked a 28-yard field goal to give Washington a 17–16 victory.

An easy win over Buffalo, 27–7, was countered by a loss up in Philadelphia to the Eagles, 31–27. The roller coaster continued the next two weeks, with the Redskins triumphing over the Detroit Lions, 20–13, then losing to the Rams, 30–26. In the Detroit game, Doug Williams came off the bench to replace Schroeder, who had fallen into Coach Gibbs' disfavor. Williams threw two touchdown passes, one to Kelvin Bryant and the other to Gary Clark, to ensure the win and to assure himself the starting role at quarterback the following week.

After the loss to the Rams, the Redskins had a record of 7–3–0. But there was little pressure from their division neighbors. The Cowboys were in second place at 5–5–0; the Eagles and Cardinals were tied for third with records of 4–6–0; and the disheveled Giants had an ignominious 3–7–0 record.

There would be no competition from any of these teams as the season ran through its final third. Jay Schroeder was back as starting quarterback in the confrontation with the Giants, but only because Doug Williams had sprained his back in practice that week. Schroeder managed to rouse the Redskins from a 16–0 deficit at the half to a 23–19 victory at day's end, the winning score coming on a

28-yard pass to Ricky Sanders. Behind Schroeder the following week, Washington had little trouble with the Cardinals, thrashing them 34–17, but lost perennial All-Pro receiver Art Monk to a knee injury in the process.

In two close games, the Redskins nipped the Cowboys, 24–20, and then dropped one to the Miami Dolphins, 23–21. The last game of the season was with the Vikings up at the Metrodome in Minneapolis, and it was a repeat of the thriller the two teams had staged the year before. Again Washington had to come from behind in the fourth quarter to tie the game. This time the hero was Doug Williams, brought in during the second half when Joe Gibbs again decided to bench Jay Schroeder. Williams found Ricky Sanders for a 46-yard touchdown pass in the third quarter, and then engineered two scoring drives in the final period, one ending with a 37-yard field goal from Ali Haji-Sheikh and the other with a 51-yard touchdown pass to Sanders. The game went into overtime, just as it had the year before. And again the Redskins won the toss, received, and marched. Instead of winning it on a touchdown on their first possession this year, they did it with a Haji-Sheikh 26-yard field goal.

The Redskins' record of 11–4–0 easily took the divisional crown in a year when all four of the other NFC East teams turned in losing records. Doug Williams had earned the starting position at quarterback for the playoffs, Coach Gibbs announced. Rookie running back Timmy Smith would be on the bench at the start of the playoffs, but would see a lot of action, Gibbs also said.

Once again Washington's first opponent in the playoffs was the Bears, this time at wind-chilled Soldier Field in Chicago. The year before the Skins had upset the title-holding Bears; this year the game was rated a toss-up.

Chicago appeared to be on its way to enacting revenge for the previous year's ouster by taking a 14–0 lead in the first half. But the Redskins were far from demoralized. Williams got them moving, directing a 69-yard touchdown drive, capped when George Rogers knifed in from the 3-yard line. Shortly thereafter, Williams led another march, this one climaxed by an 18-yard touchdown pass to tight end Clint Didier. At the half, the score was 14–14.

In the third quarter, Washington moved ahead in a dramatic fashion. Cornerback Darrell Green, back to return a Chicago punt, took it on his own 48-yard line, raced down the sideline, hurdled a diving Bears defender, then cut back toward the middle and took it all the way.

The 21 points that Washington logged by the end of the third quarter proved to be enough. The defense handled the rest. Key interceptions in the

Site:	Jack Murphy Stadium, San Diego, California	
Date:	January 31, 1988	
Weather:	60°, sunny	
Attendance:	73,302	
Gross receipts:	$27,100,000	
Player shares:	$36,000 winner, $18,000 loser	

STARTING LINEUPS

WASHINGTON REDSKINS	OFFENSE	DENVER BRONCOS
Ricky Sanders	WR	Vance Johnson
Joe Jacoby	LT	Dave Studdard
Raleigh McKenzie	LG	Keith Bishop
Jeff Bostic	C	Mike Freeman
R. C. Thielemann	RG	Stefan Humphries
Mark May	RT	Ken Lanier
Don Warren	TE	Clarence Kay
Gary Clark	WR	Mark Jackson
Doug Williams	QB	John Elway
Clint Didier	TE/RB	Gene Lang
Timmy Smith	RB	Sammy Winder
Ali Haji-Sheikh	K	Rich Karlis
	DEFENSE	
Charles Mann	LE	Andre Townsend
Dave Butz	LT/NT	Greg Kragen
Darryl Grant	RT/RE	Rulon Jones
Dexter Manley	RE/OLB	Simon Fletcher

Mel Kaufman	LB/ILB	Karl Mecklenberg	
Neal Olkewicz	MLB/ILB	Rickey Hunley	
Monte Coleman	LB/OLB	Jim Ryan	
Darrell Green	CB	Mark Haynes	
Barry Wilburn	CB	Steve Wilson	
Alvin Walton	S	Dennis Smith	
Todd Bowles	S	Tony Lilly	
Steve Cox	P	Mike Horan	

COACHES

Joe Gibbs	Dan Reeves

SCORING

	1st Qtr	2nd Qtr	3rd Qtr	4th Qtr	Final Score
Redskins	0	35	0	7	42
Broncos	10	0	0	0	10

fourth quarter by Barry Wilburn and Dennis Woodberry and two sacks in the waning minutes by defensive end Charles Mann destroyed the Bears. All told, Bears quarterback Jim McMahon was sacked five times and intercepted three times. The final score was Washington 21, Chicago 17, and for the second consecutive year the Redskins had served as spoilers to the Bears' Super Bowl aspirations.

For the second year in a row as well, Washington would attend the NFC championship game, this one in its hometown. Facing the Skins would be the all-too-familiar Minnesota Vikings, foes in the team's last two overtime games. Minnesota had gotten into the playoffs as a wild-card team with a record of 8–7–1, but they had been less than impressive in losing three of their last four regular-season games. In the playoffs, the Vikings were decided underdogs, but still managed to decimate the rejuvenated New Orleans Saints, 44–10, and then overwhelm the highly regarded San Francisco 49ers, 36–24.

The Vikings had shown offensive strength in their two playoff games. Wade Wilson replaced Tommy Kramer at quarterback, and with his passing and scrambling was beginning to remind Minnesotans of Fran Tarkenton, who had so entertained them with his versatility in the seventies. Anthony Carter had developed into one of the most electrifying wide receivers in the game, and running back Darrin Nelson was a proven ground gainer.

The Washington defense, on the other hand, had been devastating through the season and the playoffs and seemed to be getting better with every game. When the Vikings came to RFK Stadium, it was the NFL's senior defensive lineman, 37-year-old Dave Butz, who rallied his fellow defenders and made the plays that stopped the otherwise surging Vikes.

Washington started the scoring in the first quarter when Doug Williams connected on a 42-yard touchdown pass play to Kelvin Bryant. The Vikings came back to tie it at 7 apiece before the half, but it was becoming clear that this game would be decided on the relative merits of the defenses of the two teams.

Washington went ahead in the third quarter when Ali Haji-Sheikh booted a 28-yard field goal. But Minnesota countered with one of its own in the fourth quarter. It was after that that the Redskins made their first truly concerted drive of the day. Doug Williams, having one of his poorest days ever, had been beleaguered by the Minnesota defense, but suddenly things began to come together. He moved Washington 70 yards, culminating the drive with a 7-yard touchdown toss to Gary Clark, and the Skins were ahead, 17–10. The Vikings came right back. Wade Wilson brought them all the way to the 6-yard line of the Redskins. It was fourth down, 56 seconds were remaining, and every fan in RFK Stadium was on his or her feet. Wilson dropped back and rifled the ball to running back Darrin Nelson, who was seemingly open on the goal line. But Nelson bobbled it momentarily, and then cornerback Darrell Green collided with him, sending the ball fluttering to the ground. The Redskins defense had prevailed.

With a final score of 17–10, Washington was able to win primarily because the Redskins' defenders had chased, frustrated, and feloniously assaulted the Vikings all afternoon. Wade Wilson had been sacked eight times, one short of the NFL playoff record. Two of those had been dealt by the aging Dave Butz. The Redskins were on their way to the Super Bowl, their third appearance at that classic in the eighties.

A legion of Washington fans filled every seat on flights from National and Dulles airports in late January 1988 to San Diego, site of Super Bowl XXII. Their Redskins were treating them to a third Super Bowl of the decade.

The oddsmakers, however, looked on them as three-point underdogs. The reason was a simple one, they said. Their opponent, the Denver Broncos, had John Elway at quarterback. He was considered the league's most potent weapon, commonly pulling off the big play to break open a game just when the Broncos needed it. He had three wide receivers used to streaking downfield to gather in his bombs: Vance Johnson, Ricky Nattiel, and Mark Jackson. Denver also had a fine running back in Sammy Winder, as well as All-Pros in linebacker Karl Mecklenberg and defensive end Rulon Jones. In addition, Elway had taken the same team to the Super Bowl the year before.

It was a beautiful Sunday afternoon in sunny Southern California on January 31, 1988, with a mild but cooling breeze wafting about Jack Murphy Stadium. The arena was filled to capacity, some fans sporting war paint, others bright orange cowboy hats, each faction taunting the other. The pregame was over, and the players were on the field. Former Green Bay great and Hall of Famer Don Hutson handled the formalities of the honorary coin toss. Washington won and chose to receive.

With the Redskins punting after getting nowhere on their first possession, John Elway came out to take command at his own 44-yard line. He promptly demonstrated why he carried the reputation of a game breaker. On the first play from scrimmage, he dropped back and rocketed the ball down the right

Redskins cornerback Barry Wilburn leaps to intercept a John Elway pass in Super Bowl XXII. Washington annihilated the Denver Broncos on that January day at Jack Murphy Stadium in San Diego by the score of 42–10. Wilburn had two interceptions in the game. The intended receiver is Denver's Ricky Nattiel.

You can be right some of the time. . . . Dr. Z, Paul Zimmerman, in *Sports Illustrated:*

> **The brightest star going into the game is, of course, Denver quarterback John Elway. . . . [Doug] Williams is tough physically and emotionally . . . a streak thrower, and when he gets hot, few people can gobble up yards as quickly. . . . But the guess here is that Denver will win 38–31 in a shootout.**

And you can be very close. . . . Beano Cook of ESPN: "I predict the Redskins to win it, 41–10 [the final was 42–10]." When asked why he predicted an underdog to win by such a decisive margin, he said with a shrug, "The Redskins are the only team in Washington without too many lawyers."

Doug Williams, after the 1,000th time he had been reminded of his race during the media-blitz week preceding Super Bowl XXII:

> **Joe Gibbs and Bobby Beathard didn't bring me in to be the first black quarterback in the Super Bowl. They brought me in to be the quarterback of the Washington Redskins.**

Jack Kent Cooke:

> **I was petrified almost to the point of immobility. I thought, "What has happened to our Washington Redskins? Down 10–0." Then it turns out to be better than anything in my sports career. . . . Joe Gibbs is a hell of a coach. What a job he did.**

John Elway, when asked afterward what was the single worst moment in the game for him: "The second quarter."

sideline, where Nattiel was a step ahead of Washington cornerback Barry Wilburn. Nattiel took it in stride and streaked the rest of the way into the end zone for the first score of the day. Less than four minutes later, Elway moved the Broncos to the Redskin 7-yard line, where Rich Karlis kicked a field goal. A little later, a leg injury forced Doug Williams to leave the game; Jay Schroeder replaced him, but he could not get the Skins moving either. At the end of the first quarter, it was Denver 10, Washington 0, and it looked like the oddsmakers had been right on target.

And then there was the second quarter—the wildest 15 minutes in Super Bowl history and surely one of the most entertaining and gratifying in all of Redskins history. Williams came back to quarterback the Redskins. With a first and 10 at his own 20-yard line, Williams lofted a bomb toward the right sideline. It was snagged by Ricky Sanders, who took it all the way in for an 80-yard touchdown.

Redskins quarterback Doug Williams (No. 17) rolls out in Super Bowl XXII. Williams set two Super Bowl records that day: throwing four touchdown passes in a quarter (the second) and gaining 340 yards on his 18 (of 29) completions. He was named the game's MVP as the Redskins romped to a 42–10 victory over the Denver Broncos. *Photo courtesy of Vernon Biever Photography.*

Tight end Clint Didier (No. 86) is hoisted in triumph by center Jeff Bostic (No. 53) after catching a touchdown pass thrown by Doug Williams in Super Bowl XXII. Coming over to join the celebration is wide receiver Ricky Sanders (No. 83).

The Redskins' defense allowed the Broncos three downs and a punt. Then Williams hit tight end Don Warren for nine yards, Timmy Smith broke through the middle for 19 yards, and a few plays later Williams teamed with wide receiver Gary Clark on a 27-yard touchdown pass. The lead was now in the hands of the Skins, 14–10.

Two minutes later, Washington had the ball again. Timmy Smith took a hand-off and sliced off tackle, broke to the sideline, and raced 58 yards for another touchdown.

The Washington defense allowed the Broncos another three plays and a punt. Then once more Williams found Ricky Sanders on the right sideline, where he was again beating the Denver defender. The result this time was a 50-yard touchdown.

After the fourth Washington kickoff of the quarter, the Skins' defense allowed Denver only three plays, the last of which ended with an Elway pass into the hands of Washington defensive back Barry Wilburn. With the ball on the Skins' 22-yard line, Timmy Smith broke off left tackle and sped 43 yards before he was finally run out of bounds. Williams completed two passes to Sanders, having his greatest day ever catching the football, then tried a different receiver, tight end Clint Didier, who caught it in the end zone. With Ali Haji-Sheikh's fifth extra point of the quarter, the Redskins led 35–10.

The quarter finally and mercifully came to an end for the Broncos, who had just suffered the ignominy of having allowed the most points ever scored in a single quarter, not just in Super Bowl annals, but in the entire history of the NFL playoffs. Even the Chicago Bears, when they demolished the Redskins 73–0 in 1940, did not accumulate 35 points in a single period of play.

TRIVIA

Advertisers had to divvy up $1.35 million a minute for commercial time during Super Bowl XXII, the highest amount ever paid in the history of television advertising (prime evening hours on regular television ordinarily sold for about $120,000 a half-minute). To the advertisers' chagrin, however, the game drew only a 41.9 rating and a 62 percent share of all TV in use, making it the lowest-rated Super Bowl since the 1974 matching of the Minnesota Vikings and Miami Dolphins.

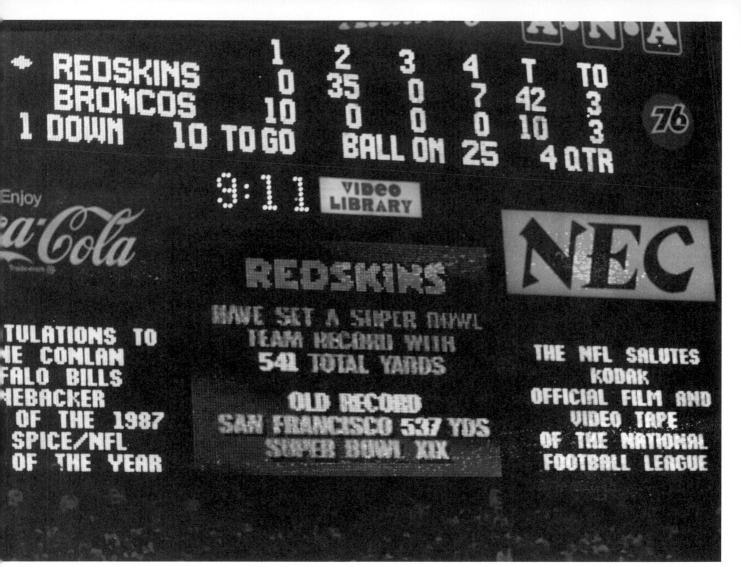

The kind of scoreboard Washington fans like to see.

None of the 73,302 spectators in Jack Murphy Stadium, nor the several thousand in the press boxes, expected the Broncos to come back after such a second-quarter humiliation. And they did not. The Washington defense held them scoreless through the final two periods of play. Washington added one final score in the fourth quarter when Timmy Smith carried the ball three times for 32, 7, and 4 yards and a touchdown. The final score: Washington 42, Denver 10.

The record books needed a lot of updating as the jubilant Redskins left the field for the locker room and the traditional postgame celebrations. Besides the incredible second-quarter team stats, Doug Williams had passed for more yards than any player in the history of the Super Bowl (340); Ricky Sanders had caught many of those passes for 193 yards, another Super Bowl mark; and Timmy Smith had gained more yards rushing than any other runner since the Roman numerals had begun back in the sixties (204 in all). When all was said and done, the first African American to quarterback a team in the Super Bowl, Doug Williams, was also recognized as the game's Most Valuable Player.

Inside the locker room, the Vince Lombardi Trophy was accepted by exuberant owner Jack Kent Cooke and exhilarated Coach Joe Gibbs. It was the Washington Redskins' second NFL world championship of the decade.

SUPER BOWL XXVI: 1992

The 1990–1991 football season was destined to endure in the minds of Redskins fans as one of the most satisfying ever. For the first time since winning Super Bowl XXII, the Redskins had made it to the playoffs in 1990, this time as a wild card. With a regular-season record of 10-6, they went to Philadelphia, where they dispatched the Eagles, 20–6, in the wild-card game; unfortunately, they were eliminated the following week in San Francisco by the 49ers, 28–10.

All the key players were back for 1991. Quarterback Mark Rypien had passed for over 2,000 yards in 1990, and his three top receivers were among the most feared in pro football: Art Monk, Gary Clark, and Ricky Sanders. Veteran Don Warren was still a mainstay at tight end. Running back Earnest Byner was coming off a 1,219-yard rushing season; Gerald Riggs and Ricky Ervins were also still on the team. The offensive line still featured All-Pros like Joe Jacoby, Russ Grimm, Jeff Bostic, Raleigh McKenzie, and Jim Lachey. On defense Charles Mann was there at end, Wilber Marshall at linebacker, and Darrell Green at cornerback. Place-kicker Chip Lohmiller, who had contributed 131 points on 30 field goals and 41 extra points in 1990, was headed for a Pro Bowl year in 1991.

JOE GIBBS

This team had great chemistry, a great feeling for each other. From day one, no one was fighting for individual goals.

The Redskins opened at RFK Stadium against the Lions and gave a preview of what the season was to be like, blowing out Detroit 45–0. Next on the agenda was the archrival Cowboys, who—with Troy Aikman throwing to Michael Irvin and Emmitt Smith carrying the football—were predicted by some to go all the way in 1991. In the first half, Dallas, in front of a hometown crowd, looked like a true contender, with a 21–10 lead. But Washington came back to take control of the game. With four field goals from Lohmiller, including one for 53 yards and another for 52, the Redskins posted an important, come-from-behind, 33–31 victory. The next opponent, Phoenix, was no more successful at RFK than Detroit had been two weeks earlier; they could not get on the scoreboard either, falling 34–0 to a red-hot Redskins team.

With an average of more than 37 points a game, Washington then traveled to Cincinnati, where they were a heavy favorite. The Bengals were unimpressed and took the game down to the final minute; tied 27–27, Gerald Riggs burst through for a game-winning touchdown, and Washington remained undefeated at the close of the season's first quarter.

The second quarter of the season was no less successful. It began with a record of sorts; the Redskins held their opponents scoreless for the third straight home game, defeating the Eagles 23–0. They followed with two easy wins, 20–7 over the Bears in Chicago and 42–17 over the Browns, who, in the seventh game of the season, became the first team in 1991 to score a point against Washington at RFK Stadium. Waiting for the Redskins, however, were the ever-pesky intradivision rival, the Giants, who in 1991 were more than just an annoyance: they were the reigning NFL champions, having defeated Buffalo in Super Bowl XXV back in January. Although they were only 4–3 when they lined up to play Washington at the Meadowlands, the Giants looked like champs—at least during the first half, which they totally dominated, holding the Redskins scoreless while scoring 13 points themselves. Washington reversed the tide in the second half, however, not yielding a point. Rypien then took offensive command, throwing two touchdown passes to Clark to give Washington a 14–13 lead, which they would not relinquish. Lohmiller iced the cake with a field goal. At the season's midway point, Washington was 8–0, and fans were thinking playoffs, and maybe even another Super Bowl.

The following week, Houston came to RFK with a 7–1 record and almost knocked off the Redskins. For the second week in a row, the Washington offense was less than productive. At the end of regulation play, the score stood at 13–13.

The Oilers had the ball in overtime, but Green picked off a pass thrown by Warren Moon; shortly thereafter Lohmiller drilled a 41-yard field goal to maintain Washington's perfect record. The offense came alive the following week at RFK at the expense of the Atlanta Falcons. The Skins scored a season-high 56 points that day and allowed a mere 17. The following week they exploded for 41 while destroying the Steelers in Pittsbsurgh (41–14).

The Redskins were 11–0 when Dallas came to RFK to end the third quarter of the 1991 regular season. Dallas brought the Skins and their fans back to the world of mere mortals. For the first time in quite a while, Washington was completely dominated. The Cowboys built a lead and never let it get away from them. The game was not as close as the 24–21 score might indicate.

The Redskins responded with three consecutive victories in the last quarter of the 1991 season, leaving in their wake the Rams (27–6), Phoenix (20–14), and the Giants (34–17). But, with the division title and home-field advantage in the playoffs clinched, there was a surprise waiting to be dealt by the Eagles up in Philadelphia in the final game of the regular season. With Washington comfortably ahead in the fourth quarter, the otherwise unexciting Eagles erupted with 17 points to defeat the Skins, 24–22.

The first team the Redskins had to face in the playoffs was the Atlanta Falcons, the same team they had annihilated earlier in the year, 56–17. After that disaster, Atlanta had turned its season around and won six of their next seven games. But they were still no match for the Redskins, who definitively eliminated the Falcons, 24–7, in a game whose outcome was never in question.

In the NFC championship game, Washington again faced a team they had met and demolished in the regular season. The Detroit Lions came to RFK, still feeling the sting from that opening day humiliation back in September (45–0). The Lions were relying on the running of their All-Pro back Barry Sanders, but the Redskins keyed on him, shutting the great running back down; Sanders gained only 41 yards rushing all afternoon. It was another mauling, and when it was over, the Redskins were on top of a lopsided score of 41–10.

The Buffalo Bills, coached by Hall of Fame–bound Marv Levy and spurred by the running of Thurman Thomas and the passing of Jim Kelly, had triumphed in the AFC. Buffalo had been to the Super Bowl the year before and lost by a single point to the Giants; they were thirsting for revenge.

Super Bowl XXVI was played inside the Metrodome in Minneapolis, a climate-controlled 72° down on the playing field. The first quarter proved to be the most

Site:	Metrodome, Minneapolis, Minnesota	
Date:	January 26, 1992	
Weather:	Game indoors	
Attendance:	63,130	
Player shares:	$36,000 winner, $18,000 loser	

STARTING LINEUPS

WASHINGTON REDSKINS	OFFENSE	BUFFALO BILLS
Gary Clark	WR	James Lofton
Jim Lachey	LT	Will Wolford
Raleigh McKenzie	LG	Jim Ritcher
Jeff Bostic	C	Kent Hull
Mark Schlereth	RG	Glenn Parker
Joe Jacoby	RT	Howard Ballard
Don Warren	TE	Keith McKeller
Art Monk	WR	Andre Reed
Mark Rypien	QB	Jim Kelly
Earnest Byner	RB	Kenneth Davis
Chip Lohmiller	K	Scott Norwood
	DEFENSE	
Charles Mann	LE	Leon Seals
Eric Williams	NT	Jeff Wright
Tim Johnson	RE	Bruce Smith
Fred Stokes	LOLB	Cornelius Bennett
Wilber Marshall	LILB	Shane Conlan
Kurt Gouveia	RILB	Carlton Bailey
Andre Collins	ROLB	Darryl Talley

Martin Mayhew	LCB	Kirby Jackson
Darrell Green	RCB	Nate Odomes
Danny Copeland	SS	Dwight Drane
Brad Edwards	FS	Mark Kelso

	COACHES	
Joe Gibbs		Marv Levy

SCORING

	1st Qtr	2nd Qtr	3rd Qtr	4th Qtr	Final Score
Redskins	0	17	14	6	37
Bills	0	0	10	14	24

frustrating quarter that the Redskins had encountered all year. After a long march, which included two key passes from Rypien to Monk, the Redskins ended up on the Buffalo 2-yard line. On third down, Rypien again hit Monk in the end zone, but instant replay revealed that Monk had stepped out of the end zone, nullifying the touchdown. On fourth down, the snap on the field-goal attempt was mishandled. Moments later, a Kelly pass was intercepted by Brad Edwards, and the Skins had the ball on the Buffalo 12-yard line. Two plays picked up only a yard; on third down and 9, Rypien dropped back to pass only to watch the ball land in the hands of a Buffalo defender. At the end of the first quarter the score was 0–0.

JEFF BOSTIC

Jacoby, Grimm, and I sat together [in the locker room after Super Bowl XXVI] and pulled out big cigars and lit them while we were still in our uniforms. I don't think anybody would admit it, but in the back of everyone's mind, I think the idea was there that this might be the last time we get there.

Washington moved the ball in the second period of play. Rypien threw a 41-yarder to Sanders to set up a Lohmiller field goal. On their next possession, Rypien again moved the Redskins and climaxed it with a touchdown pass to Byner. Kelly tried to get the Bills moving, but one of his passes was intercepted by Green. Rypien marched the Skins to the Buffalo 1-yard line, where Riggs carried it in for the touchdown. The score at the half: Washington 17, Buffalo 0.

Buffalo and Kelly started the second half with another interception; linebacker Kurt Gouveia ran it back to the Bills' 2-yard line where Riggs carried it in for his sec-

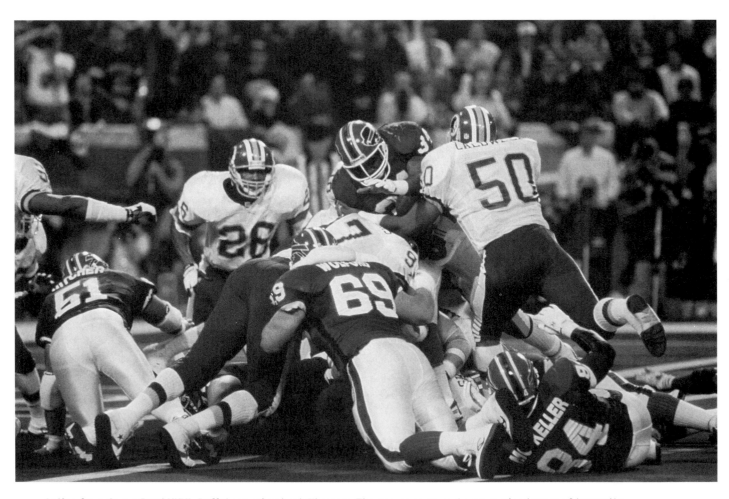

Action from Super Bowl XXVI. Buffalo running back Thurman Thomas goes up and over a mixed mass of humanity. Identifiable Washington defenders are linebacker Ravin Caldwell (No. 50) and cornerback Darrell Green (No. 28). The Skins defense held the Bills scoreless in the first half, then hung on in the second half to help Washington to a 37–24 victory and another NFL championship. *Photo courtesy of Vernon Biever Photography.*

ond touchdown of the day. Buffalo came back with 10 points of their own in the quarter, but with the score at 24–10, Rypien engineered a 79-yard drive, including a 30-yard touchdown pass to Clark. The result was never in doubt after that. Lohmiller added two field goals in the fourth quarter to put the game out of reach. The final score was 37–24, and once again the Washington Redskins were world champions.

The defense had intercepted Kelly four times; Thomas was held to just 13 yards on seven carries. Rypien, the game's MVP, completed 18 of 33 passes for 292 yards and two touchdowns. Clark had seven receptions for 114 yards; Monk had seven for 113 yards. Ricky Ervins gained 72 yards on 13 carries while Byner picked up another 49 yards on 14 carries; Riggs rushed for two touchdowns. Joe Gibbs became only the third coach in NFL history to win three Super Bowls, joining the Steelers' Chuck Noll and the 49ers' Bill Walsh.

7
The Almost Years

THE FIRST CHAMPIONSHIP GAME: 1936

George Preston Marshall, snubbing Boston for its lack of support of his team, took the Redskins to the Polo Grounds in New York for their first NFL championship game. Having won the NFL East from the New York Giants on the last game of the regular season, the 7–5–0 Redskins had to face the Green Bay Packers (10–1–1), who were a heavy favorite. Besides losing only one game all year, the oddsmakers figured, the Packers had defeated the Redskins twice during the regular season, by scores of 31–2 at Green Bay and 7–3 in Boston.

Curly Lambeau, the Hall of Fame–bound coach of the Pack, had opened up his offense by frequently passing the football, a tactic disdained by most teams in the league. Lambeau had a fine passing quarterback in Arnie Herber and two superb Hall of Famers as receivers: end Don Hutson and halfback Johnny "Blood"

1936 CHAMPIONSHIP LINEUPS

BOSTON REDSKINS		GREEN BAY PACKERS
Wayne Millner	E	Don Hutson
Charley Malone	E	Milt Gantenbein
"Turk" Edwards	T	Ernie Smith
Jim Barber	T	Lou Gordon
Les Olsson	G	"Tiny" Engebretsen
Jim Karcher	G	Lon Evans
Frank Bausch	C	George Svendsen
Riley Smith	QB	Arnie Herber
Cliff Battles	HB	George Sauer
Ed Justice	HB	Johnny "Blood" McNally
Don Irwin	FB	Clarke Hinkle
Ray Flaherty	Coach	Curly Lambeau

McNally. To augment the passing attack, the Packers relied on the powerful running of fullback Clarke Hinkle, another player bound for football immortality in the Hall of Fame at Canton, Ohio.

It was a sunny, relatively mild Sunday afternoon when the two teams squared off. The Redskins' chances faded quickly when, early in the first quarter, star back Cliff Battles lateraled to Riley Smith, who fumbled it away to Green Bay. On top of that, Battles was hurt on the play and had to leave the field for the rest of the game.

The Packers took advantage of the turnover when, shortly thereafter, Herber and Hutson hooked up on a 43-yard touchdown pass. The Redskins came back in the next period of play, mounting a 78-yard drive that culminated in a 2-yard touchdown plunge by fullback Pug Rentner. But Riley Smith, in one of his less memorable games of that season, missed the extra point and the Redskins trailed 7–6 at the half.

In the third quarter, Herber destroyed the Redskins when he teamed with McNally on a 52-yard pass play, then followed that with an 8-yard touchdown toss to end Milt Gantenbein.

In the fourth quarter, with the Skins trailing 14–6, Riley Smith was back to punt deep in his own territory, but did not get it off in time. Hinkle blocked it and recovered the ball on the Redskins' 3-yard line. Moments later Green Bay halfback Bob Monnett carried it in for the last touchdown of the game. The Packers prevailed at the whistle, 21–6.

THE HUMILIATION: 1940

After the Redskins won their first NFL title in 1937, they remained in hot contention in each of the ensuing eight years. Four times they reached the title game (1940, 1942, 1943, and 1945), and in the other four seasons they were always close in the NFL East divisional race, usually edged out by their nemesis of that era, the New York Giants.

The Redskins of 1940 were little different than those of 1939. Sammy Baugh was actually in better physical shape than he had been. And Andy Farkas was coming off a year in which he led the NFL in scoring with 68 points (11 touchdowns and 2 extra points). The defense of 1939, which had allowed only a little over 7½ points per game, was back in full force.

There was, however, the usual salary turmoil before the preseason—precipitated, according to the players, by the Big Chief's stinginess and, according to Marshall, by the avarice of the players. Whatever the reason, Wayne Millner was holding out and Frank Filchock and "Wee" Willie Wilkin turned down the contracts offered by Marshall. Baugh, who was under contract but not apparently with overwhelming satisfaction, announced that he was planning to retire at the end of the season to go into coaching on the college level. However, by the time they were ready to board the Liberty Limited in August for training camp in Spokane, Washington, all had been signed.

Around that same time, Marshall announced that seating had been increased: Griffith Stadium could now accommodate 40,000 spectators. He also added that the $1.65 tickets were to be increased to $2.20 and the $2.20 seats upped to $3.20.

The Redskins got off to a beautiful start in 1940, beginning the season with a 24–17 win over a very good Brooklyn Dodgers team led by future Hall of Fame tailback Ace Parker. The next week they sank the usually spoilsport Giants, 21–7. In fact, Washington won their first seven games of the regular season.

It was not until they traveled to Ebbets Field to face the Dodgers again that they evinced any vulnerability. That day they could not contain the versatile Parker and lost a squeaker, 16–14. In that game, Slingin' Sammy Baugh slung his way to an NFL record of 23 completions in a single game (2 were for Washington's only touchdowns).

The following week presented perhaps the biggest challenge of the season. The Chicago Bears were coming to town, leading the NFL West. From the very start of the year they had been an odds-on favorite to win the NFL title. Bert Bell, then owner of the Philadelphia Eagles, said in the preseason, "No one's going to beat the Bears this year. They're the greatest team ever assembled." They were indeed imposing, with six future Hall of Famers in the starting lineup: quarterback Sid Luckman, halfback George McAfee, center "Bulldog" Turner, tackle Joe Stydahar, and guards Danny Fortmann and George Musso. They also had All-Pros in fullback Bill Osmanski, end Ken Kavanaugh, and tackle Lee Artoe. But Bert Bell was wrong: they could be beaten. Washington proved that on a mid-November afternoon in Griffith Stadium.

The Bears scored first on a field goal by "Automatic" Jack Manders, but had great difficulty with the Washington defense throughout the rest of the first half. In the second quarter, Filchock moved the Redskins to inside the Bears' 20-yard line, then pitched out to halfback Dick Todd, who wove his way through the Chicago defense for a touchdown.

The second half was a defensive battle all the way to the last possession of the game. With the score still standing at 7–3 Washington, McAfee, who could be devastating in the open field, broke loose and made it all the way to the Redskins' 1-yard line. The Washington defense held fast, and in fact pushed the Bears back to the 6-yard line. Then, on the last play of the game, Luckman rolled out and threw to Osmanski in the end zone. Redskins defender Filchock went up and separated receiver and ball, and the final gun sounded. The Bears screamed foul. Coach George Halas rushed onto the field claiming Filchock had interfered with Osmanski. But there was no flag on the field. The final score remained: Redskins 7, Bears 3.

After the game, however, George Preston Marshall—in a state of exultation and always eager to give it to his friend and football archrival George Halas—made a statement to the press that he would come to rue. Said the Big Chief:

The Bears are front-runners, quitters. They're not a second-half team, just a bunch of crybabies! They fold up when the going gets tough.

Halas read it, then saved all the newspapers in which it appeared.

The Redskins lost to the Giants the following week, 21–7, but that year it did not spoil their title pursuit. Washington, leading the division with a record of 8–1–0 going into the Giants' game, had already outdistanced the 5–3–1 New Yorkers. All they had to do now was defeat the Philadelphia Eagles in the last game of the season, because the second-place Brooklyn Dodgers had lost three games. And at Griffith Stadium they did just what was required of them, beating Philadelphia 13–6.

The Redskins, with a record of 9–2–0, the most games they had won thus far in their history, were the NFL East champs for the second time since moving to Washington in 1937. Sammy Baugh had reasserted himself as the team's premier passer, completing 111 for league highs of 1,367 yards and 12 touchdowns. Filchock added another 460 yards passing. With Andy Farkas out for the season with a knee injury, Dick Todd led the team in rushing in 1940, picking up 408 yards, with a 5.4-yard average. He also gained more yards on pass receptions (402) than any other Redskin. Baugh made All-Pro for the second time in his then-four-year Redskins career.

Meanwhile, over in the NFL West, the Bears had apparently dried their tears and defeated the Cleveland Rams, 47–25, and the Chicago Cardinals, 31–23, to clinch their division title.

The NFL championship game of 1940 was scheduled for the home stadium of the NFL East titleholder. So the Redskins and the Bears would meet in the same

arena where they had battled so defensively a few weeks earlier. Despite the fact that Washington had won that encounter, the bookmakers favored the Bears; so did most of the sportswriters. Bob Considine of the *New York Times-Herald* suggested 9-5 odds. Shirley Povich of the *Washington Post* was a bit more conservative: he thought 7-5 was more appropriate.

Neither Marshall nor Halas agreed with the oddsmakers. According to his wife, Corinne Griffith, at the breakfast table in his Washington home the day of the game Marshall remarked:

> **The so-called experts make us a slight underdog today. That's ridiculous. . . . We already beat them. Why, we only lost two games this year. The bookmakers must be crazy.**

Halas, adopting a different psychological strategy, said:

> **Those guys [the oddsmakers] must be crazy. This game is an even-money game or nothing at all. Sure, we've got power, but look at the Redskins—they have Sammy Baugh and Dick Todd, a combination we have to stop if we're going to win this championship.**

Whatever the odds, it was pegged by all to be a battle royal. Robert Ruark, a sportswriter in those days before he began to write about Africa, described it this way:

> It says right here in the paper that 35,000 tickets have been sold for the football game Sunday between the Bears and the Redskins and that there isn't a spare pew in Pa Griffith's ballpark. You know what all those people are paying to see? Not a football game. A fistfight.

Coach George Halas was the first Bear in the locker room that December Sunday at Griffith Stadium. Still in his psychological mode, he had with him the newspaper clippings of Marshall's remarks after the Redskins defeated the Bears earlier that season. He taped them all over the locker room. Later, as the Bears donned their uniforms, they had ample time to reflect on Marshall's description

1940 CHAMPIONSHIP LINEUPS

WASHINGTON REDSKINS		CHICAGO BEARS
Bob Masterson	LE	Bob Nowaskey
"Wee" Willie Wilkin	LT	Joe Stydahar
Dick Farman	LG	Danny Fortmann
Bob Titchenal	C	"Bulldog" Turner
Steve Slivinski	RG	George Musso
Jim Barber	RT	Lee Artoe
Charley Malone	RE	George Wilson
Max Krause	QB	Sid Luckman
Sammy Baugh	LH	Ray Nolting
Ed Justice	RH	George McAfee
Jimmy Johnston	FB	Bill Osmanski
Ray Flaherty	Coach	George Halas

In the NFL championship game of 1940, Redskins fullback Jimmy Johnston (No. 31), in the arms of quarterback/defensive back Sid Luckman of the Chicago Bears, is also in the middle of a hostile crowd of Bears: Bill Osmanski (No. 9), Joe Stydahar (No. 13), George McAfee (No. 5), Danny Fortmann (No. 21), and John Siegal (No. 6). The Bears embarrassed the Redskins that day by the highest score in NFL history, 73–0. Four of the Bears in this picture are in the Pro Football Hall of Fame (Luckman, Stydahar, McAfee, and Fortmann). *Photo reprinted courtesy of the Associated Press.*

of them. Then, just before they were to take the field Halas confronted them and, pointing at the clippings, said:

Gentlemen, this is what George Preston Marshall thinks of you. I think you're a great football team, the greatest ever assembled. Go out on the field and prove it.

Halas proved that crisp, sunny Sunday afternoon that he was the psychological equal to Sigmund Freud, and the Bears provided irrefutable evidence that they were the battlefield equivalent of Caesar's legions.

Washington fans prefer not to dwell on the cataclysm. But for the sake of historical reference, here is what happened. With the game only 55 seconds old, Bears fullback Osmanski broke out around left end and ran 68 yards for a touchdown. Later in the first quarter, Luckman quarterback-sneaked in for another Chicago touchdown. Then halfback Joe Maniaci eluded all Washington defenders on a 42-yard scamper for another score. In the second period Luckman connected with end Kavanaugh for still another Bears touchdown. The score at intermission: Chicago 28, Washington 0.

In the second half, Bears defender Hampton Pool picked off a Baugh pass and ran it 15 yards for a touchdown. Then halfback Ray Nolting ran 23 for another score. Redskins tailback Roy Zimmerman threw, unfortunately, to Bears defender McAfee, who carried it back 34 yards for a touchdown. Minutes later it was linebacker Turner's turn; he grabbed another Zimmerman pass and toted it 21 yards for a touchdown. Halfback Harry Clark, on a double reverse, then ran 44 yards for a score. Fullback Gary Famiglietti followed with a 2-yard plunge. And lastly, if not mercilessly, Clark bucked in from the 1-yard line.

The score was 73–0, Bears, when the final gun sounded, the piercing report of which prompted one press box wag to observe to the sportswriter sitting next to him: "Marshall just shot himself."

George Preston Marshall was neither dead nor speechless after the slaughter:

What can I say. We needed a 50-man line against their power. We had the greatest crowd in Washington's history and we played our poorest game. I am mortified to think what we did to that crowd.

Some thoughts and comments after the carnage, better known as the NFL championship game of 1940:

Sammy Baugh, when asked if the outcome might have been different had Charley Malone caught what appeared to be a touchdown pass in the first quarter with the score a mere 7–0, Bears:

> **Hell, yes, the score would have been 73–6.**

Bob Considine, in his column "On the Line":

> **The Chicago Bears massacred the Washington Redskins 73–0 yesterday. . . . The unluckiest guy in the crowd was the five-buck bettor who took the Redskins and 70 points.**

Shirley Povich, in his column "This Morning" for the *Washington Post*:

> **If you're wanting to know what happened to the Redskins yesterday, maybe this will explain it: the Bears happened to 'em.**
>
> **It reminds us of our first breathless visit to the Grand Canyon. All we could say is: "There she is, and ain't she a beaut." When they hung up that final score at Griffith Stadium yesterday, all we could utter was: "There it is, and wasn't it awful."**

Bill Stern, famous sports broadcaster:

> **It got so bad that, toward the end, the Bears had to give up place-kicking the extra points and try passes instead because all the footballs booted into the stands were being kept by the spectators as souvenirs. And they were down to their last football.**

Red Smith, in his column "Sports of the Times" for *The New York Times*:

> **George Preston Marshall, the mettlesome laundryman who owns the Redskins, looked on from the stands—except when he turned his back to charge up the aisle and throw a punch at a dissatisfied customer—and when his ordeal was over, every hair in his raccoon coat had turned white.**

George Preston Marshall:

> **We were awful and you don't need to ask me if we are going to clean house. Some of the boys are going to be embarrassed when the time comes to make contracts for next year.**

GEORGE HALAS

> Some observers said the Bears were a perfect football team that day. I can't quite agree. Looking over the movies, I can see where we should have scored another touchdown.

THE BEARS AGAIN: 1943

It took the Redskins until 1942 before they were able to shed the shroud of that 1940 title game in which they sat, humiliatingly, at the zero end of a 73–0 score. And, of course, they did it with a certain panache, wreaking revenge on the perpetrators of that disaster, the Chicago Bears themselves, in the championship game of 1942, beating the Bears by the score of 14–6 and securing for Washington its second NFL crown.

What the Big Chief wanted now was a repeat: back-to-back championships. Up to that time, only the Chicago Bears had won two consecutive titles (1940 and 1941). Marshall confronted the sports press:

> We have proven we are the team to beat. We will now show just how true that statement is by launching a string of championships unprecedented in the National Football League.

World War II had depleted the rosters of most teams in the NFL by the start of the 1943 season, to the degree that the Philadelphia Eagles and the Pittsburgh Steelers were forced to combine their two teams in the NFL East and became known around the league as the Phil-Pitt Steagles.

The Redskins were not as badly drained of talent as many teams. They still had Baugh, Farkas, Wilbur Moore, Joe Aguirre, Bob Masterson, and Wilkin, among others. They had, however, lost to military service such regulars as Todd, Filchock, Millner, Charley Malone, Ed Justice, Ed Cifers, and Fred Davis. In fact, 44 Redskins in all would serve in World War II at one time or another during the years 1942 through 1945. Only one did not return: halfback Keith Birlem, who was killed in battle May 7, 1943.

The most noticeable absence, however, was Head Coach Ray Flaherty, who was now in the U.S. Navy. Replacing him on the sideline was Arthur J. "Dutch" Bergman, who was well known around the nation's capital, having coached at

Catholic University during the thirties. Dutch had also served as Marshall's chief scout for the Skins the year before, traveling to the various NFL cities and bringing back reports to Flaherty. Bergman was helped out in his newfound job by former Redskins great Turk Edwards, who handled the defense.

The Redskins, as they had each year since coming to Washington, got off to a strong start in 1943. They demolished the Dodgers 27–0 and the Packers 33–7 in the first two games of the season. Then came the Chicago Cardinals, the league pushover (they would lose all 10 of their games that year), who at Griffith Stadium almost surprised Marshall and his tribe, with the Redskins eking out a 13–7 victory in the last moments.

There were actually only two teams who offered the Redskins any problem that year. The first was the Phil-Pitt Steagles, a team with hardly a single recognizable football name on its roster, who held them to a 14–14 tie in Philadelphia and then defeated the Skins 27–14 in Washington. The second was, predictably, the consistently pain-provoking New York Giants. Tuffy Leemans had been converted to a quarterback in New York, and Bill Paschal was now doing most of the running for the team. On the line, 34-year-old veteran Mel Hein was still walking off with All-Pro honors at center each year and youthful Al Blozis was proving that he was one of the best tackles in the pros. The schedule pitted New York and Washington against each other on the last two Sundays of the regular season, and the Redskins, with a record of 6–1–1 as opposed to New York's 4–3–1, clearly held their football destiny in their own hands when they went up to Manhattan to face the Giants. But they fumbled it up there, losing 14–10.

The following week they had the opportunity to retrieve their fate in the friendlier confines of Griffith Stadium, but instead were stunned, 31–7, by the New Yorkers. The two losses brought the two teams into a tie for the NFL East crown with identical records of 6–3–1.

The playoff game was scheduled for the Polo Grounds on December 19, and the Redskins, who had been a marked favorite when they had traveled up to New York two weeks earlier, were now a distinct underdog.

It was bitterly cold that Sunday afternoon and the frozen turf of the Polo Grounds, according to Baugh, "made you think you were playing on a sidewalk."

Baugh, who had had one of his finest years as a pro that season, leading the league in passing, punting, and interceptions, was smarting worse than anyone

Several decades after the 1943 playoff game between the Redskins and the Giants to determine the NFL East title, Dutch Bergman explained to Washington *Evening Star* columnist Lewis F. Atchison how he tried to spur the Skins after they had lost two consecutive games to the Giants on the two preceding Sundays. Atchison duly reported it in his column in 1964:

> It was a cheerless, dispirited group when Bergman entered the room for his pre-game. A definite "let's get it over with" atmosphere was in the air and he sensed it.
>
> "I just want to say," he began in slow, precise words, "that we have some good ballplayers on this squad and we have some yellow-bellied, gutless ones too. I know that some of you already have bought train tickets and are leaving for home right after the game. You're going out there, take your beating, and slink home like whipped dogs. You don't want to play the Bears. You're yellow, gutless. . . ."
>
> "Wait a minute there, you can't call me yellow," Sammy Baugh angrily broke in. "Nobody's gonna call me a quitter."
>
> The rangy quarterback took a couple of menacing steps forward, but Dutch held his ground.
>
> "All right, Sam, if you want to fight, go out and fight the Giants," he calmly replied. "I'll be here in this room after the game. I'll be waiting for you."

It worked. The Redskins went out and scalped the Giants 28–0, and Baugh's passing is credited with having led them to the victory.

from the two previous losses to the Giants. As the confrontation would prove, he was obviously determined to regain his and his team's respectability.

In the second quarter, Baugh got the offense moving. Behind his passing the Redskins marched, and from the 2-yard line Farkas bulled in for the game's first score. Baugh engineered a similar drive a little later that also ended up on the 2, and Farkas again toted the ball in for a touchdown, enabling the Redskins to retire to their locker room with a 14–0 halftime lead.

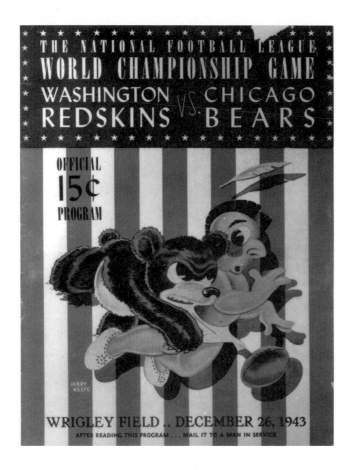

THE NATIONAL FOOTBALL LEAGUE
WORLD CHAMPIONSHIP GAME
WASHINGTON vs. CHICAGO
REDSKINS BEARS

OFFICIAL
15¢
PROGRAM

WRIGLEY FIELD .. DECEMBER 26, 1943
AFTER READING THIS PROGRAM . . . MAIL IT TO A MAN IN SERVICE

In the third quarter, the Giants' offense came alive and moved the ball to the Washington 32, but there the Washington defense doused the drive, and the period remained scoreless. In the fourth quarter, New York's Leemans dropped back and rifled a pass that Baugh intercepted and carried 28 yards to the New York 1-yard line. Farkas plunged in for the touchdown on the next play. And finally, to add the proverbial icing to the cake, Baugh tossed a touchdown pass to Ted Lapka. The final score: Redskins 28, Giants 0, and Baugh had his revenge. He completed 16 of 21 passes that day for 199 yards.

With the win, the Redskins earned the right to play in their fourth NFL championship game in seven years. And for the fourth time, they were to face the Chicago Bears.

While Baugh was having one of his finest years, so was Bears quarterback Luckman. Both, in fact, were named All-Pro, Luckman at quarterback and Baugh at halfback. Luckman had set several NFL records that year when he became the first quarterback ever to pass for more than 400 yards in a game (433) and to throw seven touchdown passes in one game, both of which he accomplished in a 56–7 decimation of the New York Giants. He had also set single-season standards by passing for 2,194 yards and 28 touchdowns.

Because the Bears had lost a good number of their regulars to the war effort, they induced Bronko Nagurski, now 34 years old, to end his five-year retirement and once again don a Bears uniform. He was still an awesome force.

The Bears had ended their season with a record of 8–1–1, their only loss dealt to them by the Redskins, 21–7, a game in which Coach Bergman surprised the Chicagoans with the old Statue of Liberty play: end Wilbur Moore snatched the ball from a poised-to-pass Baugh and ran 20 yards for a touchdown.

1943 CHAMPIONSHIP LINEUPS

WASHINGTON REDSKINS		CHICAGO BEARS
Bob Masterson	LE	Jim Benton
Lou Rymkus	LT	Dominic Sigilio
Clyde Shugart	LG	Danny Fortmann
George Smith	C	"Bulldog" Turner
Steve Slivinski	RG	George Musso
Joe Pasqua	RT	Al Hoptowit
Joe Aguirre	RE	George Wilson
Ray Hare	QB	Bob Snyder
Frank Seno	LH	Harry Clark
George Cafego	RH	Dante Magnani
Andy Farkas	FB	Bob Masters
"Dutch" Bergman	Coach	Hunk Anderson
		Paddy Driscoll
		Luke Johnsos

The NFL championship game was set for Sunday, December 26, at Wrigley Field in Chicago. Both teams figured they had something going against them before they even took the field. Because the Bears had begun their season two weeks before the Redskins and because the title game had to be pushed back a week to accommodate the NFL East playoff game, Chicago had not played a football game in a month. On the other hand, the Redskins were coming off three crucial, pressure-filled games. The gamblers wondered which fact would dull the edge, or if perhaps both might exact a toll.

When the day had ended, it was safe to say that three intense games in succession had been more damaging than four weeks of rest and relaxation—that and the fact that Baugh had staggered to the sideline after the opening kickoff when

Chicago Bears quarterback Sid Luckman finds a big hole in the Redskins line during the 1943 NFL title game at Wrigley Field in Chicago. Washington could not contain the Bears during most of that dismal, cold afternoon, and finally lost 41–21. *Photo reprinted courtesy of Bettmann Archive.*

someone had kicked him in the head. He remained there with a mild concussion for the rest of the first half, replaced by George Cafego. Add to that a game in which Luckman could virtually do no wrong for his Bears, and the outcome became exceedingly, if uncomfortably, predictable.

The game began stodgily. Neither team could post a score of any kind in the first quarter. The first major drive came in the second quarter, when Cafego hit Moore for a 34-yard pass play and then followed with a 24-yarder that Moore could not handle—the reason being that the Bears defender had interfered with him. It gave Washington a first down at the Chicago 2-yard line. Two plays later Farkas burst through for the touchdown. It was, unfortunately, the only lead the Redskins would enjoy that cold and gloomy afternoon.

The Bears came right back. With Luckman passing and Nagurski plunging, Chicago made it to the Washington 31-yard line, where Luckman flicked a little screen pass to halfback Harry Clark, whose blockers paved his way into the end zone. Another Luckman-led drive brought the ball to the 3-yard line of the Redskins, where Nagurski took it and bulldozed in for another score, the last

Georgе Preston Marshall was always known as a person who made his presence known—and sometimes in the most unlikely of places, such as this one described in *The Chicago Bears, An Illustrated History* by Richard Whittingham (Simon and Schuster, 1986):

The Bears were moving toward a touchdown as time was running out in the first half during the NFL championship game of 1943 against the Washington Redskins. Ralph Brizzolara, acting president of the Bears while George Halas was in the navy, looked down the Bear bench and suddenly noticed that the person sitting at the end of it was not wearing a Bear uniform. He was, in fact, dressed in an elegant raccoon coat and a homburg hat.

"My god, it's Marshall," Brizzolara shouted, as he stormed down to confront the owner of the Washington Redskins. George Preston Marshall began to explain that he had merely been on his way down to the Redskins' locker room and decided to pay a quick half-time visit to the Bears as well. Brizzolara, sure that Marshall was there for some nefarious reason, like stealing signals or listening in on the Bear coaches' instructions, summoned Jack Goldie, the team's equipment manager. "Physically remove Marshall from this area," he told him. Goldie clutched the fur-covered arm of the Redskins' owner and roughly escorted him back into the grandstand. There an usher demanded to see his ticket stub, which Marshall could not produce. The usher then called two policemen. Grasping Marshall by the arms, the lawmen were about to lead him from the ball park when he finally managed to convince them that he actually was who he said he was.

After the game, Brizzolara said: "I didn't want Marshall there eavesdropping. . . . A championship and a great honor were at stake. . . . That's the lowest way there can be of trying to win a game. . . . Yes, we threw him out—not invited him out."

Regarding the incident, Marshall said: "Fiddlesticks! It was a first-class bush-league trick." And then added: "You can say for me that Brizzolara is not a gentleman. And I'll never speak to him again!"

Later the following week, Elmer Layden, the NFL commissioner, also had something to say. He fined Marshall and Brizzolara $500 each for "actions not reciprocal of the public confidence in the National Football League."

touchdown he would score in an illustrious pro football career. The score at the half was 14–7, Chicago.

In the third period, Luckman teamed up with halfback Dante Magnani for two touchdowns, the first a 36-yard pass and the second a 66-yarder. The Redskins, with Baugh now back in the game, got on the board in the same period when Slingin' Sammy spotted Farkas open and drilled a 17-yard touchdown pass to him.

For Washington, the fourth quarter was an unfortunate repeat of the third. Luckman threw to end Jim Benton for a 26-yard touchdown, then came back and hit Clark with a 16-yarder. The Redskins got a token touchdown late in the fourth quarter when Baugh threw a 25-yard TD pass to Aguirre. But by then the game was well out of sight. At the end the score stood Bears 41, Redskins 21.

To the chagrin of Washington fans, it had truly been Luckman's day, while their own Baugh had sat dazed through the first half and then, despite the fog that hung in his head, had tried gamely, but hopelessly, to get his team going in the second half. Slingin' Sam did complete 8 of 12 passes for 123 yards and two touchdowns after he returned to the game, but Luckman could count 15 of 26 for 286 yards and an NFL championship game record of five touchdowns (previously three, set by Baugh in the 1937 title tilt).

The Redskins and the Bears would have to settle for two titles apiece in their four encounters for the NFL crown.

THE LAST FOR A WHILE: 1945

Marshall was thoroughly disenchanted with the 1944 season, as he made clear in a variety of statements to the press, but not enough so to replace Dudley DeGroot as his coach. He made it abundantly clear, however, that he expected a better showing in 1945.

Coach DeGroot accommodated him—almost, anyway. Baugh helped considerably, having now fully mastered the profession of T-formation quarterback. He felt so comfortable in the role by 1945 that he quipped, "I could play it in top hat and tails."

The Redskins opened up in Beantown against the Boston Yanks, a team that had joined the NFL just the year before. Washington was a heavy favorite to beat the NFL neophytes from Boston, who had turned in a meager record of 2–8–0 in their maiden season. But the Boston Yanks—who apparently had not been informed that they were the underdog and had not heard Marshall's statements to the press that the Redskins were the clear favorites to win the NFL East that year— stunned the Redskins, 28–20.

After that, however, there was nothing to stop the marauding Skins. They knocked off their next six opponents, including a fine Philadelphia Eagles team that showcased All-Pro halfback Steve Van Buren; the always difficult New York Giants, in a game in which Baugh completed 20 of 24 passes for 265 yards and two touchdowns; and the perennially powerful Chicago Bears.

Their success was founded around the skills of Baugh, who was no longer being platooned with Filchock and was having one of his best years ever as a Redskin. Baugh's unsurpassed passing was supplemented by the powerful running of fullback Frank Akins, the fleetness of rookie halfback Steve Bagarus, and the place-kicking of Aguirre. In those six victories, the Redskins averaged 25 points a game.

1945 CHAMPIONSHIP LINEUPS

WASHINGTON REDSKINS		CLEVELAND RAMS
Wayne Millner	LE	Floyd Konetsky
Fred Davis	LT	Eberle Schultz
Al Lolotai	LG	Riley Matheson
Ki Aldrich	C	Mike Scarry
Marvin Whited	RG	Milan Lazetich
Earl Audet	RT	Gil Bouley
Doug Turley	RE	Steve Pritko
Sammy Baugh	QB	Steve Nemeth
Dick Todd	LH	Fred Gehrke
Merlyn Condit	RH	Jim Gillette
Frank Akins	FB	Pat West
Dudley DeGroot	Coach	Adam Walsh

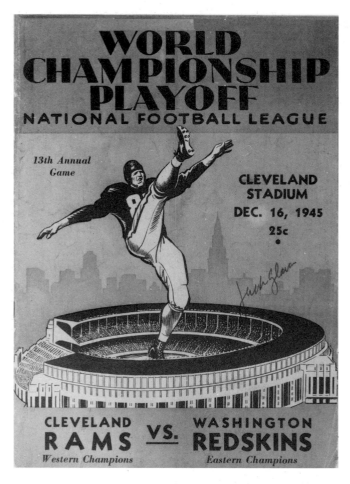

WORLD CHAMPIONSHIP PLAYOFF

NATIONAL FOOTBALL LEAGUE

13th Annual Game

CLEVELAND STADIUM
DEC. 16, 1945
25c

CLEVELAND **RAMS** VS. WASHINGTON **REDSKINS**

Western Champions *Eastern Champions*

Their offense failed them, however, when they went to Philadelphia to face the Eagles in a crucial game; if they had won it, they would have practically wrapped up the NFL East title. Washington was 6–1–0 and Philadelphia was 5–2–0, while the normally pesky Giants were out of the running with a record of 2–4–1. But the Eagles mounted a fortification that day that even Baugh could not breach, and the Redskins fell, 16–0.

The defeat proved of little importance, however, because Washington rebounded and shut out their last two opponents of the year, the Steelers, 24–0, and the Giants, 17–0, while the Eagles lost to the Giants. With an 8–2–0 record, Washington had earned its fifth NFL East title.

Baugh, enjoying his first selection as an All-Pro quarterback (his previous such honors were as a halfback), had set an NFL record by completing 70.3 percent of his passes. Slingin' Sam's 128 completions were the most in the NFL that year, and only Sid Luckman of the Bears gained more yards passing than Baugh's 1,669 yards (1,725).

Akins was second in rushing to Philadelphia's Steve Van Buren, gaining 797 yards, the most a Redskin had earned since Cliff Battles ran for 897 in 1937. Akins also posted an impressive average of 5.4 yards per carry. Bagarus led the team in pass receptions with 39 and in yards gained receiving with 637, both Washington records at the time. And Aguirre led the league with seven field goals and was successful on 23 of 24 conversion attempts, both setting new team marks.

The Redskins would not be facing the Chicago Bears as they had in their four previous title-game appearances. Instead they were to meet the Cleveland Rams, who, with a record of 9–1–0, had glided through the NFL West. The Rams were quarterbacked by rookie Bob Waterfield, destined for the Pro Football Hall of Fame, who was third that year in yards gained passing behind Luckman and Baugh. Waterfield also led the league in touchdown passes (14) and in yards

PRIORITIES

The late Jack Mara, former president of the New York Giants football team, often told the story of George Preston Marshall and his football priorities.

The Giants were in Washington one year in the mid-forties to play the Redskins when a freak snowstorm left the field under about a foot of snow. An hour before the teams were to take the field for pregame warm-ups, Mara was surveying the situation from the sideline, wondering if indeed it would be possible to play a game in all that snow.

His thoughts were interrupted, however, when he saw Marshall trudging across the field in the knee-high snow. As he approached, Marshall shook his head. "Don't worry, Jack, they're coming," he said. "They'll be here in plenty of time."

"Snowplows?" Mara asked.

"Snowplows, hell," Marshall said with a look of great disbelief. "I'm talking about overshoes for the band."

gained per pass attempt (9.4), and was a distinct threat with his bootleg runs around end.

The game was set for Municipal Stadium in Cleveland, an amphitheater that could seat 80,000. The setting was less than comfortable, however. Five inches of snow were on the ground the day before the game. And, on the day of the game, as Shirley Povich described it in his *Washington Post* column:

> Pretty soon they'll line up for the kickoff but the heroes of this Redskins-Rams game for the pro league championship are already established. They're the 32,178 fans who paid as much as $6 to watch this thing in zero weather. They're peddling hot coffee in the stands, and the lucky fans are getting it spilled all over 'em. When one clumsy vendor attempted to apologize, he was told, "Never mind, the pleasure is all mine."

On that gelid afternoon in Cleveland, the Rams were the first to march. Halfback Fred Gehrke picked up 16 yards on a crossbuck, then Waterfield connected with All-Pro

Two Washington defenders (No. 17 is tackle Fred Davis) converge on Cleveland Rams halfback Jim Gillette in the 1945 NFL championship game, played at Memorial Stadium in Cleveland in bitter cold (six degrees above zero at game time). The Redskins, after failing on two field-goal attempts in the fourth quarter, came out on the short end of a 15–14 score that day. *Photo reprinted courtesy of Bettmann Archive.*

end Jim Benton on a 30-yard pass to the Washington 14-yard line. Cleveland bulled it down to the 5, but disdained a field-goal attempt and was held on fourth down.

Instead of the three points the Rams might have gotten, they managed to get two. Baugh dropped back into the end zone to pass, but when he threw the ball it hit the goal post crossbar and bounced back at him, which, according to the rules of the day, constituted a safety, so the Rams took a 2–0 lead into the second quarter.

Worse than that, Baugh did not appear on the field for the second period, benched with some badly bruised ribs and replaced at quarterback by Filchock. But it was not all bad news in that period of play. Redskins linebacker Ki Aldrich intercepted a Waterfield pass. Moments later Filchock threw down the sideline to Bagarus at the Cleveland 20, and the halfback scooted around the Ram defender and took it in for a touchdown. Aguirre's conversion was good and Washington had a 7–2 lead.

It did not last long, however. Balancing his offensive attack, Waterfield handed off to halfback Jim Gillette, who picked up 18 yards. He hit Benton for 14 yards, and then Benton again, this time for 37 yards and a touchdown. Waterfield's extra point was tipped by a Washington defender and hit the crossbar, but it still caromed over into the end zone, and the Rams reclaimed the lead, 9–7.

In the third quarter, the Rams struck again. Waterfield went to Gillette, 32 yards in the air, and the halfback then carried the ball the remaining 12 yards for the score. This time Waterfield missed the extra point.

The Redskins came right back. Filchock threw to Bagarus for a 50-yard gain to the Cleveland 8-yard line. Then Filchock tossed one in the end zone to fullback Bob Seymour. Aguirre's kick was good and the Redskins trailed by a single point, 15–14.

The raw, freezing weather took its icy toll in the fourth quarter. Both teams were noticeably slowed. The Redskins managed to get within field-goal range twice, but both times Aguirre's kicks were wide. The game ended with the score 15–14, the Redskins being denied a victory by the crossbar that had stopped Baugh's pass in the first quarter, and being deprived of a tie by the crossbar that did not stop Waterfield's extra point in the second quarter.

For their toil in arcticlike Cleveland that December Sunday, each Redskin received $903.47 while each Ram took home $1,469.74.

SUPER BOWL VII: 1973

After a losing season in 1970, the Redskins' chief of staff, Edward Bennett Williams, and other powers of note in the organization decided on still another coaching change. Available was just the kind of leader they wanted, a coach with a history of single-handedly turning a poor team into a consistent winner.

George Allen had that reputation; controversy, however, was also part of his portfolio. In Chicago, where he had served as defensive coordinator for the Bears under George Halas, he had been given the game ball when the team's tough defense had systematically thwarted the Giants' offense in the 1963 NFL title game. The Bears won it, 14–10. But he was known around town as a "contract breacher" because he broke his contract with Halas and the Bears in order

Columnist Steve Guback of the *Sunday Star* and the Washington *Daily News* concocted this quiz for fans of the Redskins in 1972. "How well do you REALLY know the Redskins?" he asked. Not very well, he implied, if you could not match the following players with the nicknames they are known by in the confines of Redskin Park and the locker room at RFK Stadium.

Jerry Smith	Sweet-Pea
Jack Pardee	Grumpy
Roy Jefferson	Whisky
Ron McDole	Gabby
Brig Owens	Rubber-Man
Chris Hanburger	Twiggy
Larry Brown	Babycakes
Charlie Harraway	Pigpen
Billy Kilmer	Rap
Terry Hermeling	Rev.

Answers to the Nickname Quiz:

Smith	Babycakes
Pardee	Gabby
Jefferson	Sweet-Pea
McDole	Rubber-Man
Owens	Twiggy
Hanburger	Grumpy
Brown	Rap
Harraway	Rev.
Kilmer	Whisky
Hermeling	Pigpen

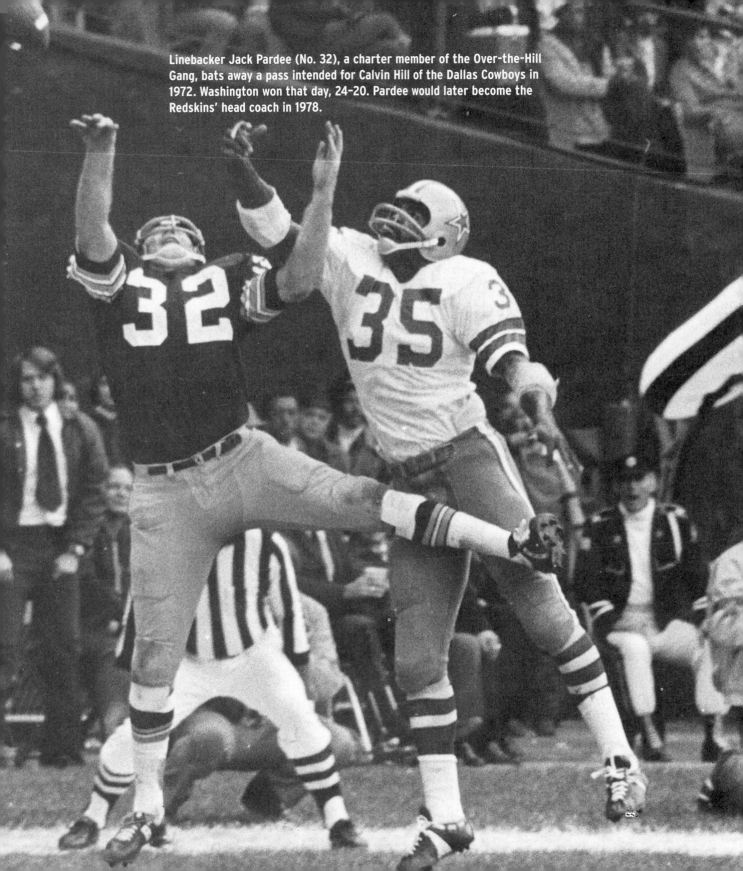

Linebacker Jack Pardee (No. 32), a charter member of the Over-the-Hill Gang, bats away a pass intended for Calvin Hill of the Dallas Cowboys in 1972. Washington won that day, 24–20. Pardee would later become the Redskins' head coach in 1978.

to take the head coaching job for the Los Angeles Rams. Halas sued Allen and won the suit in court. Then, with his point made, he released Allen from the contract.

As the 1972 football season approached, there was more excitement wafting about Washington and the surrounding environs than at perhaps any time since Sammy Baugh had gone back to Texas.

Preseason predictors, however, were touting the Cowboys, who had defeated the Miami Dolphins, 24–3, in Super Bowl VI the preceding January to again capture the NFC East crown. The Cowboys were an awesome force led by Roger Staubach at quarterback (although a shoulder injury would keep him on the bench most of the year), ably backed up by Craig Morton. They also had running back Calvin Hill, wide receiver Bob Hayes, tight end Mike Ditka, defensive tackle Bob Lilly, defensive backs Herb Adderley and Cliff Harris, and linebackers Lee Roy Jordan and Chuck Howley, to name just a few who often appeared on the All-Pro listings.

Allen was undismayed, however, and announced before the season, "This is the year Dallas falls from grace, and the Redskins are going to be the ones doing the pushing."

As it turned out, he was correct.

Sonny Jurgensen was healthy again at the start of the season, but he was now 38 years old. Despite his reverential regard for aged ballplayers, Allen decided that the 32-year-old Billy Kilmer would lead the tribe. Charley Taylor and Larry Brown were back in first-rate shape, and the defense—old, wily, gritty, and menacingly experienced—seemed ready for any offensive onslaught.

And so the Redskins charged into the season with the same vivacity they had the year before. Granted they did not win their first five straight, but they won four of them, defeating the Cardinals twice, the Eagles, and the Minnesota Vikings, who had stormed through the NFC Central the year before. Their only loss was a frustrating, depressing surprise at the hands of the New England Patriots. Curt Knight had kicked a field goal in the waning minutes of the game hoping to tie the score at 24. But an overzealous Patriot defender had bumped into Knight. The penalty gave the Redskins a first down if they chose to take it. Coach Allen said to go for the win, so the Redskins canceled the field goal and set out to score a touchdown for the victory. But they did not get the ball into the end zone. Knight came back onto the field after three fruitless downs, but

Chris Hanburger (No. 55) works out on the blocking dummy under the eyes of assistant coach Sam Huff at training camp in 1970. Hanburger was in the middle of his 14-year career with the Redskins that summer. Huff, a linebacker with the Redskins 1964–1967 and 1969, left the coaching staff after the 1970 season. He himself had an illustrious career with the New York Giants before coming to Washington and was inducted into the Pro Football Hall of Fame in 1982.

this time he missed the field goal and the Redskins succumbed of their own volition, 24–21.

The sixth game of the season brought the Cowboys to Washington. Dallas, like the Redskins, came into the game with a 4–1–0 record. Jurgensen was Washington's starting quarterback now, with Kilmer benched after the loss to New England. And Morton was the Cowboys' full-time quarterback while the injured Staubach watched from the sideline. Morton, though, appeared to be on the way to one of his best seasons ever. Despite Washington's home-field advantage, the oddsmakers favored Dallas by a touchdown.

It looked as if they were correct, at least through the first half. A field goal and a Morton touchdown pass gave Dallas a 10–0 lead at the end of the first quarter, which was extended to 13–0 in the second period. Jurgensen led a Washington drive that climaxed with a pass to Larry Brown for a touchdown, but at the half the Redskins trailed by the oddsmakers' six points.

Another seven points were added to the lead in the third quarter when true-life cowboy and Dallas Cowboy Walt Garrison burst in for a touchdown. But then, true to Allen's preseason prediction, the Cowboys began their fall from grace, and the Redskins were doing the pushing.

Larry Brown broke one for 34 yards and a touchdown to bring the score to 20–14. Knight kicked a 42-yard field goal to make it 20–17. Charlie Harraway barreled 13 yards to make the score 24–20, Redskins. And during all this offensive

SUPER BOWL VII

Site:	Memorial Coliseum, Los Angeles, California
Date:	January 14, 1973
Weather:	84°, clear and sunny
Attendance:	90,182
Gross receipts:	$4,180,086.53
Player shares:	$15,000 winner, $7,500 loser

STARTING LINEUPS

WASHINGTON REDSKINS	OFFENSE	MIAMI DOLPHINS
Charley Taylor	WR	Paul Warfield
Terry Hermeling	LT	Wayne Moore
Paul Laaveg	LG	Bob Kuechenberg
Len Hauss	C	Jim Langer
John Wilbur	RG	Larry Little
Walt Rock	RT	Norm Evans
Jerry Smith	TE	Marv Fleming

Roy Jefferson	WR	Howard Twilley
Billy Kilmer	QB	Bob Griese
Larry Brown	RB	Jim Kiick
Charlie Harraway	FB	Larry Csonka
Curt Knight	K	Garo Yepremian

DEFENSE

Ron McDole	LE	Vern Den Herder
Bill Brundige	LT	Manny Fernandez
Diron Talbert	RT	Bob Heinz
Verlon Biggs	RE	Bill Stanfill
Jack Pardee	LB	Doug Swift
Myron Pottios	MLB	Nick Buoniconti
Chris Hanburger	LB	Mike Kolen
Pat Fischer	CB	Lloyd Mumphord
Mike Bass	CB	Curtis Johnson
Brig Owens	S	Dick Anderson
Roosevelt Taylor	S	Jake Scott
Mike Bragg	P	Larry Seiple

COACHES

George Allen		Don Shula

SCORING

	1st Qtr	2nd Qtr	3rd Qtr	4th Qtr	Final Score
Redskins	0	0	0	7	7
Dolphins	7	7	0	0	14

derring-do, the "Over-the-Hill Gang" defense totally shut down the Cowboys. At the final gun, Washington had defeated the despised Texans and was in sole possession of first place in the NFC East.

The Skins continued their winning ways, taking the next six games in a row. With two games remaining, Washington was 11–1–0, and more importantly had clinched the NFC East title. Ensuing losses to the Cowboys and the Buffalo Bills were meaningless. It was the first time since 1965 that the Dallas Cowboys had not triumphed in the NFC East. And the Redskins' 11 victories would remain their most ever until another Super Bowl–bound Washington team won 14 in 1983.

The entire team contributed to the 1972 regular-season glory. The defense gave up the fewest points in the NFC, 218, for a per-game average of 15.6. Larry Brown led the NFL by gaining 1,216 yards rushing, which was also a new club record.

Kilmer, who had regained the starting job at quarterback after Jurgensen suffered a season-ending injury in the seventh game that year, was the fourth-ranked passer in the league. Charley Taylor gained 673 yards on 49 receptions, and Roy Jefferson picked up 550 on 35 catches. Six Redskins earned invitations to the Pro Bowl: Brown, Kilmer, Taylor, Len Hauss, Chris Hanburger, and "Speedy" Duncan.

The playoff alignment for 1972 pitted Washington against the Green Bay Packers, who had won the NFC Central Division with relative ease and a 10–4–0 record. The Pack was far from the powerhouse it had been during the sixties in the Lombardi years, when Paul Hornung, Bart Starr, Jim Taylor, and all the others had terrorized the league. The Packers did have a brute of a fullback in John Brockington and a good runner/receiver in halfback MacArthur Lane, but they had not looked all that impressive in falling to the Redskins at RFK

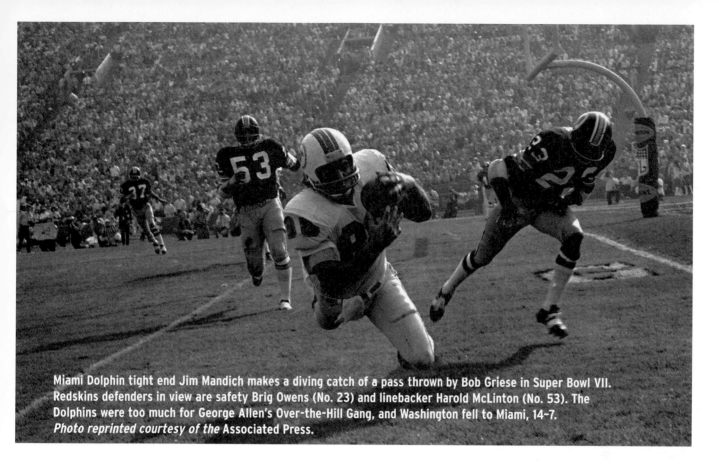

Miami Dolphin tight end Jim Mandich makes a diving catch of a pass thrown by Bob Griese in Super Bowl VII. Redskins defenders in view are safety Brig Owens (No. 23) and linebacker Harold McLinton (No. 53). The Dolphins were too much for George Allen's Over-the-Hill Gang, and Washington fell to Miami, 14-7. *Photo reprinted courtesy of the* Associated Press.

Stadium, 21–16, earlier in the year. Their second meeting was also scheduled for RFK Stadium, on Christmas Eve.

George Allen's game plan focused first on stopping the Green Bay running game. He had great faith in his defense, but he added nose guard Manny Sistrunk to help stifle the Packers rushing attack. Offensively he wanted a ball-control game: keep it on the ground, use the pass only when needed or as a surprise.

The plan worked perfectly, although Green Bay was the first to get on the scoreboard. But Chester Marcol's field goal in the second quarter provided the only points the Packers would score all afternoon.

The Redskins came right back, and Kilmer did indeed surprise the Pack, with a 32-yard toss to Roy Jefferson for a touchdown. A Washington field goal just before the half lifted the lead to 10–3. Knight added two more field goals for the Skins in the fourth quarter, and the final score was Washington 16, Green Bay 3. The defense had done just what George Allen had asked of it. The Packers rushed for only two first downs and a meager 78 yards all day.

After Super Bowl VII, both coaches summed up their sentiments. George Allen:

> It doesn't do any good to play in the Super Bowl if you don't win. Miami is not a team that impresses you on film because they execute so well. Our kicking game was not up to par. We just lost to a team that played a better game. . . . I can't get out of here [Los Angeles] fast enough. We will stay overnight and leave tomorrow morning. There will be a lot of hours of agony tonight.

Don Shula:

> When you do not go all the way, there is an empty feeling, even if you are Coach of the Year. But there is no empty feeling this year. This is the ultimate. . . . This is the greatest team I have been associated with.

The victory, of course, sent the Redskins to the NFC championship game. They would not have to travel very far, however. It, too, was to be played in RFK Stadium.

The opponent was none other than the Dallas Cowboys, a wild-card entry, the most veteran of veterans in terms of the NFL playoffs during the late sixties and early seventies. The Cowboys, who had been runner-up to the Redskins in the regular season, had put on their postseason game face and defeated the NFC West champs, the 49ers, 30–28, when a recovered Staubach came off the bench to throw two touchdown passes in the waning minutes of the game.

The title tilt took place on New Year's Eve afternoon, a chilly, damp, overcast day in D.C. Staubach was in the saddle, so to speak, for the Cowboys, and Dallas fans were thrilled to have him back, especially after he'd plucked victory from the claws of defeat the week before.

But it was not Staubach's star that would shine in the darkened sky above RFK Stadium. It was the quarterback on the Redskins side of the line of scrimmage, Billy Kilmer. After a Knight field goal got the scoring started for Washington,

Kilmer connected with the ever-reliable Charley Taylor on a 15-yard touchdown pass and took a 10–3 lead into the locker room at halftime. In the fourth quarter, Kilmer again went to Taylor, this time for a 45-yard touchdown. Knight added three more field goals that period, and the Over-the-Hill Gang defense was as stingy as it had been in the playoff game the week before, allowing only a second-quarter field goal. The final score was Washington 26, Dallas 3.

Next stop: that most glittering of sports events, the Super Bowl.

When the Miami Dolphins arrived in Los Angeles, they brought with them a note of distinction. They had won all 14 of their regular-season games. Only one other team in the history of the National Football League, which had been in operation for over half a century, had posted a perfect regular season. The Chicago Bears had done it twice, in 1934 (13–0–0) and 1942 (11–0–0). The Bears, however, had lost the title game in both of those years, to the Giants in 1934 and to the Redskins in 1942.

Miami, who by Super Bowl time had won 16 straight games, including its 2 playoff triumphs, stood on the threshold of making NFL history by becoming the first championship team with a totally unblemished record.

Surprisingly, however, the Dolphins were not the favorites. The oddsmakers favored Allen's Over-the-Hill Gang by two points. Coach Allen raised his eyebrows more than once when that fact was brought up in the two hype-filled weeks before the Super Bowl game. Allen knew he had to contend with Miami's explosive passing game, which featured Bob Griese throwing to the likes of Paul Warfield, Howard Twilley, and old vet Marv Fleming. Then there was the powerful running attack, centered on Larry Csonka, Jim Kiick, and Mercury Morris. And the Miami defense was ranked the best in the entire NFL, yielding the least number of points per game (12.2), the least number of first downs (186), and the second-least number of yards rushing (1,548, or a mere 111 per game). Allen, as was his nature, remained steadfastly positive and confident. Experience would prevail in this most pressure-packed of games, he told the assembled press and media corps, whom he found quite distracting and annoying.

It was a sunny but typically hazy day in smoggy Los Angeles, and uncomfortably hot for a football game (84° at kickoff), that mid-January afternoon when the Redskins and Dolphins took the field at the Coliseum to decide the 1972 NFL title.

The ball exchanged hands five times before any real action took place. There were just under three minutes to play in the first quarter when the Dolphins began to march. They ate up yardage on the ground; then Griese connected on a

14-yarder to Warfield. At the Washington 28-yard line, Griese threw a perfect strike to Twilley near the goal line, who carried it in for the game's first score. Garo Yepremian's extra point gave the Dolphins a 7–0 lead.

The Redskins had as much trouble moving the ball in the second period as they had had in the first quarter. At the same time, the defense was holding its own, shutting down the Miami attack, with the exception of a 47-yard touchdown bomb from Griese to Warfield that, fortunately for the Skins, was called back because of a penalty.

The Redskins were not so fortunate in the last two minutes of the period. Kilmer dropped back to pass but threw into the hands of Miami's All-Pro linebacker Nick Buoniconti, who returned it 32 yards to the Washington 27. After a pair of running plays, Griese picked up a first down by hitting tight end Jim Mandich on the Redskins' 2-yard line with a little less than 30 seconds to go in the half. Moments later, Kiick bulled it in for the touchdown, and Miami took a 14–0 halftime lead.

The Redskins had a chance to score early in the third period when they got within field-goal range, but Knight's attempt was wide. The Dolphins also had a chance to put some points on the board in the same quarter after Csonka broke free and carried the ball 49 yards to the Washington 16-yard line. But a Griese pass into the end zone was picked off by Redskins safety Brig Owens.

In the fourth quarter, the Skins marched 79 yards to the Miami 10-yard line. But when Kilmer threw into the end zone, the ball was snared by Dolphins safety Jake Scott, who ran it all the way back to the Redskins' 48-yard line. Miami moved the ball into field-goal range and Yepremian lined up for a 42-yarder. Then, in one of the classic football follies of all time, Yepremian booted the ball straight into the hands of onrushing Redskin Bill Brundige. The blocked kick rolled around before Yepremian picked it up, juggled it in panic, and then—in a mixture of lob and bobble—threw it right into the hands of Washington cornerback Mike Bass, who raced 49 yards with it for a Redskins touchdown.

Washington got the ball back with a little more than a minute to play at its own 30-yard line. Kilmer, however, could not overcome the Miami defense, which had been outstanding all day. When the game ended the Skins were back on their own 15 and the scoreboard read Miami 14, Washington 7.

Miami had made football history at the Redskins' expense. It was a game best summed up by Washington linebacker Jack Pardee after it was over. "We were never really in the game . . . and we were never really out of it." So, with disappointment but the notion that they were a certifiable contender, Allen and his Over-the-Hill Gang headed home to begin preparations for the 1973 season.

SUPER BOWL XVIII: 1984

The Super Bowl championship rings for the 1982 Redskins were not even cast before innuendos in the press and among the media implied that perhaps Washington won it only because of a strike-shortened, playoff-convoluted season. After all, before the season, the team was not even considered a contender. The season itself then proved to be an anomaly. One local newspaper, while still in the wake of the championship celebration, made a point of reminding everyone that no Super Bowl champ in the previous three years had made a return visit to the season-ending classic.

At Redskin Park the negativism was ignored, and preparation for the 1983 season got under way. Once again Joe Gibbs and his scouting system drafted wisely and well. In the first round they selected cornerback Darrell Green from Texas A&I, and following him were defensive end Charles Mann of Nevada at Reno and running back Kelvin Bryant out of North Carolina.

The preseason was a little better than the year before, with Washington defeating Cincinnati and Buffalo but falling to Atlanta and Super Bowl–foe Miami. But the regular season did not begin on the note that Coach Gibbs would have liked. The Cowboys, pegged to be the biggest threat in the NFL East, came to town to open the football year and set the Super Bowl champs down, 31–30.

Even in defeat, the Redskins illustrated clearly that they could indeed score points. At that particular time, however, no one knew that Washington was on its way to setting an NFL record for the most points scored in a single season.

After that initial setback, Gibbs got his Hogs, his running game, his passing attack, and his defense on the right track. They easily knocked off the Eagles, Kansas City, and Seattle before facing the Los Angeles Raiders, who were leading the AFC West with a 4–0–0 record and were reputed to be the best that conference had to offer in 1983.

It turned out to be one of the most exciting games ever staged at RFK Stadium. Behind the passing of Jim Plunkett, the Raiders built a 35–20 lead midway through the fourth quarter. And they had done it in a spectacular fashion. Plunkett had thrown four touchdown passes, one a 99-yarder to Cliff Branch that tied the NFL record for the longest pass play in history. Greg Pruitt ran a punt back 97 yards for a touchdown, 1 yard shy of the all-time NFL mark.

There were seven and a half minutes left when Joe Theismann set about reversing the momentum of the game. He threw a simple screen pass to Joe Washington, who raced 67 yards with it to the Los Angeles 21-yard line. Two plays later, Theismann pitched it to Charlie Brown in the end zone for a touchdown. An onside kick was recovered by the Redskins and Theismann moved his offense to the Raider 17, where Mark Moseley kicked a field goal to bring Washington within five points of Los Angeles. The Redskins defense also rose to the occasion and held, forcing Los Angeles to punt with just under two minutes left in the game. Theismann went into the two-minute drill and completed three straight passes to Brown that brought the Redskins down to the Raiders 6-yard line. On the next play, Theismann hit Washington in the end zone for the game-winning touchdown. The final score: Redskins 37, Raiders 35.

The following week the Redskins demolished the Cardinals and then went to Green Bay, where they were a heavy favorite to wreak another demolition on the mediocre Packers. But the Packers proved far from mediocre that Monday night at Lambeau Field. They jumped out in front in the first quarter when linebacker Mike Douglass scooped up a Redskins fumble and ran it 22 yards for a touchdown. Thus began one of the wildest offensive games in NFL history.

With Lynn Dickey throwing three touchdown passes for Green Bay, Theismann tossing two, and John Riggins running for another pair for the Skins, among various other methods of scoring, the score was 47–45 in favor of Washington with less than a minute remaining. But then Jan Stenerud aced a 20-yard field goal for the Pack to give them the lead. Washington came back, however, with Theismann's now one-minute drill bringing the Redskins to the Green Bay 20-yard line. With one second remaining, Moseley put foot to ball, but—to the surprise and chagrin of his legion of fans—missed the field goal. And Washington suffered its second loss of the season.

In the 48–47 loss to Green Bay, two Redskins records were set: the two-team total of 1,025 yards of offense (Redskins 552, Packers 473) and the two-team total of 771 yards passing (Redskins 368, Packers 403). In addition, of 12 possessions in the second half, the two teams scored on 10 of them.

After the pyrotechnics in Green Bay, however, there was no stopping the Washington express, which was rolling nonstop toward Tampa, Florida, where Super Bowl XVIII was scheduled to take place. Amassing large scores in every game, the Redskins handily won their last nine games, including a delightful revenge over the Cowboys in the next to last game of the year, 31–10, which also clinched the division title for Washington. When the regular season finally ended,

Defensive end Charles Mann brings a New York Giants ball carrier to the turf at RFK Stadium. Looking on are Redskins tackle Dexter Manley (No. 72) and Giants quarterback Phil Simms (No. 11). Mann, who played for Washington from 1983 through 1993, and Manley, from 1981 through 1989, proved to be one of the finest pairs of defensive linemen in Redskins history.

the Skins had a record of 14–2–0, the best in the entire NFL and the most wins in the team's history.

The total of 541 points that the Redskins scored that year remains their highest ever in an NFL regular season. The team averaged nearly 34 points a game. Moseley led the league in scoring with 161 points, the most ever by a kicker in a single season. The only player to score more points in a season up to that time was Green Bay's Paul Hornung, who set the NFL mark in 1960 when he tallied 176 points (15 touchdowns, 15 field goals, 41 extra points).

Riggins set the club record for rushing yardage (since broken) with 1,347, as well as number of carries at 374. Theismann again topped 3,000 yards passing, his 3,714 falling only 30 short of the club standard set by Sonny Jurgensen in 1967. His 276 completions out of 459 attempts (60 percent) and 29 touchdowns helped to give him a ranking of No. 2 in the NFC. Charlie Brown became only the third Redskin receiver to surpass 1,000 yards gained on receptions, with 1,225 (the first two were Bobby Mitchell and Charley Taylor). And, needless to say, the Hogs clearly controlled the trenches, or "trough," as it was now being called around Washington.

With the best record in the league, the Redskins again could treat their fans to home games throughout the playoffs. Their first opponents were the Los Angeles Rams, a wild-card entry who had eliminated the other wild-card team, the Cowboys, a week earlier.

The Rams, who were 9–7–0 in the regular season, had a major weapon in running back Eric Dickerson. He had led the league in rushing with 1,808 yards on an average carry of 4.6 yards and had picked up another 404 yards on his 51 pass receptions.

Washington's game plan was obviously geared to stopping the Los Angeles running game, which in effect meant stopping Dickerson. Joe Gibbs also said he wanted to get some points on the board early so that the Rams would have to resort to passing to get back in the game.

Washington accomplished both its goals. Dickerson was totally stopped, gaining a paltry 16 yards all afternoon on 10 carries. And the Skins were on the scoreboard early. They marched on their first possession, and Riggins burst in for the first touchdown of the day. The next time they got the ball Theismann threw to Art Monk for a 40-yard touchdown play. On the ensuing possession Moseley kicked a 42-yard field goal. The score at the end of the first quarter: Washington 17, Los Angeles 0.

CHARLEY CASSERLY (REDSKINS GENERAL MANAGER)

That was the greatest team in the history of the Redskins, in my opinion. We led the league in scoring [485 points]. We were second in defensive points allowed [224]. We were 14–1 going into the final game of the year. We're ahead of Philadelphia, and Joe [Gibbs] pulls [Mark] Rypien from the game. The Eagles come back and beat us on a field goal. That's how close we were to 15–1.

In the second period, Riggins ran in two more for touchdowns and Monk caught a 21-yarder from Theismann for still another score. The Rams managed to post seven points when Vince Ferragamo threw a TD pass to Preston Dennard, but at the half they trailed by an insurmountable margin of 38–7.

Moseley added a pair of field goals in the third quarter. Then, in the final period, Darrell Green grabbed a Ferragamo pass that bounced off Dickerson's hands and streaked 72 yards for the last touchdown of the day. The Redskins' defense was virtually impenetrable during the second half. The final score, in one of the most lopsided games in NFL postseason history: Redskins 51, Rams 7.

The victory earned the Skins the right to host the team that had edged the Rams out of the NFC West title, Bill Walsh's San Francisco 49ers. Frisco had won 10 games and lost 6 during the regular season, and its method of attack was considerably different from that of the Rams. Walsh liked to pass, and one of the chief reasons was that he had Joe Montana at quarterback. He also had All-Pros Dwight Clark and Freddie Solomon on the receiving end, as well as rookie Roger Craig, who had proved to be a distinct threat coming out of the backfield. Clark, however, was injured and therefore unavailable for the title game.

More than 55,000 filled RFK Stadium for the NFC championship game January 8, 1984, the Redskins' 132nd consecutive sellout there. The Redskins did not come raging out of the chute as they had the week before against the Rams, but then neither did the 49ers. Both teams fumbled the ball to the other to stop scoring drives in the first period, and as the clock ran out there were only a pair of goose eggs on the scoreboard.

In the second quarter, Washington finally made its move. Theismann passed to tight end Clint Didier for a 46-yard gain. With the ball at the San Francisco 4, Riggins got the call and blasted in for a touchdown. It and Moseley's conversion were the only points of the period.

The Redskins did come on with a rage at the start of the second half, however. Defensive back Green jarred the ball loose from the 49ers' Freddie Solomon, who had caught a Montana pass deep in his own territory, and then recovered it for Washington. The Skins capitalized on it when Riggins eventually bucked in from the 1-yard line. Then, on their next possession, the Redskins seemed to have iced the game when Theismann tossed a 70-yard bomb to Charlie Brown. With the help of Washington's outstanding defense, the score going into the last period of play was 21–0, Washington.

The fans were not leaving the stadium to celebrate what appeared now to be imminent victory, but they were complacent, and visions of Super Bowl XVIII were dancing in a lot of their heads. The least complacent person in RFK Stadium, however, was Joe Montana. He had been stymied and stifled through three quarters of play.

With pinpoint passing, Montana moved the ball for the 49ers, and from the Washington 5 hit wide receiver Mike Wilson for San Francisco's first score of the day. On the 49ers' next possession, Montana dropped back from his own 24-yard line and rifled the ball to a speeding Solomon, who took it all the way downfield for another touchdown. Suddenly the 49ers were within a touchdown of the Redskins. And Montana was not through. After the 49ers forced a Washington punt, Montana conducted another successful drive, then threw his third touchdown in

SUPER BOWL XVIII

Site:	Tampa Stadium, Tampa, Florida	
Date:	January 22, 1984	
Weather:	68°, cloudy	
Attendance:	72,920	
Gross receipts:	$20,002,390.28	
Player shares:	$36,000 winner, $18,000 loser	

STARTING LINEUPS

WASHINGTON REDSKINS	OFFENSE	LOS ANGELES RAIDERS
Charlie Brown	WR	Cliff Branch
Joe Jacoby	LT	Bruce Davis
Russ Grimm	LG	Charley Hannah
Jeff Bostic	C	Dave Dalby
Mark May	RG	Mickey Marvin
George Starke	RT	Henry Lawrence
Don Warren	TE	Todd Christensen

Art Monk	WR	Malcolm Barnwell
Joe Theismann	QB	Jim Plunkett
Rick Walker	RB	Marcus Allen
John Riggins	FB	Kenny King
Mark Moseley	K	Chris Bahr

DEFENSE

Todd Liebenstein	LE	Howie Long
Dave Butz	LT/NT	Reggie Kinlaw
Darryl Grant	RT/RE	Lyle Alzado
Dexter Manley	RE/OLB	Ted Hendricks
Mel Kaufman	LB/ILB	Matt Millen
Neal Olkewicz	MLB/ILB	Bob Nelson
Rich Milot	LB/OLB	Rod Martin
Darrell Green	CB	Lester Hayes
Anthony Washington	CB	Mike Haynes
Ken Coffey	S	Mike Davis
Mark Murphy	S	Vann McElroy
Jeff Hayes	P	Ray Guy

COACHES

Joe Gibbs		Tom Flores

SCORING

	1st Qtr	2nd Qtr	3rd Qtr	4th Qtr	Final Score
Redskins	0	3	6	0	9
Raiders	7	14	14	3	38

The Super Bowl has never been known for understatement or its lack of conspicuous consumption, pizzazz, hype, and pageantry, much less its endless parade of celebrities. As Ira Berkow wrote for *The New York Times* regarding Super Bowl XVIII:

> Not since 1539, when Hernando de Soto arrived with the greatest sea armada ever assembled for the New World exploration, has Tampa Bay experienced anything like Super Bowl week.
>
> An estimated 80,000 people, pachyderms, and football players trooped in to participate in the numerous events of the week, many of which were centered in the small banner-strewn downtown section of this town of about 300,000.
>
> Frank Sinatra crooned, Jesse Jackson orated, Bob Hope joked, and belly dancers gyrated.
>
> Jane Fonda was here, Ted Koppel was here, but a former college lineman, Ronald Reagan, was a no-show. He was receiving the "leather-helmet" award at the National Football League alumni dinner Saturday night but called in his regrets and appreciation.

Why were they all there, or almost all? Because it was, in the vernacular of Sid Caesar, the "Show of Shows." It lasts a week, until Super Bowl Sunday finally dawns. And even then, the show still goes on—before, in, and around the game itself. This excerpt from the official program of Super Bowl XVIII gives an idea of the last act of the show—the Super Sunday crescendo:

PREGAME AND HALFTIME ENTERTAINMENT:
LOGISTICAL SPECTACULARS

> Super Bowl XVIII pregame festivities will begin at Tampa Stadium 90 minutes before kickoff with highlights of the past 17 Super Bowls, which will be shown on the Diamond Vision scoreboard. . . .

One of the world's most popular recording artists, Barry Manilow, will be singing the National Anthem today. Manilow has an incredible string of 25 consecutive "Top 40" hits and 10 straight platinum albums (given for sales of one to four million). To date, he has total international sales of 50 million records. Manilow, who has won an Emmy, a Grammy, and has been voted the American Music Award's Top Male Pop Vocalist, also has been selected the United Way of America's National Chairman for Youth and Voluntarism.

During the National Anthem, a color guard from MacDill Air Force Base near Tampa will be stationed on the field. As the anthem is being played, a huge (160' x 97') American flag donated by Thomas "Ski" Demski will be unfurled. The flag will stretch from the goal line to the 50-yard line.

One of the NFL's most famous figures, Bronko Nagurski, will be today's honorary coin tosser prior to kickoff. The legendary Chicago Bears fullback (who played with the Bears from 1930 to 1937 and in 1943) was elected as a charter member of the Pro Football Hall of Fame in 1963.

Walt Disney World in Orlando, Florida, promises the Super Bowl's most spectacular halftime show yet, which is titled "Super Bowl XVIII's Salute to the Superstars of the Silver Screen."

The show will feature all of the favorite Disney characters, as well as 1,200–1,400 other performers, the bulk of whom are made up of local students from the Hillsborough School District in Tampa.

Disney held auditions in October at local schools and any interested student in the district was encouraged to participate. The students who were selected began group rehearsals at 11 area high schools late in December. The individual groups rehearsed three or four times in a three-week period, and last Sunday Disney brought the groups together for a walk-through practice. On Friday, January 20, a full-scale dress rehearsal was held at Tampa's Laito High School.

Getting all the various elements and performers to the game will be a challenge for Walt Disney World. A platoon of 50–60 buses will be used to transport the performers to Tampa Stadium. The buses will arrive after kickoff in an attempt to avoid the traffic prior to the game. After the buses have arrived, all the performers will assemble outside the stadium and wait for halftime to begin. During the show, a stage crew of 200 will be on hand to help facilitate set changes.

John Madden, former Raiders coach and now color commentator on CBS pro football television broadcasts, predicted that Super Bowl XVIII would be an unpredictable game:

> I compare it to Duran-Leonard [boxing bout]. Nobody knew who would win. That's what makes it such a great matchup. And there are a lot of reasons why.
>
> Both teams are built to play on their grass home fields, and the field at Tampa Stadium is grass.
>
> It'll be the Raiders defense versus the Hogs. Neither group will be intimidated. Can you imagine Russ Grimm and John Riggins intimidated?
>
> Both are physical teams. There'll be no finesse out there.
>
> Both teams have the great running back, Marcus Allen with Los Angeles and the Redskins' Riggins. . . .
>
> Both teams have a great coach. Washington's Joe Gibbs is known for his offensive talents, but Tom Flores also has done an outstanding job. . . .
>
> It will probably come down to the number of turnovers.

Well, you can't be right all the time, John.

seven minutes, a 12-yarder to Wilson. A stunned crowd became dismally aware that the ticket to the Super Bowl they thought they had in hand had been snatched away.

However, now it was Theismann's turn to go to work. No longer could he settle for handing the ball off in hopes of eating time off the clock. The Skins needed a score. Starting from his own 22-yard line, Theismann engineered the perfect drive, moving the ball steadily and slowly down the field. Granted, he was aided by two controversial penalties against the 49ers, a pass-interference call on a toss intended for Monk and a holding call against All-Pro safety Ronnie Lott. Still, Theismann used up a crucial six minutes and 12 seconds before he turned the attack over on a fourth down to the foot of Mark Moseley at the 49ers' 8-yard line.

It was a chip shot, as they say. But Moseley uncharacteristically had missed four field-goal attempts earlier. The usually reliable kicker was having the worst day of his football life. But Moseley redeemed himself, booting the ball straight through the uprights. The defense held. And the game ended with Washington on top, 24–21, and breathing a collective sigh of relief after finally thwarting one of the most exciting comebacks in NFL playoff history. Riggins gained more than 100 yards rushing, making it six playoff games in a row that he had broken the century mark, an NFL record. And it was the second playoff game in a row in which Charlie Brown caught passes for more than 100 yards.

So, it was on to Tampa and Super Bowl XVIII, with Joe Gibbs gleefully reminding the naysayers that a team could indeed make a return trip to the championship classic two seasons in a row.

The matchup in Tampa for the 18th Super Bowl had all the prerequisites for a wild, exciting, offensive football game. Neither Redskins nor Raiders fans could forget the 37–35 thriller that Washington had won in RFK Stadium back in early October. Both teams were explosive, the Redskins having scored the most points in NFL history during their regular season and the Raiders not far behind, having scored at least 20 points in every game that year.

Under Coach Tom Flores, the Raiders had produced a record of 12–4–0 and had easily triumphed in the AFC West. They had an excellent passing game anchored by the arm of Jim Plunkett, who had completed 230 of 379 passes for 2,935 yards and 20 touchdowns that year. His favorite receiver was tight end Todd Christensen, who had pulled in 92 receptions for 1,247 yards. The Raiders also had a potential game breaker in speedy wide receiver Cliff Branch. And, of course, they had All-Pro running back Marcus Allen, who had gained 1,014 yards rushing in 1983. The defense was formidable, with linemen like Lyle Alzado and Howie Long, linebacker Ted Hendricks, and defensive back Lester Hayes.

Los Angeles had had little trouble sailing through the AFC playoffs. It whipped the once mighty Pittsburgh Steelers, 38–10, and then squelched the Seattle Seahawks, 31–14. Marcus Allen had rushed for over 100 yards in each game, and Plunkett had passed for more than 200 in each as well.

As dominant as the Redskins had been all year, and despite the fact that they had won two more games than had the Raiders, and had defeated them, the game was viewed as a toss-up by the oddsmakers. Former coach turned broadcaster John Madden was in agreement:

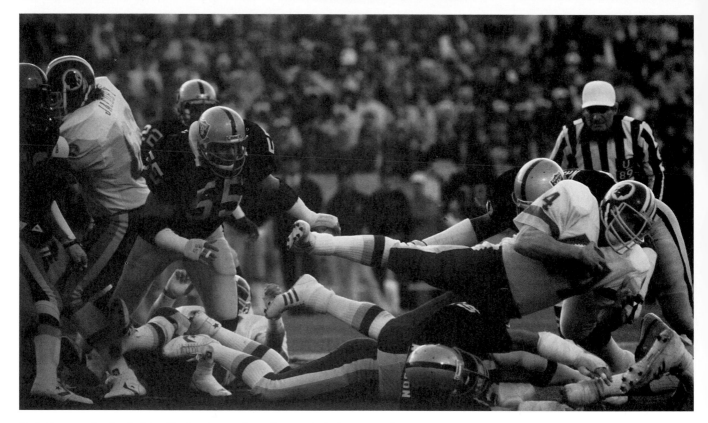

Redskins running back John Riggins lunges for a few yards in Super Bowl XVIII, against the Los Angeles Raiders, played at Tampa Stadium in Florida. Riggins was held to 64 yards rushing that day and the Raiders shut down the rest of the otherwise heralded Washington offense (the most prolific in the NFL that year). The final score: Raiders 38, Redskins 9.
Photo courtesy of Vernon Biever Photography.

Last year I predicted the Redskins to upset the Dolphins. But in this game between the Redskins and Raiders, I can't say who will win.

Well, he probably could have by halftime. The cloudy afternoon turned to pure gloom for the Redskins early in the game. Jeff Hayes was back to punt in his own end zone, but the Hogs were asleep at the trough. Derrick Jensen slithered through, slapped the ball to the turf, and then fell on it for a touchdown.

The Raiders tried to be fair about the whole thing and fumbled a punt back to the Redskins, but Washington could only move to the Los Angeles 28-yard line. Moseley, so good for so much of the regular season—his 33 field goals were the third most in NFL history—came on, but missed the three-pointer.

Washington went to the reliable Riggins, but the holes were not there and the Redskins were not getting anywhere. Theismann was having difficulty locating a receiver when he needed one. To make matters worse, Plunkett stung the Redskins with a toss over the middle to Branch that resulted in a 50-yard gain. Several plays later, Plunkett drilled one to Branch in the end zone, and the Raiders had a 14-point lead.

The Skins finally got a drive going midway through the second quarter, but it bogged down at the Los Angeles 8-yard line. Moseley came on and this time connected to put Washington on the scoreboard. But then the gloom got gloomier for Redskins fans. With only 12 seconds left in the half and the Skins deep in their own territory, almost everyone assumed Washington would simply run the clock out. Instead, Theismann faked a handoff and threw the ball toward the sideline to running back Joe Washington. But Raider linebacker Jack Squirek was not fooled. He streaked in front of Washington and snatched the ball at the 5-yard line, then continued on into the end zone. At the half it was 21–3, Raiders.

Washington came back in the third period with a concerted drive that ate up 70 yards and was climaxed by a 1-yard plunge by Riggins into the end zone. Moseley's extra point was blocked, however. Then the Raiders countered with a 70-yard march of their own on the next possession, culminated when Marcus Allen carried it in from the 5-yard line.

As the third quarter was about to close, Allen took a pitchout from Plunkett and headed around left end, saw an opening, cut back, and then broke away on a dazzling 74-yard touchdown run. It was a Super Bowl record. The score going into the fourth quarter was Los Angeles 35, Washington 9.

It was, in effect, all over at that point. A dull fourth quarter saw only one score, a 21-yard field goal for the Raiders by Chris Bahr. The final score: Raiders 38, Redskins 9, at the time the widest margin of victory in Super Bowl history.

It had been a surprise to the oddsmakers, John Madden, and especially the Redskins themselves and their loyalists. In the locker room after the game, a weary and disconsolate Joe Gibbs said:

The season is so long. You go 17, 18, 19 games without a break; it's hard on a team to go through it. We were emotionally spent. We just weren't up for it today.

The Redskins, however, had made it to back-to-back Super Bowls, joining such select company as the Green Bay Packers (Super Bowls I and II), Dallas Cowboys (V and VI, XII and XIII), Miami Dolphins (VII and VIII), Minnesota Vikings (VIII and IX), and Pittsburgh Steelers (IX and X, XIII and XIV).

8

The Great Coaches

RAY FLAHERTY

After the Redskins had, with sweet revenge, won the 1942 NFL championship by defeating the Chicago Bears, they also suffered a loss. Coach Ray Flaherty put down his whistle and clipboard and left for the U.S. Navy and World War II.

Flaherty, who had been at the helm of the Redskins since 1936, led them to their first title in 1937 and their second in 1942, and logged an enviable record

Head Coach Ray Flaherty poses with his championship team after the Redskins defeated the Chicago Bears in the 1942 NFL title game. No. 33 is Sammy Baugh, who threw a pass for one touchdown, then on defense intercepted a pass in the end zone to stop a crucial Bears drive. In his seven years as head coach of the Redskins, Flaherty compiled a record of 54-21-3. His winning percentage of .712 is the best in Redskins history.

of 54–21–3 (.712). Only subsequent pilots Joe Gibbs and George Allen have won more games for Washington than Flaherty.

Ray Flaherty returned from World War II and coached in the new All America Football Conference for the New York Yankees (1946–1948) and the Chicago Hornets (1949).

This tribute in the 1942 championship game program summed up the feelings for Flaherty of fans and team alike:

> **They call him the Knute Rockne of pro football. The guys in the know . . . they say that Ray Flaherty, head coach of the Washington Redskins, is the smartest coach in football today.**
>
> **The thousands of Washington fans, who in every game have seen Ray play as hard from the bench as most of the boys do on the field, will miss him next year when he's playing that real tough ballgame for Uncle Sam. . . .**
>
> **The big redhead from Spokane, Washington, will be missed by the fans, but he'll be missed even more by the Redskins players. There is not a man on the squad who wouldn't fight his heart out for Flaherty. . . .**
>
> **Flaherty is big and tough and hard; but he's fair and he's kind. He's going into a tough scrap. He will take with him the admiration and respect and good wishes of every Redskin fan and player.**

VINCE LOMBARDI

In spite of their extraordinary aerial attack, the Redskins were not able to win more than 5 of their 14 games in 1967, and their record of 5–6–3 left them ahead of only the first-year Saints in the NFL Capitol Division.

It was surely not the fault of Sonny Jurgensen, who turned in a record-setting year. The "rotund rifle," as one scribe referred to him, set NFL records by completing 288 passes (in 508 attempts) for 3,747 yards and established a club record of 31 touchdown passes. Jurgensen's three favorite receivers were still Charley Taylor (70 catches, the league high, for 990 yards), Jerry Smith (67 receptions for 849 yards), and Bobby Mitchell (60 snares for 866 yards).

In 1968, middle linebacker Sam Huff retired and All-Pro safety Paul Krause was traded to the Vikings for linebacker Marlin McKeever. Washington acquired Heisman Trophy–winning quarterback Gary Beban, who had shone at UCLA but,

Head Coach Otto Graham (with the whistle around his neck) poses with his assistant coaches in 1967. In his three years leading the Redskins, 1966-1968, Graham was 17–22–3.

as it would turn out, could not maintain that luminescence as a pro. Jurgensen was plagued with rib injuries for much of the season, and the running game was practically nonexistent. The result was a disappointing 5–9–0 season.

It was time for a change, decreed Edward Bennett Williams, and it was one that reverberated through the nation's capital. It was not the departure of Otto Graham, which had in fact been expected. It was the hiring, as head coach and general manager, of the legendary Vince Lombardi, who had engineered the Green Bay Packers' turnaround from the disaster of the fifties to the dynasty of the sixties. Fans referred to it as the "coming of St. Vince" and looked forward to a plethora of miracles.

But with the arrival of Lombardi, there was also the departure of George Preston Marshall. The Big Chief, after a long illness, died in August 1969.

The first miracle Lombardi pulled off was the drafting and development of running back Larry Brown from Kansas State. Brown would add life to a running attack that had been stagnant for more than a decade.

Next he took an uninspired, undisciplined group of players, integrated them with some new blood, and turned the entire mixture into a well-trained, motivated football team. The result was a heightened level of excitement and a renewed anticipation of winning among Redskins fans, feelings that had rarely been there during the previous 20 years.

The Redskins got off on the proverbial right foot in 1969 by defeating the New Orleans Saints. But by the time they made their debut that year at D.C. Stadium, they were 1–1–1. It did not deter a sellout crowd from watching Lombardi's Skins devour the St. Louis Cardinals, 33–17, and make believers of fans and skeptics alike.

The team was truly the most exciting in many years and the fans were more exuberant than they had been in an age. It lasted through the entire season, and when it was over a grinning, gap-toothed Vince Lombardi celebrated a 7–5–2 record and a second-place finish in the Capitol Division.

By 1969, after 24 lackluster years, Redskins fans were ready for a savior.

The legend, Vince Lombardi, barks some instructions to his Redskins during calisthenics. Lombardi coached only one year, 1969, a season in which he turned a loser into a winner; the teams' record for that season was 7-5-2. As Hall of Famer Bobby Mitchell recalled, "He scared us into winning."

Lombardi had successfully developed a balanced offensive attack and had inspired the defense to be intimidating, although it was clearly not as strong as he would have liked. At season's end, Lombardi vowed it would be better in 1970. No one doubted their sainted leader.

Jurgensen had been allowed to do what he did best and had ended up the league's top passer in 1969, completing 274 passes for 3,102 yards and 22 touchdowns. Taylor caught the second-most passes in the NFL that year, 71 for 883 yards. Rookie Larry Brown rushed for 888 yards and Charlie Harraway ran for 428. All told, six Redskins went to the Pro Bowl, the most in some time: Jurgensen, Brown, Jerry Smith, Chris Hanburger, Pat Fischer, and Len Hauss.

The emphasis on defense for 1970 was apparent in the draft, when Lombardi took defensive end Bill Brundige of Colorado as his first pick, followed by defensive tackle Manny Sistrunk from Arkansas A&M.

Just when everything seemed to be going right for the Redskins, tragedy struck. The seemingly immortal Vince Lombardi proved only too mortal when he

Coach Vince Lombardi (right), linebacker Sam Huff (No. 70), and defensive back Rickie Harris (29) on the sideline in a downpour during the 1969 preseason. Lombardi brought Washington its first season above .500 since 1955.

was struck down by cancer. He would not be with the team for training camp, he explained, and the head coaching duties would be handled by his chief assistant, Bill Austin. Two weeks before the 1970 regular season, Lombardi died, and a football nation mourned the passing of one of the game's greatest coaches and most inspiring figures.

Bill Austin (foreground) was in his first year as a Redskins assistant coach in 1969 when this photo was taken. The following year he served as a bridge between head coaches Vince Lombardi (looking on from the left here) and George Allen, who took over in 1971. Austin was 6-8-0 as head coach in 1970. Also observing here is assistant coach Sam Huff (right).

LONE STAR DIETZ'S TRICK PLAYS

William "Lone Star" Dietz was a team-mate of Jim Thorpe's at Carlisle in the early 1900s. After coaching a U.S. Marine Corps team in World War I, he coached on the college level at Washington State, Purdue, Louisiana Tech, Wyoming, Haskell, and Albright before taking over the Redskins in 1933. During his two years with the Skins (1933–1934), he won 11 games, lost 11, and had 2 ties.

Lone Star Dietz was a colorful coach in many ways, from his costumes to his trick plays—which, incidentally, almost never worked. Cliff Battles described the plays in an interview with Bob Curran for his book *Pro Football's Rag Days:*

He had a fondness for trick plays. One of these was the Fake Fumble. On the Fake Fumble play the tailback would get the pass from center and then fake a fumble. At this the defense was supposed to relax. Then the tailback would either leap into the air and throw a pass or he would run with the ball.

Then there was the Broken Shoelace play. One of our players would pretend he had a broken shoelace and we would all pretend we had taken a time-out. When the defense relaxed, we would do almost anything.

We didn't like these plays. I didn't especially because I always ended up getting pounded harder than usual by the other team. Lone Star used to take our quarterbacks aside and bribe them. He'd give them money out of his own pocket if they would call these special trick plays.

When I found out about the bribes, I told him that he was going to give me special compensation for the pounding I took on those plays. Nothing came of that, of course.

But the best was a thing Lone Star called the "squirrel cage." It was for a kickoff. In those days no one kicked from a tee, and therefore the ball would usually come low and fast, a line drive. Well, with the extra time that afforded us we would sometimes use the "squirrel cage." After the ball was kicked to us, we would all run back to about the 10-yard line and form a huddle. The man who had caught the kickoff would hand it over to another player. Then we would all break out running as if we had the ball hidden behind our backs. The player we usually gave the ball to was Turk Edwards, who was over 250 pounds and the biggest man on the team. No one would think that he was carrying the ball. They would tackle all of the backs and the ends and the like, and Turk would lumber up the field with the ball hidden behind his back. He got 50 yards or more on a couple of occasions, and the crowd used to love it.

He [Coach Allen] *is* different. I've never met anyone in my life so determined to win. As you know, people who are "different" irritate other people. I also think you'll have to agree that most people are negative-minded, and it is natural for these people to dislike George. He's a winner, and winners antagonize negative-minded people. His system is the best, his practice program is the best, his training camp is the best . . . George is the best-organized coach I've ever been around.

Austin, who had been second in command to Lombardi for many years at Green Bay, had a difficult job trying to carry on in the wake of Lombardi. After they lost the first two games of the 1970 regular season and then five in a row later in the year, it appeared that the Skins had reverted to their pre-Lombardi doldrums. Their record of 6–8–0 left them in fourth place in the NFC East, clearly outclassed by the Cowboys, the Giants, and the Cardinals.

But the clouds that had shrouded Griffith Stadium and D.C. Stadium since 1946 were about to be swept away. The first blast of wind would come with the hiring of the volatile and victory-oriented George Allen.

GEORGE ALLEN

When George Allen took over as head coach and general manager of the Washington Redskins in 1971, he decided immediately that the future indeed had to be *now*. The last two and a half decades had produced a dizzying series of failures, with only four winning seasons

Head Coach George Allen talks strategy with a member of his "Over-the-Hill Gang," linebacker Jack Pardee, in 1971. Pardee himself went into coaching after his playing days were over, and he became the Redskins' head coach in 1978.

Was George Allen the perpetrator of clandestine deeds, the employer of surreptitious agents? Only Allen himself knows—or if he was, only Allen and his undercover army know—but many an NFL coaching rival would swear that Allen and/or members of his coaching staff were prone to spying on the closed practice sessions of his upcoming opponents.

There was the time in Philadelphia, for example, when Eagles trainer Otho Davis swore that he saw a member of Allen's staff, dressed in dungarees and wearing a welder's hat, lurking about the otherwise empty stands of Veterans Stadium while the Eagles were preparing for a game against Washington.

Another incident of similar repute occurred when Allen was guiding the Rams in 1967. It seems Tex Schramm, then Dallas Cowboys general manager, announced to the press that a suspicious-looking yellow Chevrolet had been parked across from the team's practice field. He had taken down the license number and after a little investigation had determined that it was a Hertz rental car that had been rented to, of all people, Johnny Sanders—then chief of the Rams' scouting system.

Allen immediately retorted with a countercharge. He said that his coaching staff had observed a man, sitting up in a eucalyptus tree with binoculars, spying on the Rams' practice session. They had chased the man but had not caught him. According to Allen, however, the man looked an awful lot like Frank "Bucko" Kilroy, the former Philadelphia Eagles All-Pro guard who was now employed by the Cowboys as a scout.

If the two teams were spying on each other, Allen's secret service must have been more adroit, because the Rams annihilated the Cowboys the following Sunday, 35–13.

since 1945. The present was hardly any better, with Allen inheriting a young team that had lost five of its last seven games the previous season.

After five winning years as head coach of the Los Angeles Rams, Allen signed a contract with Washington that made him the highest-paid coach in NFL history. His annual salary of $125,000 was also supplemented by a variety of perks and incentive bonuses.

One of Allen's first moves was to initiate the construction of Redskins Park, a $750,000, multiuse training facility and office complex that featured two practice fields, one with natural grass and the other with an artificial surface.

Then came the trades. Allen's philosophy was to build a team around proven veterans. And he went after them with gusto. As author David Slattery observed:

He sent future draft choices around like pellets from a shotgun. When he finished, he had taken the team from a young, rebuilding group to a covey of veterans soon known as the "Over-the-Hill Gang."

In 1971, Allen's bartering activity totaled 19 trades, involving 24 draft choices and 33 players (8 of whom had played for Allen in Los Angeles). The most notable oldster/newcomers were quarterback Billy Kilmer from the Saints, linebackers Jack Pardee and Myron Pottios and defensive tackle Diron Talbert from the Rams, wide receiver Roy Jefferson from the Colts, defensive ends Verlon Biggs from the Jets and Ron McDole from the Bills, and defensive backs Richie Petitbon from the Rams and "Speedy" Duncan from the Chargers. Allen even managed to talk former Green Bay Packers star receiver Boyd Dowler out of retirement.

Allen also arrived in the nation's capital with his mouth full of inspirational slogans: "Every year is the most important year." "What we do in the off-season will determine what we do in the regular season." They were carefully logged by everyone from the beat sports reporter to columnist Art Buchwald. Said Allen:

When I came to Washington, I had to *sell* winning. Even whether or not I had to, I felt it was proper and the time to do it was right away. If not, it would not become a way of life, and I believe that it must. I found cooperation in this respect, though some people weren't used to working hard to achieve it. To have a job and not be one of the best . . . well, in my mind, there is something wrong with anyone who thinks that way.

The roots of Allen's enthusiasm for football and devotion to winning can be traced to his undergraduate college days at Alma College in Michigan and Marquette University, where he played end. (Allen also received a master's degree from Stanford.) He began college-level coaching at Morningside in Iowa (1948–1951), then moved to Whittier College in California in 1952 and remained there for five years.

George Allen (with the football), surrounded by his assistant coaches, was famous for his statement "The future is now" and his preference for seasoned veterans. He brought to Washington a group of NFL old-timers who acquired the nickname the "Over-the-Hill Gang," although they were far from over the hill—they carried the Redskins to Super Bowl VII in the 1972 season. Allen is the second-winningest coach in Redskins history; only Joe Gibbs has won more games. In his seven years with Washington, Allen was 67-30-1. His win percentage of .689 at Washington is second only to Ray Flaherty's .712.

In 1957, Allen began his NFL coaching career as an assistant to Sid Gillman with the Los Angeles Rams. The following season he went to the Chicago Bears to assist "Papa Bear" George Halas as defensive coordinator. In 1963, Allen's league-leading defensive platoon with the Bears battered and stifled every opponent and proved to be the key ingredient in bringing the Bears that year's NFL crown (so instrumental that Halas awarded Allen the championship game ball).

A *WASHINGTON POST* EDITORIAL ON COACH ALLEN

His single-minded insistence on unstinting, unquestioning reinforcement from everybody—fans, football writers, and owners alike—also prompted him to petty, self-pitying outbursts when things went wrong, as witness his embittered parting shots (he called club president Williams "Devious . . . deceitful . . . a Jekyll and Hyde"). And that is why, while applauding his accomplishments and wishing him well, we look upon his parting with emotions that are mixed.

In 1966, Allen accepted the head coaching job with the Rams and was promptly sued by George Halas for breach of contract; after taking Allen to court, the Bears' legendary owner and coach finally relented and released Allen from his contract.

With the Rams, Allen developed the reputation of being a "player's coach," one which served him well when team owner Dan Reeves tried to fire him after the 1968 season. A player revolt forced Reeves to reinstate Allen, who then led the Rams to the playoffs in 1969. Said Allen:

I think I can handle all my players. I treat them like I hope I would be treated. I take time and I spend time with them. Part of the misunderstanding that grows up in this business is not doing that, not helping them better themselves.

Ted Marchibroda (left), talking here with quarterback Norm Snead, was the offensive coach of the Redskins from 1961 to 1965 and from 1971 to 1974. Snead quarterbacked the Redskins from 1961 through 1963.

While Allen will be forever remembered as a champion of veterans, he also pioneered the free-agent camps that gave unknowns and the overlooked a chance at playing in the NFL.

Allen turned down offers from the Green Bay Packers and the Houston Oilers to accept the Redskins job in 1971. He added a new coaching staff, three of whom would later become NFL head coaches themselves: Marv Levy, Ted Marchibroda, and Mike McCormack.

The Over-the-Hill Gang provided the seasoned squad that Allen felt would lead Washington back into contention. Allen's emphasis on discipline and defense, coupled with his many-faceted motivational tactics, spurred the Redskins to a 9–4–1 record his first year on the job and earned Washington its first playoff berth since 1945. Allen was a unanimous selection as NFC Coach of the Year, an award he would also receive the following year, and again in 1976. After that first winning season, Allen explained:

An aging team is the least of my worries. If you do things right at the start of any football operation, you don't have to build and rebuild. We have a solid club in Washington. They win because they want to win.

Winning, of course, has a way of unifying a team and its fans, and the Redskins found faithful support for their new coach and his unorthodox philosophy.

In 1972, his second season, Allen gave Washingtonians their first conference title in 27 years. With an 11–3–0 record, the Redskins and the now-famous "Ramskins" defense held playoff foes Green Bay and Dallas to just three points

A chalk talk in the Redskins locker room administered by Coach Joe Gibbs.

apiece and advanced almost effortlessly to the team's first Super Bowl before falling to the AFC champion Miami Dolphins.

In his seven years as head coach at Washington, Allen posted a record of 67–30–1, making him the winningest coach in Redskins history, at least until Joe Gibbs came along in the eighties. Allen took his Over-the-Hill Gang to the playoffs five times. His winning percentage (including his years with the Rams) of .684 is high enough to rank him among the top 10 coaches in NFL history.

JOE GIBBS

Joe Gibbs likes strike-stressed seasons. That is not to say he likes the idea of his players (or any NFL players for that matter) going out on strike. But every time they do, he wins a Super Bowl for Washington.

In the strike-shortened season of 1982, only his second as head coach, Gibbs brought the Redskins through it with eight wins in nine games and then added three decisive victories in the playoffs before knocking off the Miami Dolphins, 27–17, in Super Bowl XVII.

With his regular squad flanking a replacement team in the discombobulated season of 1987, Gibbs guided the strikers and the scabs to a divisional title with a record of 11–4–0 (one game was lost to the strike), through the playoffs, and into Super Bowl XX. There his marauding Redskins decimated the Denver Broncos, 42–10.

Needless to say, those two striking seasons, along with the 1991 Super Bowl season, have been the highlights of Gibbs' career as head coach in Washington. Overall, however, since taking over the team in 1981, Gibbs became the winningest coach in Washington Redskins history. His teams won 124 games against 60 losses, breaking the mark George Allen set when his teams won 67, lost 30, and tied 1 game in the seventies. His record in the playoffs stands at 16 victories and just 5 defeats. He left after the 1992 season and began a successful career as a race-car owner.

Gibbs began his coaching career at San Diego State in 1964, as assistant to Don Coryell. In 1967 he was tapped for the job of offensive-line coach at Florida State under Bill Peterson, and the team compiled a record of 15–4–2 in the two years he was there. In 1969 he went to work for John McKay at Southern Cal as an assistant and stayed at USC for another two years, the teams winning 15 of their 20 games while he was there. After that, it was on to Arkansas to work under Frank Broyles, another two-year stint, during which the Razorbacks posted a record of 14–8–1.

Jack Pardee, an outstanding linebacker when he played for the Los Angeles Rams (1957-1970) and then the Redskins (1971-1972), first became the head coach of the Chicago Bears (1975-1977), then moved to Washington, where he guided the Redskins from 1978 through 1980. With the Skins he was .500: 24-24-0.

In 1973 Gibbs moved to the pros. It was his former coach and mentor, Don Coryell, who made the transition possible. Coryell, who was the head coach of the St. Louis Cardinals at that time, hired him to handle the offensive backfield. From 1973 to 1977 the Cards were 42–27–1 and took two NFC East titles. In 1979, Coryell moved to San Diego to direct the Chargers, and he brought Gibbs with him. During both of the years that Gibbs worked with Coryell in San Diego, the Chargers triumphed in the AFC West.

After Washington had lived through more than a decade of defense-oriented football under George Allen and Jack Pardee, the front office decided it was time for somebody more concerned with honing an offensive attack. After all, the Redskins had Joe Theismann and John Riggins in the backfield and the Hogs up front. Gibbs had never held a head coaching position before, but he was highly regarded as an offensive innovator who had tutored the pass-prolific Dan Fouts out in San Diego. The Redskins brass decided to take a chance and hired him to direct Washington's destiny in the 1981 season.

After Gibbs' team lost its first five games that year, one Washington positive thinker observed, "Well, don't forget, Tom Landry lost his first five *seasons* down in Dallas and Clint Murchison didn't fire him; hell, he gave him a 10-year contract." After that awful start, Gibbs rallied the Redskins and the team became one of the true powerhouses of the decade. In his second and third years as chief of the Redskins, he took the Skins to back-to-back Super Bowls.

COACH GIBBS BY THE NUMBERS

YEAR	REGULAR SEASON	PLAYOFFS	STANDING
1981	8–8–0	N/A	4th, NFC East
1982	8–1–0	4–0	Super Bowl champion
1983	14–2–0	2–1	NFC champion
1984	11–5–0	0–1	Division champion
1985	10–6–0	N/A	2nd, NFC East
1986	12–4–0	2–1	NFC runner-up
1987	11–4–0	3–0	Super Bowl champion
1988	7–9–0	N/A	4th, NFC East
1989	10–6–0	N/A	3rd, NFC East
1990	10–6–0	1–1	3rd, NFC East
1991	14–2–0	3–0	Super Bowl champion
1992	9–7–0	1–1	3rd, NFC East

In so doing, he was also named Coach of the Year by the Associated Press both years, the first time that had happened since the legendary Vince Lombardi of the Green Bay Packers was so honored in 1961 and 1962.

Under the offense-minded Gibbs, the Redskins set a then National Football League record for points scored in a season (541 in 1983). His philosophy:

> I make up my game plan to try to confuse the opponent's defense. If you can take away what their defense has worked on, what they learned about you from studying films of your games, you can confuse them. It's kind of like a chess match.

As writer Gary Pomerantz of the *Washington Post* put it, "Gibbs is a man of perception and a coach of deception."

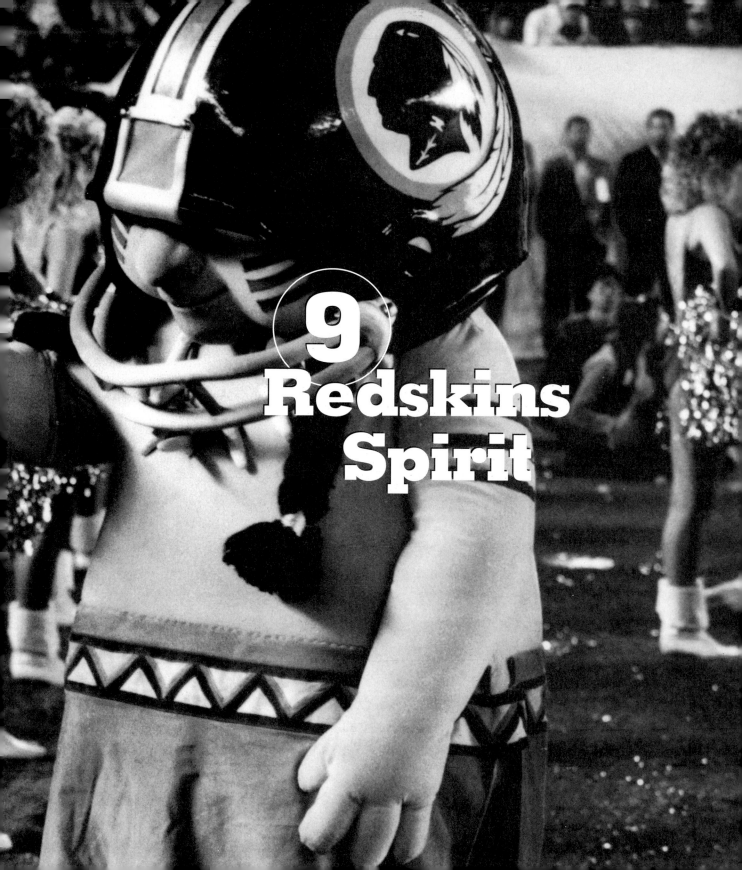

9
Redskins Spirit

THE SONG

What is *the* song? "Hail to the Redskins," of course. It was not, however, the first fight song penned for a pro football team, as George Preston Marshall often claimed: the Chicago Bears and the Frankford Yellow Jackets had adopted their own inspirational music and lyrics in the twenties. But it is arguably the most famous.

As Morris Siegel wrote in an article about the song in a 1983 edition of *Game-Day* magazine:

> It was sung badly, if enthusiastically, on the White House lawn by Secretary of State George Shultz.
>
> It was performed nightly for a week in the Kennedy Center for the Performing Arts by the National Symphony Orchestra under the direction of Russian-born conductor Mstislav Rostropovich.
>
> It was proposed as the official song of the nation's capital, which now is identified as much as the headquarters of the Super Bowl XVII champions (the Washington Redskins, naturally) as the seat of the federal government.
>
> It was extolled by a unanimously adopted resolution of the Maryland State Senate, a display of bipartisanship at its highest level.
>
> In Washington, it continues to be number one on the people's charts regardless of which Top 40 show they listen to. It remains a unifying battle cry at restaurants and bars on Capitol Hill.
>
> However poorly it is sung or played, "Hail to the Redskins" immediately brings Washingtonians to attention.

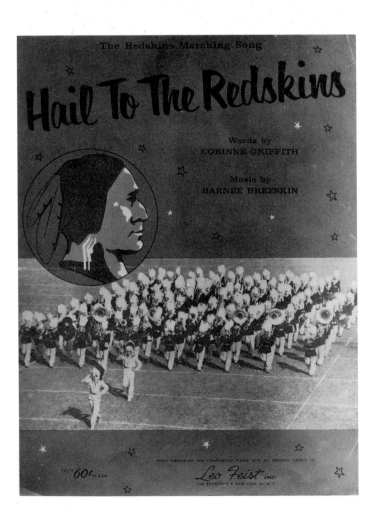

"HAIL TO THE REDSKINS"

The original lyrics penned by Corinne Griffith in 1937:

Hail to the Redskins.
Hail victory!
Braves on the warpath.
Fight for old D.C.
Scalp 'um, swamp 'um, we will
Take 'um big score.
Read 'um, weep 'um, touchdown, we want heap more.
Fight on, fight on, 'til you have won, sons of Wash-ing-ton.
Rah! Rah! Rah!
Hail to the Redskins. Hail Victory!
Braves on the warpath.
Fight for old D.C.

How did this paean to George Preston Marshall's noble Redskins come about? Let Corinne Griffith, the Big Chief's wife and the fight song's lyricist, tell the story, as she did in her book *My Life with the Redskins* (A. S. Barnes, 1947):

We returned to the Shoreham Hotel in Washington after leaving Dallas early in the summer of 1937. Things were fairly quiet one morning, when the telephone rang. It was Barnee [Breeskin], leader of the Shoreham orchestra. Since the Redskins were going to be in Washington, he said, he thought they should have a song and he had written one, which he wanted us to hear. He was calling it "Hail to the Redskins."

I turned from the telephone, held my hand over the receiver, and asked George (whose nose was, as always, buried in a newspaper) if he wanted to hear the number. Without even looking up or missing a line of what he was reading, he said, "If I listened to every song written for the Redskins since moving to Washington I wouldn't have time to do my washing—I mean attend to my laundry. Tell Barnee "No."

"Hello, Barnee? He says he'll be delighted." Barnee thanked me and asked me to thank George, which I did. At a quarter of eight that night, we heard for the first time the music of "Hail to the Redskins."

The music was sent to Buddy De Sylva, who wrote the lyrics for "A Kiss in the Dark," "When Day Is Done," "You're a Sweetheart," and other fine songs. His answer about a Redskin song was: "How could one write anything romantic about pro football?"

Then it was sent to Bob Considine, now on the *New York Mirror*. Bob returned it, saying, "Love, Bob."

After that affectionate outburst, George concluded, "I guess you'll have to write the lyrics; no one else will.

THE COMPOSER

The composer of "Hail to the Redskins," Barnet "Barnee" Breeskin, had been a friend of George Preston Marshall's before Washington's most famous laundryman ever got into professional football. At the dawn of the thirties, Marshall lived in the Shoreham Hotel in D.C., where Breeskin conducted the dance band.

As Breeskin explained to feature writer Tom Yorke for *The Washington Times* in 1988, "I used to sit with him every night between sets at the Shoreham, and then in 1932 he started fooling around with the Boston Braves football team." After learning that Marshall was going to bring his team to Washington, Breeskin said, "It inspired me. I went downstairs early in the morning and wrote it [the music] in three or four minutes."

Breeskin explained that he wanted to give the fight song a Southern flavor:

So for the first and last parts I used the basic chords of "Dixie" and interpolated a different melody. For the chorus I wanted a Redskin or Indian theme so I gave it some tom-tom effect, which conjures up a picture of an Indian war dance.

The song Barnee Breeskin composed for Marshall was originally titled "The Redskins March," but after Corinne Griffith Marshall wrote the words to it the title was changed to "Hail to the Redskins."

Breeskin remained the bandleader at the Shoreham from 1930 to 1956 and served as leader of Marshall's Redskins Marching Band from 1938 to 1951. The latter was always an experience. During those years, Marshall communicated by phone from his box not only to his coach on the sideline, but also directly to bandleader Breeskin regarding song selections during the game and at halftime. Marshall felt the band and its master were such an integral part of the Redskins' framework that he often had Breeskin sit in during the team's Monday morning meetings, where the previous day's game was assessed. Breeskin recalled one such meeting in 1943:

> One time when the team lost . . . the Monday meeting started and Marshall was really set to raise hell . . . when [Coach] Dutch Bergman turned around and said, "Mr. Marshall, did you notice that the trombones were a little flat?" Well, Marshall turned to me and talked for 20 minutes about how the band has got to be improved, and that the damn drunks in the stands were doing this and that. This was a ploy that Dutch used. Consequently, the meeting would get over, Dutch would be off free and easy, and I'd be sitting there wondering if I still had a job.

Barnee Breeskin also enjoyed telling the story of the morning after his marriage in October 1945:

> Dolores and I were on our honeymoon at the Waldorf-Astoria in New York . . . when I received an early-morning telephone call from Marshall, telling me to get back down here to Griffith Stadium for the game. My wife never would go back to another football game after that.

THE BAND

The Redskins Marching Band made its inaugural appearance in Washington on the same September evening in 1937 that George Preston Marshall introduced his newly relocated franchise in the National Football League to football fans in the nation's capital.

At the bandstand podium that night, just before the Redskins were to take on the New York Giants, Barnee Breeskin conducted his Shoreham Hotel band as it played the National Anthem. Marshall also gave Breeskin the additional responsibility of entertaining the fans with music throughout the game.

But that was only the start for music lover Marshall. He also wanted his own marching band to entertain at halftime of the Redskins' home games. So he

The Washington Redskins band, the pride and joy of George Preston Marshall, shown here at Griffith Stadium. The band made its debut on September 1? 1937, the same Sunday tha the Redskins played their first home game in Washington, D.C.

Football is a game of pageantry. It derives as a spectacle from the gladiator shows of the Romans. It is strictly amphitheater. Its great success is due to the color surrounding it. It needs music and bands. Football without a band is like a musical without an orchestra.

Part of the pageantry: the Redskins cheerleaders.

merged several smaller brass bands—one, it is said, was from a dairy, another from a local reform school. When he was through, he had a 150-piece brass band.

The band and halftime entertainment were so deeply embedded in the Big Chief's heart that it prompted one writer to observe:

It could be said that when George Preston Marshall put on a football game, the two halves were merely bookends to keep the halftime show standing tall.

During the championship years and through the lean ones as well, whether wearing flowing headdresses or Redskins stocking caps, the band has been around ever since that first fateful night in Washington. In fact, the Redskins band, at least according to recorded history, was silenced only once. And it was the night of one of the team's most glorious victories.

For the last game of the 1937 regular season, which would decide the NFL East title that year, Marshall brought his marching band along with the team to New York, where the game was being played at the Polo Grounds. The band, all wearing white headdresses and appropriate costumes, marched down Seventh Avenue in Manhattan with the Big Chief at the head. Inside the Polo Grounds, its rendition of "Hail to the Redskins" so inspired the team that they decimated the Giants 49–14, thus earning the right to play in the NFL title game against the Bears.

After the game, the band, the team, Marshall, and his entourage boarded the last train back to Washington. At Union Station in Washington at about 11:00 that

night, some 10,000 fans were waiting to welcome home the victors. Marshall thought it only proper for his beloved band to lead a little march up Pennsylvania Avenue.

The Washington police, less musically inclined than Marshall, especially just before midnight, told him that he could not stage his victory march without an official city license. Marshall argued vehemently with them. The police stood firm: "No license, no parade."

Marshall left angrily, but not in defeat. He marshaled as many members of the band as he could find and guided them up the avenue, out of sight of the police—or so he thought. There they would march a single block to the tune of "Hail to the Redskins."

As the first few bars of that famous fight song lilted into the balmy Washington night air, the police reappeared. The music stopped and the police threatened to arrest the entire band. But, having only one patrol wagon with them, they settled for merely collaring the drum major.

A deprived, frustrated Marshall grumped that hostile New York had allowed his band to march on its streets while his own hometown was denying him and his triumphal team that very same, simple honor. But to no avail. He followed the paddy wagon down to 1st Precinct headquarters and came up with the $25 to bail his drum major out of jail.

SIEMENS
FedExField
SIEMENS
FedExField
SIEMENS
FedExField

10
The Modern
Redskins

In 1999 Daniel M. Snyder became the fourth majority owner in Washington Redskins history, following franchise founder George Preston Marshall and subsequent owners Jack Kent Cooke and his estate (administrated by John Kent Cooke). Snyder purchased the organization for $800 million, the most money paid to that date for a sports franchise in the United States.

Snyder received in return a team that, in 1998, posted a disappointing 6–10 season. He promised a turnaround; he told the fans that Washington was going to have a winner again, and soon.

Stephen Davis bursting through the Carolina Panthers defense. *Photo reprinted by permission Peter Read Miller/TimePix.*

Norv Turner, who had been at the helm since 1994, was kept on as head coach, but Snyder made it clear that with or without Turner, he was intent on seeing the Redskins return to the glory of their Super Bowl days in the eighties and early nineties.

In 1999 there was indeed a turnaround, with the Redskins reversing their regular-season record to 10–6— good enough to claim their first NFC Eastern Division title since 1991. After defeating the wild-card Lions 27–13, the Skins met the Buccaneers in Tampa Bay in the NFC divisional playoff game, but came away on the short end of a 14–13 score.

It had been a good year. Stephen Davis rushed for 1,405 yards (a Redskins record, eclipsing Terry Allen's 1,353 in 1996); Brad Johnson posted a quarterback rating of 90.0, completing 316 of 519 passes for 4,005 yards and 24 touchdowns. Michael Westbrook was the top receiver with 65 catches for 1,191 yards and nine touchdowns. Davis, Johnson, and offensive guard Tré

Receiver Michael Westbrook trying to fight off St. Louis Ram Taje Allen (No. 20) and Toby Wright (No. 32). *Photo reprinted by permission Bob Rosato/TimePix.*

Johnson went to the Pro Bowl. Snyder was named the NFL's Owner of the Year by *Sport* magazine.

For the year 2000, Snyder moved the team's training camp to Redskins Park in Ashburn, Virginia. He also added one of the more glittering names in professional football to the team's roster: "Neon" Deion Sanders, cornerback, kick returner, and sometimes wide receiver. Also added were perennial All-Pro defensive end Bruce Smith (11 Pro Bowls during his 15 years with the Buffalo Bills);

Redskins cornerback Deion Sanders eludes the Dallas Cowboys' Wayne McGarity. *Photo reprinted courtesy of the Associated Press.*

Irving Fryar, one of the game's outstanding wide receivers (ranked seventh on the all-time NFL receiver chart going into the 2000 season); and back-up quarterback Jeff George, who was coming off his best season yet in the NFL (a quarterback rating of 94.2 in 1999). The draft produced two players who would soon become Redskins of note: linebacker LaVar Arrington, an All-American from Penn State drafted in the first round, and offensive lineman Chris Samuels, another first-round pick, out of Alabama.

With Washington's impressive season in 1999 and the new acquisitions, it was not surprising that many of the preseason prognosticators predicted that the Skins would represent the NFC in the Super Bowl at the end of the 2000 season. Despite all the high hopes, however, Washington got off to a rocky start; after defeating Carolina in the season opener, they lost to the Lions and then the

Cowboys. After that, however, they appeared to be on their way to fulfilling the preseason predictions, winning their next five in a row. But losses to Tennessee and Arizona followed, bringing their record to an unsatisfying 6–4. A win over St. Louis was followed by consecutive losses to the Eagles and the Giants.

With the Redskins at 7–6 and the chances of a playoff berth—much less a Super Bowl appearance—fast diminishing, Snyder relieved Norv Turner of his duties as head coach and replaced him with interim coach Terry Robiskie. Robiskie, in his seventh year on the Redskins coaching staff, had been the team's passing game coordinator. Losses to Dallas and Pittsburgh followed. A win over Arizona in the final game left the Skins with a disappointing 8–8 record and no invitation to postseason play.

Individual performances were also less than inspiring, although Stephen Davis had another 1,000-plus year, gaining 1,318 yards on 332 carries. But neither Brad Johnson nor Jeff George had a year as good as the previous one. Despite the lackluster season, four Skins earned a trip to the Pro Bowl: running back Stephen Davis, cornerback Champ Bailey, tight end Stephen Alexander, and defensive end Marco Coleman.

Despite the team's lackluster performance, the fans were more supportive than ever. Attendance for the 2000 regular season in Washington was 647,424, a new National Football League record. The average home attendance at FedEx Field was 80,928.

In January 2001 the Redskins announced the hiring of Marty Schottenheimer as their new head coach. Schottenheimer ranked No. 12 at the time among NFL coaches with more than 100 victories, and his overall record was an impressive 150–96–1. Coming from the Kansas City Chiefs, where he'd won 101 games in 10 years against only 58 losses and one tie, he carried the credentials of a winner—which was exactly what Daniel Snyder had promised the fans.

In 2001 the Redskins returned to Dickinson College in Carlisle, Pennsylvania, for training camp, reinstating what was a 32-year tradition that began in 1963 and ended in 1994. What followed, however, was totally unexpected: the Skins lost their first five regular-season games, a start almost as bad as 1998, when they dropped the first seven games in a row. But they rallied, winning the ensuing five games against the Cardinals, Giants, Seahawks, Broncos, and Eagles. It was the first time in NFL history that a team turned around and won its next five consecutive games after losing its first five. At 5–5, thoughts of the playoffs were rekindled— but not for long. Washington continued to play .500 ball for the remainder of the

In four seasons as a Redskin, LaVar Arrington has emerged as one of the league's most feared linebackers. *Photo courtesy of AP/Wide World Photos.*

year, with losses to the Cowboys, Eagles, and Bears, and victories over Arizona (twice) and New Orleans.

For the second year in a row a record of 8–8 was not good enough to make the playoffs. It wasn't good enough for Marty Schottenheimer, either—he decided to bow out after the season. It was, however, a year in which Stephen Davis broke his own all-time Redskins single-season rushing record by gaining 1,432 yards. He did it on 356 carries for an average of 4.0 per carry. Davis also became the first Washington ball carrier to rush for more than 1,000 yards in three consecutive seasons.

Tony Banks, who had been released by the Cowboys and picked up by Washington, had earned the starting quarterback job for 2001 and posted a rating of 71.3 with his completion of 198 of 370 passes for 2,386 yards and 10 touchdowns. His primary receiver was Michael Westbrook, who snared 57 of those passes for 664 yards, 4 for touchdowns. The ever-reliable Bruce Smith led the team in sacks with five. Three Redskins went to the Pro Bowl that year: linebacker LaVar Arrington, cornerback Champ Bailey, and offensive tackle Chris Samuels.

Just as he had the year before, team owner Daniel Snyder celebrated the New Year by announcing the hiring of a new head coach—Steve Spurrier, the 25th in the team's long and illustrious history. Spurrier, an All-American quarterback and Heisman Trophy winner at the University of Florida in the mid-sixties, had been a successful head coach at his alma mater, where he established himself as one of the winningest coaches in college football history. In his 12 years leading the Gators (1990–2001), he compiled an overall record of 122–27–1, winning seven Southeastern Conference titles and the national championship in 1996 and taking his team to 11 bowl games. Known for his aggressive offensive style of coaching (his Florida teams averaged 35 points per game with an average of 310 passing yards and 460 total yards per game), his arrival signaled the reinstatement of a wide-open brand of football for the Washington franchise. In the words of owner Daniel Snyder, "Steve Spurrier will bring a supercharged, exciting, and dynamic brand of football to our great fans. His ability to energize players and teams is unprecedented."

Steve Spurrier's "fun 'n' gun" offense never got off the ground in Washington, and the coach resigned after two disappointing seasons. *Photo courtesy of AP/Wide World Photos.*

Along with the new coach, a new quarterback also arrived: Patrick Ramsey, a 6'2", 217-pound first-round draft pick out of Tulane. With the promise offered by outstanding second-year wide receiver Rod Gardner and the always-productive ball carrying of Stephen Davis, big things were expected in 2002—especially after a preseason 4–1 romp during which the team set a club record by tallying 164 preseason points.

The regular season was less fulfilling. After a win over Arizona, the Skins fell to the Eagles and the 49ers, then defeated Tennessee before losing to the Saints and the Packers. Victories over Indianapolis and Seattle gave the ballclub a record of 4–4 at midseason. The second half of the year was less fulfilling; wins over the Rams, Texans, and Cowboys were offset by losses to the Jaguars, Cowboys, Eagles, and Giants (twice). The final record of 7–9 was as disappointing as it was unexpected.

Stephen Davis gained only 820 yards rushing, the first time in four years that he was under the 1,000-yard mark for the season. Patrick Ramsey, trading off the quarterbacking duties throughout the season with veteran Shane Matthews,

Wide receiver Laveranues Coles went to the Pro Bowl in his first season in Washington after being signed away from the New York Jets prior to the 2003 campaign. *Photo courtesy of AP/Wide World Photos.*

managed a quarterback rating of 71.8 (117 completions of 227 passes thrown, 1,539 yards, and nine touchdowns). Rod Gardner was the leading receiver, snagging 71 passes for 1,006 yards and eight touchdowns. On the defensive side, linebacker LaVar Arrington recorded 11 sacks and defensive end Bruce Smith another 9. Arrington, Champ Bailey, and Chris Samuels again went to the Pro Bowl.

One game in 2002—December 29, the last game of the season, a victory over the Dallas Cowboys—was especially memorable not because it was a victory, but because it was cornerback Darrell Green's last game. At 42 years old he was retiring after 20 seasons in a Washington Redskins uniform. A first-round draft pick in 1983 out of Texas A&I, he left with legendary status. Among his many accomplishments, Green set the NFL record for consecutive seasons with an interception (19) and shared the league mark with two others for most career interceptions

(54). He went to seven Pro Bowls and set Redskins longevity records by playing in 295 games (and starting in 258 of them).

All the promise of an exciting, postseason-bound Redskins team under offensive wizard Steve Spurrier sadly dissipated in 2003. The third most productive running back in Redskins history, Stephen Davis (only John Riggins and Larry Brown have gained more yards rushing than Davis' 5,790), was lost for salary cap reasons. Hopes were high, however, after triumphs over the Jets and the Falcons in the season's first two games. But it was all downhill from there. An overtime loss to the Giants was offset by a victory over the New England Patriots, but the Skins dropped the next four in succession to the Eagles, Bucs, Bills, and Cowboys. A win over Seattle was followed by losses to Carolina, Miami, and New Orleans. After defeating the Giants, losses to the Cowboys, Bears, and Eagles brought the Redskins' season to an end. Washington was 5–11, their poorest season since 1994's dismal 3–13. Frustrated, disillusioned, and disappointed, head coach Steve Spurrier announced that he was opting out of his contract and would not be back for the 2004 season.

Running back Trung Candidate, acquired in a trade with the St. Louis Cardinals for offensive guard David Loverne and replacing the departed Stephen Davis, led the team in rushing with 600 yards on 142 attempts for an average of 4.2 yards per carry. Patrick Ramsey's 179 completions in 337 attempts for 2,166 yards and 14 touchdowns gave him a quarterback rating of only 75.8. The top receiver of 2003 was Laveranues Coles, who, after three stellar years with the Jets, was signed as an unrestricted free agent in early 2003. Coles hauled in 82 passes for 1,204 yards,

Upon returning to the team he led to three Super Bowl titles in 12 years, Joe Gibbs (right) promptly signed veteran quarterback Mark Brunell (left) and traded for Denver running back Clinton Portis (pictured on pages 272–273). *Photos courtesy of AP/Wide World Photos.*

Safety Sean Taylor, Washington's first pick in the 2004 draft (fifth pick overall), is expected to have an immediate impact on the Skins defense. *Photo courtesy of AP/Wide World Photos.*

6 for touchdowns (the best year for a Redskins receiver since the days of Art Monk and Gary Clark in the eighties). Rod Gardner caught another 59 passes for 600 yards and five touchdowns.

On the defensive side, cornerback Fred Smoot led the team in interceptions for the third consecutive year. Smoot, a second-round draft choice out of Mississippi State in 2001, picked off four passes in 2003, four in 2002, and five as a rookie in 2001. Middle linebacker Jeremiah Trotter, who started for the Eagles for three years before being acquired as an unrestricted free agent in 2002, led the team with 129 tackles, 88 of which were solos. Linebacker Jessie Armstead recorded the most sacks, 6.5, with LaVar Arrington right behind with 6. Despite the disappointing year, three Skins went to the Pro Bowl: wide receiver Laveranues Coles, linebacker LaVar Arrington, and cornerback Champ Bailey.

Calling on the philosophy that the road to success is best traveled with someone who has been there before, the Redskins wooed Pro Football Hall of Fame coach and legendary Redskins leader Joe Gibbs out of retirement, announcing on January 7, 2004, that he would be returning as head coach and team president. The man who had turned the Redskins into an NFL dynasty during his previous 12-year tenure (four Super Bowls and three NFL championships, 1981–1992) was back, and with a mission. As owner Daniel Snyder observed, "Who better to set our strategy and lead the Redskins back to the championship glory that once was ours." Who indeed.

INDEX

Page numbers are set in *italic* type when the reference is to an illustration.